EXPAT GUIDE: MOSCOW

by
MARTINE MAUREL

Copyright © 2000 Seawolf Ltd.
All rights reserved.

ISBN: 1-58112-775-8

Universal Publishers/uPUBLISH.com
USA • 2000

www.upublish.com/books/maurel.htm

Disclaimer

- All prices in this book have been quoted in US dollars and cents. These should be used only as a rough indication as the ruble/dollar rate may well have changed markedly by the time you read this book.
- Businesses and services come into existence and vanish just as rapidly. This book is intended to serve merely as a starting point for your own particular discovery of Moscow.
- Telephone numbers and e-mail addresses have not been checked.

The author and publisher cannot vouch for the veracity of hearsay information and take no responsibility for any inconvenience, actions or consequences caused by any contact that may arise between yourself and any person, or service mentioned in this book.

Acknowledgements

I thank my husband David for his patience and generosity in standing by me through thick and thin.

My gratitude goes to Oleg Ataev, who drove me around Moscow for 18 months and who never tired of pointing out the intricacies and curiosities of this remarkable city and its wonderful people.

Ian and Maria Church, and Theodora Turula are thanked for giving their time in proofing the manuscript and for their invaluable suggestions.

My dear friend Galya (Galina V. Oglobleva) also deserves my heartfelt thanks for producing the guide's cover and for showing me the secret parts of Moscow, an experience I shall forever cherish.

Acknowledgement must be given to *The Moscow Times* (*www.moscowtimes.ru*) without whose invaluable pages, much of the information in the guide would not have been available. You can subscribe (for free unless you access the archive) to the *Moscow Times* on the Internet before your move to Moscow and benefit from news that will begin to give you some indication of what is going on in Moscow.

Further acknowledgement must go to the Expat list and its over +/-1,000 strong family of mostly expatriate subscribers. Like all families this one has its colourful differences, but alongside the quips, quotes and anecdotes, is a mine of important information of great value to the newcomer to Moscow. I thank all those on the list whose information has helped to spark ideas for this guide.

Children in Moscow

Very little mention is made of children in this guide, as the majority of expats who do come to Moscow do not have children. The subject of children will be addressed in a soon-to-be published volume entitled 'Expat guide: Children in Moscow'.

The book is dedicated to
my beloved son, Christopher,
for being such a wonderful companion
and for generating so much laughter in my life.

Preface

As far as I know, this is the first attempt to write up an expat guide to Moscow in such length and detail. Others have published information in the past but not in this format, it would seem.

As a reader, and when you wish to follow up ideas or suggestions made in this guide it is important that you understand that much of the information is taken from the opinions and advice of other expatriates. Opinions are opinions and often not factual and in the light of this, you are asked to take what you read as simply a guide or indication, as opposed to a complete dearth of information on whatever subject you are considering. Such conventional wisdom is better than nothing, after all, and it's a starting point for you to make your own opinion. The main aim of this book is to help you save time and effort and ensure that your learning curve is not as steep as it surely would have been without this guide.

To establish the temporal relevance of information contained in this guide, it may be worth considering that most of the material was written in the first half of 1999.

Please send any contributions that you would like to see published in the next edition of this guide to the author at: *mmaurel@mistral.co.uk*. These will be considered for publication with due acknowledgement to yourself, if requested.

Contents

1/Moscow expats - the species 9

2/Before you arrive.........................15

3/Your first weeks 25

4/Finding accommodation..................... 31

5/Getting around........................... 51

6/Eating and drinking.........................69

7/Getting to know others 87

8/Keeping in touch......................... 109

9/Keeping busy 137

10/Staying healthy.........................167

11/Staying safe 183

12/Staying solvent 193

13/Working matters 221

14/Visitors 229

15/Weather.............................231

16/Pets 237

17/Travel from Moscow.......................243

18/Leaving 261

INDEX................................. 265

1/Moscow expats - the species

Probably the single characteristic that can define the announcement to one's friends families and colleagues that one is going to live in Moscow is the shocked reaction that accompanies this announcement. Most expats will feel as if they have just announced that they are going to live on the moon.

Before arriving in Moscow, most expats believe that the experience will be grim, depressing and hostile, surrounded, as they expect to be, by morose, xenophobic Russians. This can certainly lead you to think twice about your decision to move to Moscow. Given Russia's unremittingly bad press in the rest of the world, this reaction is not unreasonable. You would be well advised, however, to remember that the view from inside Russia, looking out, is vastly different from that outside Russia, looking in. The reality of Moscow life will confound this view. Of course, these elements do exist, but on the whole you will be pleasantly surprised to find Russians to be warm and hospitable people. They laugh, they cry, they love and they need to survive just like anyone else in the world. This is the bottom line.

The majority of expats will seek to dispel their sense of culture shock by trying to fathom what Russia and the Russians are all about. Don't expect that you will ever get near to accomplishing this task. Russia can be classed as 'a great unknown'. As Churchill said of Russia: "it is a riddle wrapped in a mystery inside an enigma". The place and its people are like the typical Russian doll known well beyond Russia's borders. Having opened up the first doll, you are surprised to see another doll, and then another, and then another and so on.

Many have a burning desire to get to the bottom of the mystery, and for them the bitter-sweet pleasure of doing so will be indefinitely prolonged. Those that want to 'suss it out' and 'sort it out' quickly will be bitterly disappointed.

You may be a seasoned expat having experienced a wide variety of hardship postings and believe that Moscow will simply be one more such posting. Don't be complacent in your views, for the culture shock you experience in Moscow will force you to thoroughly revise these beliefs and rethink your strategies. This can be deeply disconcerting to those who arrive, confident that they will be able to cope with whatever fate throws at them.

You're probably in a better position if you're a 'green' expat and are anticipating that you will face culture shock anyway. At least then you will be prepared to have your life disrupted like a thousand-piece jig-saw puzzle flung into the air. Your ability to put the pieces back into place quickly will depend on the speed with which you amass 'on-the-ground' knowledge. This book will help you to do so far more quickly than if you were left to do so simply by trial-and-error.

What generally proves to be so disorientating is the fact that you may find yourself moving from a comfort zone where you feel competent, sane,

Expat guide: Moscow   1/Moscow expats - the species

knowledgeable, capable and self-assured to feeling overwhelmed, anxious, impotent, vulnerable, and uncertain of even basic ways of coping.

Apart from making a serious attempt to learn the Cyrillic alphabet and even some basic Russian, one recommended way of trying to absorb the new culture is firstly to accept Moscow on its own terms. Try to tackle the task by taking small, bite-sized 'pieces' instead of trying to swallow the whole thing in one gulp. Realise that it takes time for things to begin to feel more familiar, even if they still don't quite make sense to you.

Russia has its own agenda, and your experience will be largely on Russia's terms. The best way of coping is to accept this fact, to go with the flow and try to fit in, rather than to impose your own views on the situation.

As recently as late 1997 it was estimated that foreign companies in Moscow numbered in the tens of thousands. Expat numbers are estimated to range from 100,000 to 200,000, though many of these are expats from former CIS states.

It is estimated that just after the 1998 financial crisis, there were about 10,000 US private citizens in Moscow and some 5,000 British citizens. There are also sizeable groups of French, Italian, German, Indian, and Asian citizens.

With Moscow's stock-exchange ranked as world's fastest growing in 1997, global confidence in Moscow and Russia grew to the extent that most foreign companies expected their foreign staff complement to continue expanding over the following five years.

The Russian Crisis of 1998 which was unleashed on 17 August, rapidly deflated these projections leading to a significant exodus of expats. Nevertheless, Moscow has always had expats and will always have expats, whether in large numbers or small. A big question mark hangs over Moscow's future, and it is not within the scope of this guide to ponder what is likely to happen after the next round of parliamentary and presidential elections.

The Moscow expat can broadly be pigeon-holed as follows: those that come to Moscow for business and support services, those that come to Moscow for humanitarian purposes, and the dependants of both these groups. These can be further subdivided into those that come to Moscow because of an enduring curiosity and love for Russia and its people, and those who simply land in Moscow because of the vicissitudes of fate. The latter are generally surprised to find themselves in Moscow and will either learn to love or hate the place.

The type of expat attracted to Russia can safely be said to be of a certain pioneering nature, and indeed this is the buzz that runs through the expat community in Moscow, the feeling that one is at the cutting edge of history rather than in a safe, predictable posting. In the early days after Perestroika, expats thrived on the perception that they were in the New Wild West, and this feeling was heightened between 1995 and 1997. Now, after the 1998 Russian Crisis, with even the necessary expats being transferred, those that are left are deemed to be truly indispensable by their companies. Undoubtedly the challenges on the staff, tax and legal and lifestyle fronts are huge and it takes a certain type of stoicism that matches Russian stoicism to make any kind of progress in this country. It's not easy, but it can be hugely rewarding.

Instead of regarding it simply as a job move, some expats turn things around by considering their move to Moscow as 'an awfully big adventure'.

Expat guide: Moscow   **1/Moscow expats - the species**

In addition to technical skills, business acumen, adaptability and motivation, followed by international experience, are ranked as the top characteristics that organisations consider essential in their recruitment drives. But this is a somewhat bald statement, as many expats testify that to succeed in Russia requires skills that will mean you will succeed anywhere else in the world.

Before you agree to come to Moscow, try to assess the posting in terms of taxation, hardship pay, housing, medical coverage, indeed whether your salary is dollar- or ruble-based and family support. Salaries may need to be adjusted for inflation, devaluation, and projected cost of living in the light of inflationary trends. The recent trend before the 1998 crisis was that the salary gap between expat and Russian managers was closing markedly, and understandably so.

When Western expertise is deemed critical, in some instances the choice is biased towards new expats coming from outside and against expats with Russian knowledge who have been in Moscow for a while and who have unrealistic expectations fuelled by the much higher salaries that were on offer during the boom times.

More than ever, and in order to capture the dwindling market, good salespeople and marketing managers are in demand as Russians by their nature are not natural salespeople.

The Soviet mentality of each fighting for his own survival and not having to consider things from the point of view of another person has led to a certain distaste for or inability to fulfil conventional selling roles. The question of integrity also arises, as Russians regard selling as a mild form of prostitution.

Before the crisis western firms facing competition from Russian firms did not stint from paying equally attractive salaries for the brightest and the best. The crisis has also meant that thousands of top-quality Russian professionals are out of work and top quality candidates are two-a-penny and also prepared to accept a much lower salary than would be accepted by their Western counterparts.

The pressure is also being put on expats to learn and speak the language as they can no longer get away with simply relying on their technical skills. The candidates who do not shy away from this tall order will be the ones who will attract the top jobs.

As Moscow is no longer currently regarded the hardship assignment it once was in terms of cost of living and supply of services and facilities, the days when expats could expect to call the tune in terms of compensation packages are rapidly receding.

Crisis times - instability

In considering the possibility of coming to live in Russia, you will no doubt take into account Russia's history of instability. Those expats who braved Soviet times and have been in Moscow for decades became integrated and thus immune to the vagaries of Russian living. However, since the early 1990s expats in Moscow have experienced an ongoing series of shock tremors which ironically, has instilled a sense of stoicism when it comes to facing new tremors. They survive (like Russians) in the knowledge that in Moscow, anything goes, and that's part of its great charm for many expats. Many expats become hooked on this instability, indeed, any posting after Moscow (except possibly for Nigeria, Iraq or North Korea) is likely to seem tame by comparison. Probably the biggest

Expat guide: Moscow   1/Moscow expats - the species

surprise you will find at the end of your time in Moscow is best summarised by what one departing expat said: "Moscow is like the Hotel California - you can check out anytime you want, but you can never leave".

Over the past decade much has changed in Moscow. The first stirrings of Perestroika instilled a sense of hope that Russia was emerging from its Soviet past and despite ups and downs, nurtured a growing sense of optimism in the first part of the decade. As things improved, this optimism came into full flower particularly from 1995.

To some, the zenith of life in Moscow was experienced in 1997 and into the early part of 1998. Very few foresaw that the bubble would burst, and burst so spectacularly. The lethal combination of Asian flu and a corrupt government coming to the end of its options toppled the entire edifice that was Russia, like a house of cards. The vast majority of expats were unprepared for the crisis and its ramifications, and although many left, new expats were still arriving as the crisis was breaking, and were still arriving a year later. No one can predict where it will lead, and for some companies, whether it will even be worth having an office in Moscow for the next year or two until things begin to stabilise and confidence grows in the new order.

The major issue at stake is the next Russian presidential election which could take place as scheduled, in the year 2000. There is no doubt that the outcome of the elections will determine the expat make-up of Russia for the next decade at least.

Deciding to move to Moscow is, in some ways, a high-risk decision, but the rewards can also be high. Are you prepared to take the gamble?

Issues to consider before you come

Terrorism

Since it became apparent in September 1999, that Moscow was the target of a terrorist campaign, security has been very tight. But whether it will ever be tight enough to prevent further attacks such as the devastating bombings that took place, is anybody's guess. This increased tension and insecurity will make anyone think twice about coming to live in Moscow and rightly so. If you do decide to move there or continue living there, you are advised to contact your embassy and ask for advice regarding the measures you should take to maximise your safety.

Racism

Note that a significant skinhead tendency exists in Moscow which targets African-Americans and people who are obviously of other cultures such as Asians. The police profess to wish to stop them. However, there is not much evidence of this being implemented. (Since the bombings in Moscow, darker-skinned Caucasians, and Chechens, specifically, have become the target of heightened security checks and in many cases, xenophobia.)

Prior to the bombing campaign, victims of attacks were mostly students, although ordinary men and women had also been attacked in public, in broad daylight. There seems to be a greater incidence of attacks in the period leading up

Expat guide: Moscow 1/Moscow expats - the species

to and for a month or two after April 20, Hitler's birthday. The Fili Park CD market Gorky Park, metros and the vicinity of foreign student residences are vulnerable areas for attacks.

Anti-Semitism

There is a deep vein of anti-Semitism in the Russians. In Moscow, synagogues have been bombed and gravestones desecrated. For all that, several very prominent members of the government are actually Jewish. (See also section on Religion).

Anti-Western feeling

The view of the Kosovo conflict from Russia was vastly different to the view from Western countries, mostly as a result of initial media manipulation. This resulted in a significant increase in anti-American feeling primarily, followed by anti-Western feeling. This feeling was by no means confined to the older Russian. Somewhat surprisingly, and to the great credit of Russians, there were only very isolated instances where Westerners were made to feel unwelcome. Anti-Western feeling subsided rapidly in the months after the resolution of the conflict.

Moscow is not Russia

It is very important that you make the distinction between Moscow and Russia, for what is outside Moscow is the real Russia, just as Monaco is not the same as Italy or France. It is regarded as an island of development. Do not think that what you see in Moscow, you will see in other parts of Russia.

Safety

Moscow's image abroad is of gangsters shooting at random as they speed through the streets of Moscow in their black Versace outfits and in cars with tinted windows. The fact of the matter is that although shootings do occur, the ordinary expat is highly unlikely to come across such an incident. Many seasoned local expats are adamant that Moscow is far safer than New York or London.

Standard of living

Despite the devastating effects of the crisis, and the anti-Moscow bias of Western television, Moscow has certainly not regressed to the days when queues formed outside bread shops. Most things are available in Moscow and all the services you would expect to use, work extremely well. However, as always, this is subject to what happens in the next crisis!

Those expats who arrived and left in the early part of the 1990s and who return for a visit are always bowled over by the changes in the city since the early post-communism years. Indeed the pace of change in Moscow is staggering and visible from year to year. This rapid change presents part of what many expats find so exciting and stimulating about living in Moscow.

2/Before you arrive

You've been offered the job or assignment, you have made the decision to move to Moscow for a year or two or more. You know it's going to be difficult, but you don't know quite how difficult.

You've started asking around, possibly speaking to others who have lived in Moscow and asked them for their advice. The very nature of this advice is anecdotal and could be dated, but it will have helped you build up some kind of mental picture.

A ten-step guide to relocation

Careful advance planning can help to iron out this seemingly daunting task.

1. Finding a school for your children (if applicable)

As soon as you've accepted the posting, or even while your acceptance is pending, you should find out whether the school of your choice will be able to accept your child on the appointed date of your arrival. There have been long waiting lists in the past and children have sometimes been obliged to go to schools that were their parents' second choices. The move will disrupt your children's education as it is, and you can't afford to disrupt it further by not making sure that your children will be accepted by a school of your choice.

2. Determine where you are going to live

Pending your acceptance of your contract, you should try to determine what sort of accommodation will be available to you, either organised by your prospective employer or by yourself. Of course, it would be preferable if you were able to visit Moscow and check out the accommodation situation yourself or select your accommodation in advance. If you have children, you would need to tie in the location of your accommodation with the school so that you don't spend hours ferrying your kids to school and back. *(See Chapter 4 - Finding accommodation)*

3. Transport issues

Taking into account the above, it would help if you could also pre-determine the type of transport you will be able or expected to use. If you will have a car at your disposal, but the car is not available as yet, it would help if your company could organise it's purchase and registration as well as the allocation of a driver (preferably English-speaking) before your arrival to avoid any delays in using it, once you get there. If you will have to rely on metros or buses, you will need to find accommodation or schools that are easily accessible by metro. Bear in mind

Expat guide: Moscow   **2/Before you arrive**

that there are very few signs in English in Moscow and the metro is almost entirely in Cyrillic) *(See Chapter 5 - Getting around)*

4. Networking

It's always worthwhile preparing the ground for your move by talking to others who might have lived in Moscow, or might still be living there. If your sponsoring organisation can put you in touch with someone on the ground in Moscow or at home who has lived there and who would be prepared to act as a mentor, that would be a valuable contact. Don't stop at one person though, as it's always better to get a cross-section of opinion. In any case, you might build up some relationships which could prove to be helpful once you get to Moscow and need to be shown around and introduced to other expats. By joining the Expat-list *(see Chapter 7 - Keeping in touch)*, you will be able to get an idea of some of the issues of concern to expats in Moscow and also make some contacts which may prove to be helpful.

Some have found it useful to contact their embassy on arrival and inquire about any social groups or newcomers assistance programmes that may be established by fellow countrymen.

5. Planning the nitty-gritty

Once you have sorted out the above issues to your satisfaction and have agreed to sign your contract, you need to start thinking about the nitty-gritty. Even though two months might be a good benchmark for most international moves, a move to Moscow entails even earlier preparation. Depending on whether you've selected and located accommodation prior to your move, you will need to co-ordinate a move-in date with the estimated arrival date of your shipment. This includes determining whether tenants will have vacated the premises and whether all proposed alterations will have been completed. It's wise to consider contingency plans just in case your plans go awry. Obtain concrete suggestions from your employer.

Check that all visas and entry permits are in order and determine when they will be ready.

6. Selecting a shipper

Only use a company that has proven experience in moving personal effects to Russia. *(see companies listed in Chapter 18 - Leaving)*. Find out what kind of regular and up-to-date experience they have had. Ask for references from clients that match your profile. Ask who will be handling the shipment once it arrives and needs to be shepherded through Customs and to your new home. Find out which port of entry your shipper intends to use and obtain guarantees that the agency handling this possibly intermediate section of the move is reliable and regularly used by your shipper.

7. Expect delays

The regularly updated tax and Customs regulatory system make the processing of a shipment more fraught with problems even for seasoned shippers to Moscow.

16

Expat guide: Moscow   **2/Before you arrive**

Although most sea shipments take between six and eight weeks, it's better to plan for 10 weeks and then be pleasantly surprised if it arrives earlier.

8. Packing your shipment and your accompanying luggage

Before you start packing, consider the following: From 1 February 1998, foreigners were charged 50 percent duty for the importation of their household goods as a result of an IMF recommendation. This applied even if the goods are imported temporarily for the duration of the employment contract or posting.

The duty level will also vary depending on whether the shipper asks to have furniture, clothing, kitchen ware and other articles charged by type, or whether a flat rate is applied to the consignments weight or valuation.

Under the ruling, duty was charged at ECU7 or $9 per kilogram or at 50 percent of declared value. Value-added tax (+/-20 percent, confirm) is added on top.

This ruling might well have been amended by the time you read this, but it will give you some idea of how duty is calculated. Try contacting the American and British Embassies, or your own embassy in Moscow for the latest tariffs.

Whatever the situation, one of your major headaches is going to be deciding what to take and what not to take. Skimming through this guide will help to give you an idea of what is available or not.

With a possible 10-week delay that could span a season, it's wise to anticipate what sort of clothes you might need to take with you to bridge this gap. You don't want to be stuck with winter clothes in the midst of a summer-heat-wave or vice versa. Carry all precious documents such as financial and medical records with you on the plane. Consider the family who lost their worldly belongings when an entire container carrying these goods was blown overboard by a hurricane.

9. Documentation and Customs clearing

If you are bringing any items of cultural value into Moscow, remember that you will one day want to get them out again. To avoid problems with Customs clearance, see that you have all proper documentation and identification. It seems that duties are or can be levied on almost any item crossing the border into Russia, with rates and rules being applied seemingly haphazardly and almost at the whim of the Customs officers.

The Russian Customs authorities are very strict about obtaining detailed inventory lists. They are not likely to open all your boxes, but if they open one and check its contents against your list and find that the two don't tally, they'll open several more which always holds the risk of increased theft. Make sure that your list states the expected retail value of the items, especially the more expensive items.

Apart from being able to claim any items that have disappeared en route to Moscow, the list will give you a good record of what you packed and where to find it in a hurry during your first days in Moscow when boxes lie scattered and unopened around your new home.

17

Expat guide: Moscow   **2/Before you arrive**

Ensure that your shipping agent uses the services of a competent Customs clearing agent who is up-to-date with the latest Customs regulations.

Don't even think about shipping your goods yourself. Customs clearing can take days if not weeks spent in queues and getting bureaucratic stamps. Any unforeseen delay in clearing your cargo will lead to a demeurrage penalty charge which can be steep. Going via St Petersburg does not avoid problems, as you will still have to transport goods to your domicile if elsewhere, and unless you are with it every inch of the way, you have no guarantee that it will all arrive.

When people say detailed inventories are needed, they mean detailed. It's a hassle, but it's worth it and it helps with the Customs clearance for if they have checked that two or three boxes tally with the list, they are likely to let the rest through without opening them.

10. Once you arrive

Ensure before departure that you know just who you will have to deal with (on your shipper's staff) once you arrive. Find out if they will have allocated a staff member to you and that the staff member can speak English and is not likely to be away on leave when your shipment is due to arrive. Ask them to provide a contingent member of staff to help you if the appointed person falls ill or is unavailable for some reason.

It's always a good idea to find out if your company has a 'fixit' person who is accustomed to dealing on the company's behalf with Customs agents and shippers. Bear in mind that if you are working you will be trying to get to grips with a new job and will not be in the best position to try to conquer the Russian Customs system at the same time. If your partner is not working, they will also have no clue nor inclination to go out and do battle while they are trying to settle children and figure out how best to feed a family, for instance. *(See Chapter 3 - Your first weeks)*

What to bring with you

To get down to more practical matters, you will need to have a good think about what you need to bring with you. Don't find yourself moaning (after your arrival) about the things you wish you had brought with you. It's a fine balancing act, but hopefully there won't be too much that you brought that you eventually wish you'd left behind.

The best way to avoid being without something you need, which is seasonally-related, and which you can't get in Moscow, is to plan a visit to either your home country or a similarly-minded but nearer country twice a year: once in the spring to stock up on summer requirements and once in the late autumn to stock up on winter requirements.

What to bring (if health is an issue)

1. Consider bringing a sun lamp if you have young children. Vitamin D may not be added to all milk products and the lack of sunshine in winter has caused rickets in babies.

18

Expat guide: Moscow   **2/Before you arrive**

2. Bring an artificial light lamp to prevent SAD (Seasonal Adjustment Disorder) in the winter if you are prone to this disorder (depression, lethargy, etc)

3. An in-room air purifier/ioniser. This will help those who are sensitive to air pollution, which increases in summer.

4. As heaters in most homes can't be regulated resulting in dry air, a humidifier can go a long way to counteracting sore throats, dry skin and chapped lips.

5. All essential medications which you take regularly or which you may need in an emergency and which you may not be able to obtain in Moscow.

6. Bring spare contact lenses and solutions in case you can't find them in Moscow.

Clothing

Winter

You and your family will need good, thick-soled shoes for the winter. The practice in Moscow is to wear outdoor shoes and take along a pair of decent, appropriate indoor shoes for your destination, be it the office or the concert hall. There are many hat and coat check places that accept your outdoor shoes (bring a bag for your other pair); and if you are visiting people, it is usual to take your shoes off in their entrance hall. Many hosts provide slippers, but you could bring some soft indoor shoes if you don't fancy wearing other people's slippers or padding around in your stockinged feet.

Depending on how often you reckon you will be out in the snow, bring a snow suit or two. It's worthwhile having two for children, as they are expected to go to school in their snowsuits and with lots of outdoor play, one can easily become worn.

Other mandatory items are a good fleece-lined anorak or short coat for casual outdoor occasions. You'll also need a good 100% wool long coat or fur coat (many people wear fur in Moscow and it does not have the stigma it has in the West) for more formal occasions. You'll see a large proportion of women wearing fur coats and for most, it's a once-in-a-lifetime investment.

You will need a good hat to keep your head warm. It's no joke being outdoors in minus -20°C when your earlobes start to freeze and if you're wearing earrings, they start to feel as if they are burning into your flesh. Besides, *babushki* (the ever-present aged grandmothers who love to dispense advice) have been known to berate strangers for not having their heads properly covered.

It is possible to buy warm undergarments in Moscow for a reasonable price.

Summer

You can choose to wear shorts, T-shirts, mini-skirts, leggings, anything goes, though probably less way-out or casual than in the UK or States.

You'll need summer gear from about late May till mid- to late August, so don't be caught out. Moscow gets hot in the summer *(see Chapter15 - Weather)*. In June 1998 outdoor night-time temperature at 23:00 was still at 33°C. In June/July 1999, Moscow had an unbroken six-week period of temperatures in the mid-thirties, causing over 100 deaths mostly as a result of people drowning while trying to cool themselves down.

Expat guide: Moscow   **2/Before you arrive**

Sports

It's worth bringing whatever equipment you think you might need. You can buy everything in Moscow as well, but the quality might not be what you are used to, or if the quality is available, it's likely to be expensive.

Ice-skates can be purchased in Moscow for about $60 a pair, roller-blades starting at about $20, and if you shop around, cross-country skis can be bought at about $40 minimum. Sleds, bicycles and skateboards as well as footballs and basket-balls can be found anywhere. Fishing rods are available. Horse-riding gear is expensive.

Kitchen equipment

Most things can be found in Moscow. Try Ramstore for a good variety at reasonable prices.

Gardening

You can find a small variety of gardening tools as well as plastic containers for a kitchen garden or balcony garden. Seeds are available from springtime as are bags of peat and compost. Plants are more expensive than in the UK and there is nowhere near the same variety. Don't expect to find big nurseries with a wide variety of plants. These are sold instead in small florist shops which can be found all over town.

Some emergency stop-gaps

Depending on what deal has been negotiated, fully, partly or unfurnished, and depending on what you have brought with you and whether your goods have been cleared by Customs, you might land up in a place with six knives. forks, plates, pots and saucers but without the little essentials that you don't think of until you miss them. Some typical omissions are a tea strainer, a sharp knife, an egg spatula, sieve, chopping board, tea towels, bedding and pillows. which means you'll have to go out and buy them.

Beware of buying too much, as you will have to get rid of it before you leave or you may end up paying extra duty on these items and they may end up as duplicates in the place you call home.

If holiday celebrations such as Easter, Christmas and Thanksgiving are important to you and your family, bring decorations that will allow you to celebrate these occasions. This will help ward off feelings of alienation.

Bring craft supplies and a sewing machine if you won't be working and will have more free time on your hands. The IWC has a long list of craft workshops *(see Chapter 8 - Getting to know others)*. Identify those you might wish to join and obtain what you think might be the required supplies before you leave. If you need to speak to the workshop leader, call 147-2240 (Mondays 14:00 - 16:00 or Wednesday 14:00 - 16:00) and ask them to find out for you what you might need to bring.

You will easily be able to find videos of American and British movies, and expats occasionally offer to sell collections at a reduced price. However you might want to bring videos of favourite TV shows.

Audio story cassettes for children are ideal for a snowy day.

Expat guide: Moscow   2/Before you arrive

A computer midi-keyboard can help to while away the dark winter hours.

Bring your favourite American or British foods (for those down days when you want some comfort foods). From the British point of view, staples such as corned beef, Marmite, Ribena and Cadbury's Creme Eggs are not available in Moscow.

Bring English-language books to read. They can be expensive and the variety is strictly limited in the handful of English-language book-shops.

It's an idea to bring favourite bed linen which will help remind you of home.

If you're an avid cook or will have more time to bake, bring a full range of baking/cooking utensils, although most of these are available locally. You will often need to bake from scratch. Bear in mind that mixes will be in another language and often not the product you are looking for. Bring your favourite recipe books so that you can cook familiar dishes. If you're stuck you can always access the recipe sites on the Internet but be warned that many of them suggest recipes that contain products you can buy ready-made in your home country and which you will not be able to buy in Moscow, so they can be frustrating.

In addition, the mostly American recipes on the Internet use imperial measures which can be confusing if you are used to metric measures. Obtain a good conversion table for cooking (weights, temperatures). A set of measuring cups will also help.

Don't worry about ordering favourite periodicals, as these can be ordered and delivered locally at a reasonable price *(see Chapter 8 - Keeping in touch)*.

Bear in mind that it might be counter-productive to buy clothes and shoes for children in advance. Irregular 'growth spurts' might lead you to skipping several sizes in the interim.

Remember that the electricity system differs from U.S. Instead of bringing items that will require complicated transformers and converters, buy them in Moscow. Some people believe that using transformers with your 110v appliances helps to wear them out faster. Others say you should leave behind appliances that are very high energy users or generate plenty of heat such as toasters, microwaves, vacuum cleaners, etc.

If you're into music, you don't have to bring too much, as you will have a wide choice in Moscow.

Spend some time going through old albums/photographs and select those that represent the parts of your life that make you happy. You'll need them to get over the culture shock and initial depression of separation from familiar things. You might consider also scanning them onto a zip disk for ease of use and transport.

Many expats think they should bring pictures to hang on the wall, but then find they don't use them, as there is quite a good selection of street art at reasonable prices.

Children like to look at their baby pictures and periodically have to bring old pictures to school. Home videos can also help to remind your children that 'home', wherever it is, still exists. Children have short memories.

Stock up on a good supply of passport photos on matte paper, otherwise you run the risk of ink on official stamps 'disappearing' resulting in untold hassles. This will prompt immigration officials to suggest that the visa or other document is false, even though you might have used it a dozen times before in coming in or

21

Expat guide: Moscow   **2/Before you arrive**

out of the country. Bring a supply to last you for the first few months until you discover where you can have these printed in Moscow.

Language issues

You may think this is a little out of place on this list, but determining to make a start on at least learning the Cyrillic alphabet, ahead of your move to Moscow, if not making a start on Russian language lessons, will make your arrival in Moscow that much easier and less traumatic. This cannot be emphasised enough.

Countdown to your move

This list is purely a rough guide to moving and may not conform to your specific needs. Adapt it to suit them.

Task	Due date for completion		Done
Buy yourself a phrase-book or Russian learning programme and set yourself a target for learning the Cyrillic alphabet.	As soon as you know you are moving Know the alphabet by the time you leave.		
Find out about schools in Moscow, ask for enrolment forms and complete and send off.	As soon as you know you are moving		
Obtain as much information about Moscow as possible. Contact IWC and find out which interest groups you may enroll in.	As soon as you find out you are moving		
Notify your current landlord of your intention to move, or contact estate agents to let your house while you are away	As soon as you know you are moving		
Decide how you will seek accommodation in Moscow. Will the company organise or will it be up to you? If up to you, find out if you have somewhere to stay on arrival and cost, conditions, location *vis a vis* school, office	As soon as you know you will be moving		
Estimate moving costs	2 months before		
Plan a date for a garage sale or locate charity for disposal of junk	2 months before		
Once you have selected a school and been accepted, contact estate agents in Moscow and ask them to send you list of apartments in areas convenient for school, office	2 months before		
Investigate shipping your pets if taking them with you	2 months before		

Expat guide: Moscow   **2/Before you arrive**

Task	Due date for completion	Done
Research storage in your home town if necessary	1 month before	
Update address book	1 month before	
List people, companies you need to notify	1 month before	
Obtain change of address or mail-redirection from post office	1 month before	
Decide banking arrangements and direct debits while in Moscow. Find out if your bank does Internet banking and set up or make alternative arrangements	1 month before	
Find out which vaccinations/inoculations are needed and arrange to have them done in time	1 month before	
Locate an appropriate medical insurance scheme	1 month before	
Decide which credit cards you should take with you according to which companies have the best representation in Russia and take steps to increase you credit card limit if necessary	1 month before	
Purchase what you think you might need to take with you (craft supplies, baking, clothing)	1 month before	
Make your travel arrangements	1 month before	
Hold garage sale, donate to charity	1 month before	
Arrange interim accommodation in Moscow	1 - 2 months before	
Arrange new home for plants/pets	3 weeks before	
Arrange insurance for high value items you will be taking. Take photographs to prove ownership	3 weeks before	
Collate personal records and documentation you will need to take with you: medical, legal, accountants, schools religious institutions	2 weeks before	
Purchase a few adapters (round, two-pin plugs only) or power converters (Russia has a 220v 50Hz system) for essential items. You will be able to buy two pin plugs in Moscow for all other appliances.	Before packing	
Notify current utilities of disconnect or transfer dates or arrange for estate agent to notify	2 weeks before	
Settle outstanding bills	1 week before	
Cancel delivery services from date of move	2 weeks before	

Expat guide: Moscow   **2/Before you arrive**

Task	Due date for completion		Done
Obtain international driver's licence valid for six months	1 week before		
Obtain a supply of matte passport photos	1 week before		
Plan what to do with your car while away	1 week before		
Arrange for cleaning of your house	1 week before		
Take plants/pets to new homes	2 days before		
Remember to make copies of your passport and visa for immigration on arrival. It's not essential but helps your case to be processed faster.	2 days before		
Defrost fridge and dispose of perishables	2 days before		
Leave for Moscow	D-day		

3/Your first weeks

Your first weeks in Moscow will be crucial to your long-term enjoyment of the place. If accommodation and transport have been organised for you, you will be saved an enormous amount of hassle. If accommodation has not been organised, or is pending arrangement, then you will have to find interim accommodation.

Registering your arrival

The very first thing you will need to do (i.e. within 72 hours) is to register your presence with UVIR (visa registration). If you move into a hotel, the hotel, if licensed to do so, will register your passport on your behalf. However, if you move straight into accommodation, you will need to see that your sponsoring organisation registers you at UVIR *(42 Ulitsa Pokrovka).*

Staying in a hotel

Many new arrivals will be offered hotel accommodation by their companies while they find and select accommodation. Others might have been to Moscow on a 'look-see' visit prior to their arrival and have approved accommodation selections.

If the company is paying, it will usually select the hotel for the new arrival. Some of the hotels most popular with short-term long-stay residents are the Marriott, the Radisson (both inside the Garden Ring, the ring road which separates central Moscow from its suburbs), and the Meridien Country Club which is over an hour's drive away from the city centre.

Being placed in a hotel can be both a curse and a blessing. It is a blessing because it allows you to walk into ready-made accommodation where food is provided for you without you being forced to fend for yourself in terms of supermarkets and accommodation glitches in the first few weeks after your arrival. In other words, it can provide a vital cushion of security while you adjust to your new surroundings.

However, some expatriates come to regard their hotel stays as a curse exactly because it is a 'half-way house' situation.

Depending on the supply/demand situation in the residential accommodation market and if housing is tight, some expatriates might spend up to three months in a hotel while their accommodation is made ready, or while the current tenants wait to leave. The down-side of this is:

- having to eat the same food on a routine basis;
- not being free to have access to personal goods which would normally have arrived by that point and would be sitting in storage;

Expat guide: Moscow   3/Your first weeks

- not being free to start life in earnest e.g. if you've joined a group which requires certain sportswear, say ice-skates - do you go out and buy ice-skates knowing that yours are sitting in storage or do you forego the chance to enjoy yourself with newfound friends?
- this goes hand in hand with not being able to stabilise your life or beginning to build a structure of routines.

This is worth thinking about and discussing with your company before your arrival, if you fear this may severely cramp your lifestyle.

If your accommodation has to be paid by yourself and you are looking for a relatively inexpensive hotel to stay in temporarily when moving to Moscow, for the sake of access, it's best to stay within the Garden Ring, and preferably near the centre. Whatever happens, make sure you're near a metro.

Since the crisis, many hotels have become much more flexible in their pricing policy and it's worth asking around to find the best deal.

Mayor Luzhkov is intent on bridging the gap between high-priced five-star hotels and budget accommodation by focussing on the three-star range of hotels, so look out for more of these in the future.

Relatively expensive:

- **Sheraton Palace Hotel**
- **National**
- **Savoy**
- **Metropol Moscow Hotel**
- **Baltschug Kempinsky Hotel**
- **Marriott Grand Hotel**
- **Renaissance Moscow Hotel**

Relatively inexpensive:

- **Intourist** *(tel: 956-8400; Tverskaya Ulitsa)* (avoid breakfast and keep your door locked at all times) on Tverskaya Ulitsa, just up from Red Square (and due to be demolished), but recently was the target of a possibly Mafia-related bomb-blast.
- **Hotel Budapest** *(tel: 924-8820; 2 Petrovskie Linii)*
- **Hotel Ekaterina** *(metro: Paveletskaya)* close to Riverside Towers. Swedish-owned and managed. Small rooms, but clean.
- **Rossiya** *(tel: 232-5000; 6 Varvarka Ulitsa)* rather Soviet, but great location adjacent to Red Square.
- **Mayak-Park Hotel** *(tel: 142-2117; 25 Filievskaya Bolshaya Ulitsa; http://win-www.fe.msk.ru/hotels/mayak/mayak.html)* near Fili Park. Rated as clean, comfortable, friendly, reasonable restaurant, good security.
- **Ukraine Hotel** *(tel: 243-2956)* on Kutuzovsky Prospekt, with some rooms that have recently been renovated and are basic and clean. This is one of Stalin's 'Seven Sisters' buildings. **Intertur Moscovia** *(tel: 232-1039)* is a travel agent that rents a block of rooms at the Ukraine Hotel for a better price and better service than that obtainable through the hotel itself.

Expat guide: Moscow　　　　　　　　　　　　**3/Your first weeks**

- **Golden Ring Swiss Diamond Hotel** *(tel: 725-0100)* on Smolenskaya Ploschad, just near the old Arbat. The rooms (recently refurbished) and service are highly rated, and tariffs are low but climbing (about $165.00 per night).
- **Izmailovo Tourist Complex** *(tel: 166-3267; 71 Izmailovskoya Shosse)* grim-looking and Soviet, 30 or 40 minutes from the centre, but on the doorstep of the metro and the market.
- **Sovincentr World Trade Centre** *(tel: 253-2884; www.wtcmo.ru)* accommodation or Sovincentr Eridan apartment hotel)

Budget

- **Travelers' Guest House** *(50 Ulitsa Bolshaya Pereyaslavskaya, metro: Prospekt Mira, (tel: 971-4059 or e-mail: tgh@glas.apc.org)* recommended by many.
- **Russia Bed and Breakfast Home-stay** *(http://russiatravel.org/russiahomestay.html)*
- **International Bed and Breakfast** *(www.ibed.com; e-mail: ibb@dca.net; P.O. Box 823 Huntingdon Valley, PA 19006 1-800-422-5283 fax: 215-379-3363).* All accommodations are in private homes, and have English-speaking hosts. Single rates run at about $60 per night/360 per week or $75 for a double per night or $450 per week.
- **Goodwill Holidays** *(tel: 44 - 1438-716-421; fax: 44 - 1438-840-228) Manor Chambers, The Green, School Lane, Welwyn, Herts AL6 9EB UK)* will arrange home-stays with families.

Unsuitable long-term accommodation

New arrivals frequently find that the accommodation selected for them before their arrival is unsuitable and may move once or twice before they find what they are comfortable with. In this regard, it's worth considering whether the initial accommodation earmarked for you is under long-term lease which may oblige you to stay there for a year or more before you are able to move.

Clearing your goods through Customs

Both the British and American Embassies' Commercial Offices *(British: tel: 956-7477/fax: 956-7420; American: tel: 967-3412/fax: 956-4261)* hold lists of the latest rates. They will supply the information required over the phone.

Either your inviting organisation will organise to clear your goods at Customs or you will have to do it yourself. It's best to get the help of an English-speaking Russian within your organisation who has had experience in Customs clearing.

Whatever happens, don't expect an easy ride. You might be lucky, but the chances are the first problem you will encounter will be a delay, firstly in the arrival of your goods - depending on where they are coming from or in what manner they arrive i.e. air, road or sea.

Secondly, even though they might have arrived, there is likely to be a delay in clearing them. All sorts of issues come into play. for instance a change in the

27

Expat guide: Moscow   3/Your first weeks

law might hold things up, a certain member of staff may be unexpectedly on leave, there may be unexpected and premature closure of Customs clearing offices etc. All sorts of pieces of documentation will need to be taken to several different offices. You might spend one day getting through some of the offices you need to see, and then find you have to return for another day or two.

It is here that you will encounter the Russian love of bureaucracy. Whatever your feelings (and tempers do flare) remember that this is the way the Russians have done it for a long time, the officers in charge of clearing your goods are paid a pittance - which can lead to all sorts of implications, and the lack of English-speaking staff will compound the difficulty.

The best way to handle this problem is to take a relaxed, casual approach and estimate twice as long for obtaining your goods than you would normally expect. If you expect problems, at least you will be mentally prepared for them. If you don't have problems subsequently, at least you will be pleasantly surprised.

Getting around

It's also worth noting that there can be delay in obtaining registration for cars. One expat's company had purchased a second-hand car for his own use, but it spent his first month sitting in the company basement without him being able to drive it. In order to register it, it was necessary for him to fly out the country for 24 hours to renew his visa, as the remaining limit on it was too short for the registration authorities. Once that hurdle was cleared, it was then discovered that the car had a new engine in it which required a different form of registration, which almost began the entire process all over again.

If you do have a car at the ready, but no driver, you can always post a message at any of the school notice-boards asking for recommendations for drivers, or you could subscribe to the Expat-list (*see Chapter 7 - Keeping in touch*) which regularly has adverts from people offering the services of, and references for reliable drivers when they are preparing to leave the country.

Settling in

Depending on your set-up with regard to furniture and other essential supplies (pending the release of your shipment) you will spend much time coming to grips with where to buy which products (*see Chapters 4 and 12 - Finding accommodation/Staying solvent*).

One of the most important factors in settling in will be the need to establish a routine. Only then will things begin to fall into place, as routine provides a form of security against the hurly-burly of your new environment. Most expatriates will have a job to go to which helps to immediately start integration with other expatriates or Muscovites, depending on the make-up of the organisation.

Children will either go to school, or the parent who looks after them will be able to join a regular play-group (available even for babies).

The person most at risk when it comes to settling in is the stay-at-home spouse. For the purposes of this book it is assumed that the stay-at-home spouse is a woman. Women who stay at home, especially if they are in a flat or isolated in some other way, will need to make contacts quickly. The best means of doing this are to first get to know other wives whose husbands work for the same

28

Expat guide: Moscow   **3/Your first weeks**

organisation, and/or to join the IWC (International Women's Club) or other such group *(see Chapter 9 - Keeping busy)*.

If, as a stay-at-home partner, you are not in a hotel but in your own accommodation you will spend your first weeks hopefully sorting out your shipment, finding out where the best shops are for buying food and drink and other things that you find you need but have omitted to pack.

Once this is behind you, you're well and truly launched in Moscow living. Forget about the unpacking if you receive any opportunity to mix with others who are in the same boat as you are. This is crucial.

Seasoned expats will know this to be true from their experience, while newbies should hasten to adopt this approach. When you eventually leave Moscow, your most abiding memories will be of the people you have met, the friends you have made and the experiences you have shared. This is no time for you to sit behind closed doors and wait for the world to beat a path to it, for you will end up waiting an awfully long time.

The word 'network' is a reasonably new one in the business lexicon, though expats are generally expert at the practice. If you feel you want to take the initiative, you could form your own special interest group to meet at monthly intervals or more frequently.

Wherever there are expats, there is always a good reason for finding an excuse to get together.

Learning the language

So much has been thrown at you, but you will no doubt be aware (unless you speak Russian) that your major handicap is understanding Cyrillic. Learn the alphabet so that you can at least read it, and possibly learning to speak the language. Don't leave it too late to start learning the alphabet as the sooner you start to pick up words, the sooner you will start to feel integrated.

Discovery

Take every opportunity you can to visit as many different places as possible in Moscow. This will help you form a mental picture of just where you are in Moscow and distances to other places. It will also help you to gain some insight as to how the city operates. It may even help to swing things towards the positive, when you've unpacked and are without any focus. One of the best ways to do this is by taking the reasonably priced and very informative tours offered by **Patriarshy Dom Tours** *(contact in Russia: telephone/fax: 795-0927; e-mail: alanskaya@co.ru; In the United States tel: 1-413-584-9612; fax: 1-413-582-0014; e-mail: phughes (@crocker.com).*

Knowledge is mastery and the more you feel you know about your environment, the less threatened you will feel. Depending on your particular interests, you can ask Patriarshy Dom to organise a tour especially for you. The company also organises tours outside of Moscow and lectures focussing on different aspects of history.

4/Finding accommodation

There are a number of factors which you will need to take into account when looking for the right accommodation. One of the most important factors is the cost of accommodation. In Moscow, this often goes hand in hand with location, location, location. Once you have decided how much you want to pay and where you want to be, you will then need to go about finding accommodation, involving a process which can take many forms.

Whatever your criteria, remember that where you stay in Moscow will largely determine how happy your stay will be.

Cost of accommodation

If there is one reason only to be thankful for the crisis, it is that the cost of renting accommodation fell by up to 30 percent or more, putting the tenant in the driving seat instead of the landlord.

However in the first quarter of 1999, rents began stabilising as it became apparent that even though expats were leaving, there were still new ones arriving.

Nevertheless the supply of accommodation was such that expats were able to shop around and get the best deal. With many rentals (which often amount to 20 percent of an employee's package) paid for by Western companies, landlords have always been onto a good thing and know that in the plusher estates such as Serebryany Bor, they can charge an average of between $7,000 to $10,000 or more a month! In addition, smaller apartments in town can also go up to $10,000 per month, although some very comfortable accommodation is available in the $1,000 to $5,000 range. Expats such as students and those belonging to charitable organisations, as well as those whose bosses have cut their salaries, will often look at the $300 - $1,000 range.

For what is available, Moscow is more expensive, compared with other capitals, when it comes to accommodation costs. Despite this, the odd bargain can be found, such as the one with four bedrooms, Jacuzzi and open fireplace that went for $1,000. It's best to keep your ear to the ground for these deals. This amazing deal was on the market at the same time as others were expecting to get a one-bedroom or studio flat for the same amount.

Macro-economic conditions will mean that landlords prefer to focus on immediate cash-flow opportunities rather than long-term profitability, and for this they will be far more flexible in terms of accepting shorter deposits, or even no deposits at all (some of the more expensive housing estates used to demand a year's rental in advance). Tenants will also be in a position to ask for modifications at the landlord's cost rather than to simply accept a 'take-it-or-leave-it/shrug of the shoulder' attitude. Even pets may be admissible, whereas

Expat guide: Moscow   **4/Finding accommodation**

they were considered a big turn-off before the crisis, when landlords could pick and choose.

Your other option in this much more flexible market is to take a flat as an interim measure (subject to lease conditions) and look around for something better in the meantime, while you get to know the lay of the rental accommodation land.

Finding accommodation

The *Moscow Times* runs ads in all its issues for houses and apartments to let. You can also contact the estate agents who advertise in the paper or you can choose to go by word-of-mouth (a better proposition) and take on an apartment vacated or recommended by another expat. If someone is leaving, at least you won't have to pay commission and the departing expat will also probably tell you unreservedly about the down-side of the accommodation, such as whether the neighbours are noisy or the block is prone to burglaries.

If you can speak/read Russian or can ask someone to do so on your behalf, you can also consult: *Iz Ruk v Ruki* which has a wide circulation and is popular as a vehicle for advertising. You are likely to find better priced apartments in this publication without the 'expat factor' coming into play.

The Expat-list *(see Chapter8 - Keeping in touch)* is recommended for finding places vacated by expats, which might mean that commission would not be payable as an estate agent would not be involved. In addition, you could place an 'Accommodation wanted' notice and see what turns up.

Visit the following sites:

- **Russian Real Estate Net** *(www.russiarealestate.com)* and read the residential market profile published by The Western Group ONCOR International.
- **Blackwood Realty's** site at *www.blackwood.ru;*
- **Net Dvizhimost** at *www.realestate.ru;*
- **Penny Lane Realty** at *www.pennylane.ru;*
- **Sovincentr World Trade Centre** accommodation or Sovincentr Eridan apartment hotel at *www.wtcmo.ru*

Freelance 'estate agents' who are not affiliated with any company may be helpful, but remember to specify just what you want, otherwise you'll be taken to all sorts of apartments that are not to your taste and probably out of your budget specifications.

During the boom times there were many freelance 'estate-agents' around, but some expats have had bad experiences with them. One urban legend occurred where prospective tenants have been shown flats, a deal was struck, only for the new tenant to find that the owner arrived in the middle of the night to ask what the tenant was doing sleeping in his bed! Others have cited instances where the landlady expects you (after you have moved in) to put up her relatives on the couch when they visit from the country.

Russian and Moscow law oblige realtors to hold licences. In effect, therefore, you are breaking the law by not using a licensed agent, even though you may be saving yourself extra expense.

Expat guide: Moscow   **4/Finding accommodation**

Find out if the estate agent will interface between yourself and the landlord after the lease is signed. In this regard an estate agent who can speak reasonable English, is better than one who can't.

Estate agents usually offer to take you to view accommodation options in their own car, so don't work with one that doesn't. Be clear about just what charges you are liable for before you use the services of an agent.

They normally expect you to pay one month's rental upfront once you find a flat, and then they like to disappear (unless it's a company). However, bearing in mind the market situation, you might want to try to put the onus of payment on commission on the landlord (or even consider splitting), though he/she might try and get it out of you in some other way at a later stage.

Don't allow yourself to be browbeaten, nor into being forced into making a hasty choice. Speak with a number of estate agents to get a good cross-section of apartments.

Because many of the larger agencies cater to foreigners, they are often more interested in showing them higher-priced apartments. There have been incidents when an apartment for say, $1,000 is sought and only those for $2,000 plus have been shown which in effect, disregards the client's brief. Make sure that you are listened to and shown what you ask to see.

The smaller Russian-oriented agencies may not charge as much as the larger agencies in terms of commission and are more likely to show you cheaper apartments. Before you are shown an apartment, clarify whether they expect you to pay a fee for showing you the apartment and refuse to pay it if they do.

Of the smaller Russian-oriented agencies, Olga Vladimirovna at **Agency Atlantik** *(tel: 233-3015/233-5415)* has been recommended.

Sample list of estate agents and their contact details

Company	Telephone	Fax	Commission* subject to change	Short-term leases
Barin's Realty	956-2461	230-6061	one month's rent	yes
Blackwood Realty	915-1400	956-3307	one month's rent	rarely, open to negotiation
Center 2000	937-4856	937-4857	10%	no
Delight	926-4222	926-4904	one month's rent	no
HIB/Collier	258-5151	258-5152	N/a	yes
Hines	785-0500	785-0510	N/a	no
Home Sweet Home	246-0828	246-0828	one month's rent	yes
Penny Lane Realty	954-0041	237-3006	one month's rent	minimum: three months

Expat guide: Moscow   **4/Finding accommodation**

Examples of suburbs and price-range

Expensive	Moderate	Inexpensive
Arbat area	Belorussky Vokhzal	Prospekt Mira
Frunzenskaya Nab.	Tsvetnoi Bulvar	Kurskaya
Patriarch's Pond	Kuznetsky Most	Tatarskaya
Tverskaya/Pushkinskaya	Komsomolsky Prospekt	Taganka
Rosinka	Kutozovsky	
Serebryany Bor	Bolshaya Yakimanka	
Syetun	Chisty Prudy	
House on the Embankment		
Park Place		
Pokrovsky Hills		

Rentals for the above vary depending on, first and foremost, whether the economy is in boom or bust cycle. After that, apartment size, condition, seller's disposition, the negotiating abilities of both partners and the overall state of the building and its age are factors that should be considered. Condition will depend on whether it is a Western *remont**, semi-Western *remont* or Russian *remont*. (* *remont = renovation*)

Sample rent for different sized apartments*

Rooms	Western renovation	Russian renovation
1	800 - 1,000	300 - 700
2	1,000 - 1,400	500 - 900
3	1,500 - 2,500	700 - 1,400
4	2,000 - 3,500	800 - 1,900

*(December 1998; variations depend on location)

Sample guide to apartments available early 1999

Area	Size	Features	Rooms	Cost
Metro Pavaletskaya		beautiful, spacious, on banks of Moscow river, Stalin era, unfurnished	2 rooms	$700
Near Taganka	100sqm	3 balconies, two entrances, remodelled, minimum furniture		$3,400
Two blocks from Pushkin square	large	large balcony, and foyer, quiet street, Euro-*remont*, lots of light, safe, furnished/unfurnished,	3 rooms	$2,000

Expat guide: Moscow   4/Finding accommodation

Area	Size	Features	Rooms	Cost
		washing-machine		
Near metro VDNKh		fully furnished and equipped, park nearby	4 rooms	$2,000 neg
Near Chisty Prudy	120sqm	fully renovated, unfurnished		$1,800
metro Frunzenskaya	62sqm	Western *remont*	2 rooms	$1,500 neg
Olimpiskiy Prospekt	120sqm	two bathrooms extra toilet, two balconies Security guards overlooking park	3 rooms	$2000
Tverskaya		sound-proof windows washing-machine	2 rooms	$1,000
Tverskaya		warm floors, high ceilings, balcony, plenty of light	3 rooms	$3,500
Pushkin Square		washing-machine, plenty of light, secure	3 rooms	$2,000
Tverskaya		furnished, central	2 rooms	$1,000
Near Pushkin square		furnished washing-machine	3 rooms	$1,500
Olimpiskiy Prospekt	120sqm	furnished wooden floor 24 hour security two balconies	4 rooms	$2,000
Olympic Penta area	180sqm	unfurnished, or furnished to tenant's requirements; video security, three full bathrooms, sauna, Jacuzzi, panoramic view. All mod cons	5 rooms	$7,000
Patriarshy Pond	180sqm	winter garden and huge hall. Two bathrooms	4rooms	$4,500
metro Proletarskaya		colour TV, high ceilings secured entrance	2 rooms	$300
metro VDNKh		fully equipped, near park	4rooms	$2,000
Olympic Penta area	195sqm	on three levels. Latest appliances, designer furniture		$9,000 (neg)

Type of remont

The word '*remont*' roughly means 'conversion' or 'rehabilitation'. Moscow has, in recent years, climbed on the *remont* bandwagon, once landlords realised that by improving their apartments, they could obtain better rentals. When looking for

Expat guide: Moscow   4/Finding accommodation

accommodation, remember to specify to the estate agent whether you want something that is either:

- **Western *remont* (Euro-*remont*)** generally means converted to Western standards. In other words you can expect to find standards that would not be out of place in a similar apartment in the West. Indeed, some Western *remonts* are amazingly luxurious.

- **Semi-Western or semi-Russian *remont*** (same thing) is where the owner has gone part of the way to a Western standard but some typically Russian aspects remain. For instance, one expat had an apartment where the bathroom was fully upgraded including black Italian bath and basin, fully-mirrored sliding doors to the cupboard, and Western-type wall tiles. The only fly in the ointment was that Western-type materials had been installed with inferior workmanship, and within a few months of the tenant moving in, many of the tiles simply fell off the wall and smashed. In addition, the plug fittings on the wall kept coming loose, and the light switch fittings did the same.

- A **Russian *remont*** is when Russian materials have been used, so for instance even though the carpeting is new, it is not of good quality, or if the walls have been repapered, they have chosen a busy Russian pattern which is often anathema to the Westerner's eye and taste. Many Russians are coming round to the Western belief that the best way to decorate an apartment for minimal inconvenience is to have plain, sober-coloured carpets, and walls which are mostly pale, or white thus increasing the illusion of space and light which are often both needed in Russian apartments. Beware of the scam whereby the landlord agrees to requests for a certain amount of *remont*, asks for upfront payment and doesn't deliver the goods, or even disappears. This is probably less likely to occur these days, as landlords will have their eye on a longer generation of income instead of a potentially empty flat.

Remonting yourself

Opinions are divided regarding the cost of *remont* for the foreign individual and this is something that would take much, potentially costly, trial-and-error to determine.

However, stripping and painting of a 20sqm room is calculated at taking two days work for a good craftsman. Given that drivers are paid $600 per month for, say, a 40-hour week you could make a calculation that might reflect the required skill. Of course, the state of the economy and supply/demand scenarios are always crucial when judging payment.

Some might say that it takes more than two days work to strip potentially many layers of stubborn Russian wallpaper in a room of this size and paint it with one to two coats of primer plus topcoat and quality drying time. Others say it is possible to find those who would do the work for about $5sqm.

One team that offers general *remont* services has been highly rated by expats for honesty and reliability, can be contacted through Lelya *(tel: 932-5285)* Another is **Grisha & Co** who are said to be reasonably priced and reliable, can be reached at 372-7260 in the evening. They speak Russian only. A third team

Expat guide: Moscow   **4/Finding accommodation**

can be contacted at 414-2139. Juri has years of repair experience, has reasonable charges and is highly recommended.

Dima (*tel: 208-0511*) limited English, sister can translate) is highly recommended as being energetic honest, dependable, and a hard worker who can do: wallpapering, carpentry, tiles, sanitary-ware, painting, carpet/floor installation and charges in the region of $50 per day.

It's best to take on a team that has been recommended by other expats. Before commissioning them, ask to see previous work and their licences, in addition to a breakdown of costs, guarantees for workmanship. Never pay up front except for supplies.

Remember that during *remont*, the issue of asbestos fallout comes to the fore if the apartment has previously not been renovated. Ensure that the team you hire will take adequate measures to tackle any asbestos dust.

Old or modern

Old apartments usually have pleasantly high ceilings and attractive wooden parquet flooring. Rooms are also of a generally larger size and can often have attractive features. 'Modern' is more likely to be the buildings Stalin built during the 40s and 50s or the Kruschev buildings of the 60s which generally lack charm and have smaller-sized rooms. Some older-type apartments which were obviously built for the party *nomenklatura* in Soviet days are extremely spacious and well-designed. You're lucky if you get one of these.

Furnished or unfurnished

This depends on whether you are shipping over your own furniture or not. Before deciding on a furnished apartment, make sure it has everything you need. This may include dishwasher (not always included), washing-machine (often included, depending on rental), microwave (not often included), radio/hi-fi, TV and/or video system.

Don't let the landlord get away with supplying only net curtains. The best is heavier curtains (*see* **Curtains**, *below*) which will help to block out any draughts during winter and long hours of daylight in summer (especially in the early morning). Other optional items include table or floor lamps, carpets, vacuum cleaner (if you are expected to keep the carpets clean), broom, small brush dustpan, bedding, crockery, cutlery, pots and pans, kettle, toaster and glasses. Depending on what deal has been negotiated, fully, partly or unfurnished, and depending on what you have brought with you and whether your goods have been cleared by Customs, you might land up in a place with six knives, forks, plates, pots and saucers but without the little essentials that you don't think of until you miss them. You may be missing a tea strainer, a sharp knife, an egg spatula, a garlic crusher, sieve or colander, chopping board, tea towels, bedding and pillows which means you'll have to go out and buy them. Beware of buying too much, as you will have to get rid of it before you leave or they may end up as duplicates in the place you call home.

Unless you are particularly attached to your furniture, it is not really worth bringing furniture, as it can all be bought in Moscow. On the other hand, you may well be able to sell it to Muscovites or other expats if you do bring it, when you

37

Expat guide: Moscow   **4/Finding accommodation**

leave, though you will have to check the terms of your work permit to see if you are legally entitled to do so, or are expected to repatriate all your goods.

It's vital that you agree prior to signing the lease documents just what you expect to have in the apartment, as you will probably not get anywhere if you request these after you move in.

If it happens that despite everything you need to buy furniture, don't expect to find many second-hand furniture shops in Moscow. Rather try the Expat-list or go by word of mouth.

The **Domino** Stores on Pyatnitskaya, Oktyabrskaya and Komsomolsky Prospekt have some middle of the range furniture. Although the opening of the huge and first of five **Ikea** stores is planned for the first half of 2000.

For those with tighter budgets, there's a shop just past the Panasonic shop, and another between the metro and the Panasonic shop on Ulitsa Polyanka that both offer assemble-it-yourself furniture. Also try the shop with Russian-standard furniture at the bottom of Strastnoy Bulvar on the Bulvar ring.

The *khozaistvenni* store down the road from McDonald's at Kievsky Vokhzal has cheap furniture.

Mattresses are widely available: try the **Elbourg** company, located in 'Rodina' cinema, next to 'Semenovskaya' metro.

You could also try the **Grand** furniture store on Leningradsky Shosse which has Russian and Belorussian mattresses for sale. On Kutuzovsky Prospekt, there are two (Soviet style) Univermagi (i.e. Universal Magasini) and both have mattresses of different sizes available of reportedly not bad quality. It's possible to purchase orthopaedic mattresses at several major Russian department stores for between $350 - $500, depending on size.

Furniture repair

Volodia *(tel: 702-4128)* is highly recommended as a furniture repairman, but his English is limited. Another repair option can be contacted at *tel: 945-1676,* although only Russian is spoken.

Curtains and loose covers

If you're looking to make your own home furnishings, there are tailors about who would be able to make loose covers and curtains. In addition to making clothes and doing alterations, **Oleg** *(tel: 113-0356)* (he speaks only Russian) also does home furnishings. His prices are said to be reasonable and his method of work flexible, in that he will come to your home or office to do measurements, and also to drop off the finished product.

Try **Olga** *(tel: 336 8244)* who apart from being a dress designer and tailor, can also make chair covers inexpensively.

If you have not bought curtaining material (you're not likely to as you won't know the size of windows upfront) you will be able to buy curtaining material at **Dom Tkani** at Gagarin Square, Leninsky Prospekt. There are also a couple of curtaining shops on Komsomolsky Prospekt (*tkani* is the Russian word for fabric).

Boomerang, an Australian company that makes up curtains, can be contacted through Richard Mason *(tel: 954-3101 or e-mail*

38

Expat guide: Moscow   4/Finding accommodation

boomerang@glasnet.ru). The company will bring samples to you for selection in your home or office.

Gardtex on Savvinskaya Pereulok sells a variety of curtain material as do curtain shops in TsUM.

Size/number of rooms

Apartments are usually listed according to the number of rooms they have. This includes the bedrooms, living room and dining room, but not the kitchen and bathroom, so for example, a three-roomed apartment might be a bedroom, living-room and dining-room, or two bedrooms and living-room which can double as a dining-room.

Apartments are also listed by size, e.g. 100sqm which is enough to accommodate a family of four reasonably comfortably. 50 -75sqm might be suitable for a couple or single person, while 75 - 100sqm might be tight for a family with two children. Anything above 100sqm is verging on the spacious, and of course 200sqm is positively palatial.

Surroundings

Being new to Moscow, you will not know which area is better than another, but you should not go too far wrong if you judge the breakdown, given earlier in this chapter.

Being more specific, it's worth checking out the proximity of green spaces to the apartment, as this can provide much needed relief when city-living becomes oppressive. It also means that you can walk or relax there if you need to, without having to take a metro or drive by car. This is especially important if you have children or pets. In this regard, a flat near to a playground can be a boon for apartment-bound children. Look at the state of the playground and whether it has been maintained or not. This will give you a clear indication of the prosperity of the neighbourhood.

Consider also the view you get out of your window. Gazing at another grey apartment block directly opposite your living room window can get you down.

Anything that faces onto the river or a green space can help to keep your mood up when life or the weather get you down.

Consider the noise of traffic on the streets below. Major roads such as the Ring, Frunzenskaya Naberezhnaya, Leninsky Prospekt, Kutuzovsky Prospekt, Leningradsky Prospekt can be wearing if you are not used to it, as traffic starts before 06.00 continuing well into the night, until perhaps 01.00 or 02.00. If you are looking at a place in winter, remember that traffic noises are drowned by the double-glazed windows, which will be kept shut for the duration of winter. It means that in summer, when you want to open the windows, you could be in for a nasty surprise. In addition, traffic volume decreases in the winter, as many people prefer to put their cars away for the winter and take the metro instead.

Is there a restaurant or bar very near by? Can you put up with the noise of late-night revelers every weekend?

Are the surroundings either regularly cleared of snow in winter or swept daily in summer? This can give a good indication of the level of maintenance afforded to the area. Some areas are maintained so well, that throwing a cigarette

Expat guide: Moscow   **4/Finding accommodation**

butt in the gutter would be enough to induce guilt. However, there may be other poorer areas where cleanliness is not so prized.

Pets

There was a time when pets were taboo, and owners had to sneak them in or compromise in other ways. Now, the shoe is on the other foot, as landlords are far more conciliatory towards having animals. As is the same everywhere else, the larger and potentially more destructive or messy the animal, the less welcoming the landlord might be, although some are now prepared to factor in the cost of post-pet repair into rental charges.

Distance from office/school

This will, of course, be an important factor in terms of comfort and speed and general convenience. An apartment that is ten minutes from the office and which only involves taking one tram or not changing metros, is better than one that is further away. If you choose to live in a place like the Moscow Country Club, Rosinka or Serebryany Bor, you will have to take into account travelling times of 40 minutes one-way or more, depending on the weather. During heavy snowfalls, some inhabitants of these areas have been stuck in a gridlock en route to their homes for up to two hours. If you have children who will be ferried to and from afternoon activities and visits to friends, this will also be an important consideration. In general, many of the advantages of living at a place like Rosinka, such as indoor tennis court and swimming-pool, bowling, aerobics facilities, ice-rink, roller-blading facilities and residents' interest group may or may not cancel out the inconveniences of the long distance. It depends what is more important for you.

Find out what parking facilities are like if you have a car, whether it might be possible to rent a mini-garage and at what cost. Look at the cars parked in the area: are they later model cars or rusty old bangers? Are there a number of cars with yellow numberplates - indicating that there are other expats living in the area. Are there many Mercedes and other flashy cars - indicating a Mafia haunt.

How far away is the nearest metro station? A walk of up to ten minutes is optimal, but anything over that can be a little far, especially in winter.

Security

Security in Moscow is a major consideration. Apartments with an external keypad and domophone are preferable to those that don't have any. Those with concierges are worthwhile as well, as they keep an eye on who has access to the building and may be of some help in an emergency.

Look at the door of the apartment. Some can have up to seven locks. This may simply be a case of extreme precaution, or it may indicate that the flat is in a problem area and the owner expects trouble. You won't have to lock each and everyone of them whenever you go out as it will take you ages especially if you're in a hurry to go out, say, in order to take children to school on time, or if you're in a hurry to come back in (you need the bathroom/loo). Simply lock the biggest lock while you are in residence in the flat, but lock all the locks if you go away for a holiday or overnight.

Expat guide: Moscow   4/Finding accommodation

Elite complexes

There are a few elite suburbs or estates and complexes which have been colonised by expats over the past few years. Of these, **Rosinka**, with 220 houses, was one of the first housing developments to feature Western-style amenities. Its major disadvantage is that it is about an hour's drive from the centre of Moscow. Some refer to it as an 'expat ghetto', as the majority of tenants are expatriate, though there are Russian tenants as well.

If you live on such an estate you will have the benefit of a close, like-minded community with access to a sports hall, enclosed swimming-pool, shop, hair dressing salon and community activities, but you will be far from town and unable to find out what 'living like the Russians' is like, if that is your interest. In other words, it will divorce you from the Russian experience and by the time you leave, you may feel you have not really got to know Muscovites as well as you may have wanted to, because your opportunities will be that much more limited than if you had lived in town. However, if your interests lie in maximum security, sporting amenities and the opportunity to mix with expatriates, then you will not be disappointed. Rosinka (59ha) offers four types of homes ranging from 150sqm to 300sqm with rents starting at $6,500 per month up to $9,300 maximum.

The newest such project is the $100m-**Pokrovsky Hills** (15ha) in Northwest Moscow, which with 260 houses, is the largest undertaking of its kind. Adjacent to the housing estate is the new 1,200 pupil Anglo-American school, scheduled for completion in August 2000. The complex will also feature a supermarket, man-made pond and other Western amenities. Only 13km from the Kremlin, it is not as far out as Rosinka. Four styles of house will be available: the smallest (134sqm) available from $6,900 to the largest at 207sqm renting at $9,900 per month. Three- four- and five-bedroomed houses will be available.

Pine Forest Estates in the south of Moscow (12km from the MKaD) is fully secure, and with prices from about $6,000 a month, luxurious. Houses feature gas fires, saunas and Jacuzzis and the complex boasts a swimming-pool, hiking trails and tennis courts.

Syetun in South-western Moscow on Ulitsa Minskaya is the closest to the city and although it is not in a marvellous location, it is said to be more expensive than Rosinka.

Golden Keys is a complex across the road from Syetun with all modern conveniences and entertainment facilities.

Park Place located down the far end of Leninsky Prospekt (113/1) near the Anglo-American (due to move in 2000), Japanese and German schools, is not that far away from the centre. It is comprised of a number of high-rise blocks centred on a facilities section which includes hairdressing, supermarket, bookshop, café, sports club, business centre, restaurant and exchange bureau. Quite a number of diplomats live here, and living here could also help to divorce you from Russian life, if that's what you want. There is a forest across the road which is useful if you need to get out and about.

Serebryany Bor in the north west, is on a tree-filled island in the Moscow River and although not run as an estate, pockets of houses are enclosed in the form of small estates. Most of these types of houses are Swedish-designed and built in beautiful, wooded surroundings. Serebryany Bor as a whole does not have great amenities and also houses the large private dachas of rich Russians.

41

Expat guide: Moscow   **4/Finding accommodation**

There is ample opportunity to walk, and cross-country ski in the rural surrounds and in summer, boating and fishing are popular with Muscovites. It is quite a distance from Moscow, with commuters citing times of about 40 minutes travel in good conditions, though this can more than double in snowy conditions. Rents in the mini-estates for the fully furnished and maintained houses range between $6,000 and $15,000.

The **Moscow Country Club** offers wooden log-cabin type homes varying in size from 184 - 309sqm with their own fireplace, sauna and wooden floors together with use of hotel and conference centre resort facilities (including golf course) and set in a 120ha birch forest. Rentals are pretty steep, but then facilities are pretty luxurious.

Asbestos

Be careful of selecting unrenovated apartments or offices with flaking asbestos partitions as the extent to which chrysotile asbestos is used in the building industry in Russia far exceeds its use anywhere else in the world.

With the ongoing *remont* of apartments, asbestos is often ripped out without precautions being taken to prevent 'fallout'. City authorities are still said to use it for insulation of heating pipes, and old pipes can sometimes be seen lying around on pavements for months.

Heating

Heating is supplied on a subsidised basis by district authorities over the winter. Usually each apartment block has the capacity to regulate the thermostat for the building. Where weather is very variable over a few days, they might be caught short, i.e. if it's warm, the heating will be turned down and if a cold snap follows, it will not be warm enough, or if they have the temperatures on at 25 and it suddenly turns warm, you might find yourself opening windows to obtain some relief from the stifling heat. Try to get your landlord to pay the minimal heating costs. It will save you time and effort.

Gas

Mosgas *(emergency tel: 04)* is the authority to contact for any gas queries or suspicious smells. Don't risk speaking to anyone else who purports to be a gas expert. Mosgas has the experience, the licences and the know-how to deal with most of the gas problems you are likely to encounter.

Electricity

Make sure you know where the fuse box is when you move in, and what to do in the event of a power cut. Generally, electricity supply is reliable. Electricity is subsidised in Russia, hence its profligate use by many. Again, you may expect your landlord to pay the small electricity bills.

You may be in a situation (rent-wise) where you can't really expect to rely on your landlord for most breakdowns. If you seek electrical items such as fuses, check the hardware store (and the market outside this store) at the beginning of Bolshaya Dorogomilovskaya Ulitsa (metro Kievskaya). Alternately, if the fuse is

Expat guide: Moscow   **4/Finding accommodation**

also European standard, try one of the Western hardware stores such as **Abitare** on Marshal Zakharova.

Alternatively there are **SVET** stores dotted around the city while **Renlund** (Malaya Gruzinskaya Ulitsa) or **Bauklotz** (near metro Sokol) are likely to have a broader variety of goods, though they might be regarded as pricey.

If you import US-made appliances (110v), you can buy transformers from electronic kiosks, or at the electronics markets and computer stores. These will also need a couple of US power strips which offer surge-protection. This will allow you to obtain a multi-point 110v capability from one transformer.

It is suspected that voltage fluctuations in certain districts are caused by the managers of power plants who seek to 'economize' on their usage of fuel. Fluctuations will cause lights to flicker and cause a computer UPS (uninterrupted power supply) to switch on. However, most electronic items are built to accommodate a range of frequencies and most will not be damaged as a result. Nevertheless, surges which are caused by uneven spurts of power when the power is increased may damage sensitive equipment. If you notice your electronic clocks slowing in time on a daily basis, work out the deficit by taking the amount of minutes lost daily as a percentage of 24 hours x 60 minutes.

Some expats advise you to use a UPS with a surge-protector on it (or a surge-protector on its own) which should accommodate four or five electric items. Cheaper UPS/SPs are not likely to be as efficient as the more expensive ones.

There are good areas and bad areas for electrical surges and fluctuations. In the bad areas, you may encounter deep brown-outs (i.e. not quite a black-out) with 100w bulbs hardly illuminating enough to read by, and televisions that switch off. To find out whether it's only your apartment that's having the problem, ask your neighbours if their supply is sufficient.

A recommended electrician is **Yuri** *(tel: 827-6230)* who is able to rewire an apartment and who has been found to be reliable, efficient and reasonably priced.

Hot water

Remember that hot water gets turned off in city apartments for two to three weeks every summer to allow the district to clean and repair the hot-water heating system. Before you negotiate a lease, determine whether the apartment has an independent hot-water heater and if it doesn't, and the thought of three weeks of cold showers upsets you, ask the landlord to install one as part of the rental agreement.

If you accept an apartment which does not have water-heating in summer and decide to install it yourself (ask the landlord before signing), you could consider buying an 'inline' hot water heater. This would however, require up to 440v (most apartment supplies are 220v) to obtain a reasonable temperature and may require that you tap into a high-voltage line. This can be expensive and complicated and may mean that you have to obtain permits to have a meter installed that can take the higher voltage and enable you to pay for the electricity. This can cost up to $3,000.

Alternatively, you could get one of the tank types of heaters which don't heat water up instantly, but over a period of time. These supply 50 litres which would be adequate for two showers and which heats up to a temperature

43

Expat guide: Moscow　　　　　　　　**4/Finding accommodation**

regulated by a manually- controlled thermostat. They cost between $200 - 300 depending on make and size. The supplier may also be able to install them. Try the hardware market at 30 Frunzenskaya Nabarezhnaya and don't leave it till you see the dreaded notice tacked onto your apartment entrance door advising you when the water will be turned off, to avoid finding that water heaters have been sold out.

Washing-machines
(also see Chapter 12 - Staying solvent)
If you purchase a washing-machine from a large store such as **Domino**, you can specify turn-key installation and delivery. Don't turn your nose up at Russian made washing-machines, especially the Vyatka brand, which is recommended as being sturdy and reliable. They are also very cheap to buy, costing as little as $200.

In the absence of a washing-machine, visit the laundromat on Ulitsa Profsoyuznaya just a bit further down from the Interoptics building supermarket. Don't expect to find many laundromats in Moscow.

Fans

These can be purchased at many shops around Moscow (**Tisecha Meloche** near Gagarin's statue on Leninsky Prospekt, for example) or you should try the fan seller at **Gorbushka** outdoor electronics market who has about three or four varieties at prices ranging from $20 - 40. The **Univermag** outside the metro at Dobrininskaya on the Garden Ring has inexpensive fans starting at about $50.

Pest control

Many Moscow apartments are plagued by cockroaches, not only during the summer but also in the winter when apartments are kept heated. It is often the case that no matter how hard you try to keep your apartment pest-free, if your neighbours have a problem, this will keep on impacting on your apartment. There are a number of reliable pest-control firms which use safe and effective chemicals. Otherwise, if you're going to do it yourself, 'Combat' and other 'roach-hotel' type products are recommended. *(See Chapter 10 - Staying healthy)*

Humidifiers
Although these can be hard to find, they have been seen at **Global USA** and **Irish House** on Novy Arbat, **Unit Consumer Electronics**, *(tel: 956-9188/232-2444; 18 Ulitsa Yunnatov in the Sokol district)* **Planet Klimat** *(Bolshaya Lyubyanka just inside the Bulvar Ring)*. Prices range, depending on size from $60 - 500.

In the absence of a humidifier, you can fill pans with water and place them around the apartment near the heaters.

Copying keys

There are many reliable locksmiths around - look for a sign which says: *'Metalloremont'*

Expat guide: Moscow　　　　　　　**4/Finding accommodation**

Doors

A metal door with installation included should cost about $200 - 300 a time. One company that advertises its five branches as supplying and fitting doors in 24 hours, lock changing, video and audio security systems seven days a week is **Stal** *(tel: 127-9005; 5 Nagorny Proezd; 4 Novaya Ploschad; 17 Begovaya Ulitsa; 16 Kalanchyovskaya Ulitsa)*.

Pianos/piano tuning

- **Vladimir** *(tel: 575-0709)* is said to be able to move and tune pianos reliably, though he only speaks Russian.
- **Alexander** *(tel: 702-6440)* speaks Russian only and is also recommended.

Draughts

To keep draughts out, buy broad white, masking tape to seal uneven window frames. The tape is useful in that it doesn't remove paint and damage surfaces when you remove it in the summer. This is available at any builder's supply store. Some landlords will even offer to seal the windows for you themselves in order to preserve their surfaces to their liking. You could try the interim measure of filling stocking legs with rice or smaller grains as these can act as a good buffer.

Icy windows

The inner surface of your outer windows may fog and mist up and become icy as well. This is a result of warm air entering the space between the two windows. Apart from seeing that there is a tight seal on the inner window, it is recommended that you put baking soda between windows to absorb condensation. Others recommend rubbing dry white bar soap on the glass so that you achieve a good coating, and then rubbing it clear with a cloth.

Window-cleaning services

When summer comes round and you realise you can't see out your windows, nor do you want to try your hand at cleaning them yourself, **Crystal Cleaning Services** -Igor *(tel: 945-2477)* is recommended.

Using odd-job companies

If you do use someone who absconds with your money, remember that the chances are that he is not a properly registered tradesman, meaning that he may not pay all his taxes. In this case, contact him and tell him that if he does not keep to his side of the deal by a certain date, you will let the local tax inspectorate know about him and show them the receipt (remember to claim a receipt before he walks off with the money).

Signing the contract

Once you've considered all the above, and decided on an apartment, you will need to sign a contract. Not many rental contracts are notarised, but this does not

Expat guide: Moscow   4/Finding accommodation

mean that it would not be held up in a court of law. However, for numerous reasons, landlords would be reluctant to go to court. Many landlords charge more rent than what they declare in terms of tax.

To be on the safe side, you should have proof from your landlord that he has registered the lease with the tax authorities, for if your company is paying rental on a dubious contract, unpleasant investigations by the tax police could result (although the onus is on the landlord to come clean with the tax authorities). Some companies advise employees to have a rental agreement for the full amount of rent being paid, as well as monthly receipts for the payments, as this is what the tax inspectors will be asking to see.

If tax is withheld by the landlord, he may be charged a 100% concealment fee on the income together with interest, which will likely amount to more than the landlord has earned in total. It has been known during the boom period that landlords who had been outed by the tax police have taken out their wrath on their tenants by immediately attempting to hike their rental or changing locks while they were out, thus impounding their possessions.

It is probably better for the lease to be in the name of the individual employee rather than the firm, otherwise the firm, instead of the landlord, will be held liable for non-payment of taxes. By putting the lease in the individual's name, the tax obligation shifts to the landlord.

Not all landlords are money-grabbing New Russians. Many are, instead, old pensioners trying to eke out an existence by renting out an apartment while living with a relative.

It is wise to beware of any unwritten agreements between landlord and tenant. Find out what would happen in the event of you having to leave Moscow before the expected end of the lease and how much notice is required, or whether your finding a replacement tenant would be acceptable.

The more elite estates (see above) tend to impose lengthy pre-payment terms, e.g. six months to one year in advance. Unless the apartment is very expensive and desirable, it is unlikely in the post-crisis economic climate that you will be charged more than a deposit. It is very unwise to pre-pay rent in any other way than that stipulated in writing on your lease.

Agree with the landlord who shall be liable for repairs, should there be damages to the apartment, either as a result of tenant's actions, or not. Find out if you can rely on your landlord to help with repairs, whether you have to pay for them or not.

Find out whether rents are payable monthly or quarterly, and by which date they should be paid. Ask if you may terminate the lease agreement before it expires by giving 30 days written notice and whether this applies in reverse.

Determine whether your landlord will pay for water or electricity or whether you will be responsible for these very small, but time-wasting payments. This should be noted in the lease.

Note that the lease should specify the apartment number, building number and street name, otherwise the lease will not be valid. The lease should be in writing.

Check whether the landlord has the right to rent the apartment to you. If the apartment is not privatised and still owned by the state, you would need to obtain permission from the local housing committee (ZHEK) to rent it. It's also worth

Expat guide: Moscow **4/Finding accommodation**

ascertaining whether any other member of the landlord's family is registered at the same address, otherwise they may claim right of access.

Apartments rented for a year and a day or more are considered to be 'long term', whereas anything less is considered to be 'short term' and means you will not usually be allowed to sub-lease.

Prior to signing the lease you will need to examine the apartment to see that all that is promised is there. In addition, you should test all appliances to see that they are in working order.

Ask that specifications regarding the termination of contract be written into the lease.

Dachas

You could consider hiring a dacha (summer house) either as an individual or family, or together with a group of friends or colleagues. Having the use of a dacha helps to get you out of Moscow should you need a break. It's best to arrange for a dacha well in advance of the summer, as they are popular and difficult to come by in the summer. Many less sophisticated dachas will not be heated in the winter.

UPDK has excellent dachas not far from Moscow on their books. Some dacha areas to consider are: Archangelskoe, Barvikha, Gorki, Zhukovka-1, -2, -3, Peredelkino and Petrovo-Dalnee.

Also contact **Terra** *(tel: 418-7676 Russian)* which concentrates on the Rublyovsko-Uspenskoe Shosse area but occasionally finds dachas elsewhere.

A man with a van

If you need help with removals within Moscow contact:

- **Sergei** charges $10 a hour for moving you in his Gazelle *(tel/fax: 314-4730 (Russian/evening; 144-0765; or e-mail in English: iramo@com2com.ru) is* very highly recommended.
- You could also use the company **IWM-Intelorg** *(tel: 745-5154/5155)* which is also highly recommended.
- **Zhenya** *(mobile tel: 722 0893)*, is said to be careful with furniture and knowledgeable about packing goods for transit. He will assemble or dis-assemble furniture if necessary.

Domestic employees

In Moscow, you will be able to find nannies a-plenty, as well as part- or full-time cleaning help. Depending on the age of your children, and the hours you need them, some may wish to combine the job of nanny and cleaner/house-keeper. Don't be surprised if your nanny has a degree from the university or other diploma.

Babysitters charge locals about $2 per hour while American expats are said to be happy to pay $5 per hour and more. Depending on how much you want to pay, you'll have to negotiate. Some babysitters feel that they should be paid per child as well. Prices depend on supply and demand, as ever. During the crisis,

47

Expat guide: Moscow   **4/Finding accommodation**

babysitters were crying out for work and would have been happy to negotiate lower prices.

Some expats only want staff who can speak some English, while others welcome those who don't speak any English at all as they see this as an opportunity for their children to learn Russian quickly and painlessly. Though the thought of communicating by sign language until routines become familiar might be off-putting, many families have found the experience richly rewarding and satisfying.

The Expat-list and 'Kosmopolitan Kids' (delivered free locally but accessed by visiting *www.amcham.ru*) usually feature adverts for nannies and house-keepers with personal endorsements. These nannies are likely to be just as good as those supplied by the agencies. The added advantage of obtaining a nanny this way is that you will know they have worked for an expat family before.

Although word-of-mouth is the best bet when seeking a nanny, there are three nanny-agencies which you could contact if you prefer to have your nanny handpicked and your selection criteria are demanding:

- **Universal Service** *(tel: 443-0335)* Universal charges a one-off finder's fee of about $300 and about $400 per month. Individual lessons on their own, a few times a week are also available at about $8 per hour. Once a nanny is selected, hourly rates vary between $2.50 - $5.

- **Governor Class** *(tel: 250-0076)* charges $300 - 500 as a finder's fee. Hourly rates are between $2.50 and $5. The company can also locate teachers of ordinary as well as obscure subjects such as Chinese and saxophone.

- **Romashka** *(tel: 488-6175/942-0168)* charges $1,200 for a full six-month period ($350 for the first month and $170 per month for the next five months) and individual lessons cost $20 - 30 per hour. The company has been in operation for eight years and vets its nannies according to psychological selection procedures. The fee covers replacement nannies until the client is satisfied and also substitutes for nannies who unexpectedly cannot come to work.

Employing a house-keeper/nanny

Expected duties include cleaning, ironing, shopping, walking the dog, taking shoes to be repaired, cooking, washing and ironing clothes, putting them back in the wardrobes when clean and ironed, vacuuming and babysitting,

These are some of the attributes that other expats have found in their Russian housekeeping staff, so there is no reason not to expect the same:

- honesty
- kind-heartedness
- hard working
- full or part-time worker
- ability to look after pets

You will need to consider:

- how many hours a week is she willing to work
- what are her working hours

48

Expat guide: Moscow   **4/Finding accommodation**

- will overtime be extra or included in an overall salary
- salary
- rules regarding smoking
- use of the telephone
- absence due to sickness or other problems
- eating of meals in the house, either using your own food or hers
- vacation requirements
- transportation to and from work
- days off
- method of payment

Cultural quirks will mean that you will not share the same ideas as regards certain issues. One expat discovered that her nanny left her child on her own at home when she popped out to the shops, something that might be regarded as normal for Russians to do, but which might be quite unacceptable to other cultures.

Drivers

Drivers can be dedicated to a family and solely ferry around the children and non-working spouse as required. Many expats speak of happy relationships they've had with their drivers who have acted as tourist guides, messengers, translators, and even odd-job men. *(see Chapter 5 - Getting around)*
Driver's attributes:
- ability to either speak or read English, or both
- long experience and familiarity with getting around Moscow

Consider also
- if he has his own car and its use is required by you, will the amount you pay him cover petrol and repairs
- the cleanliness and good repair of his car
- how many hours a week he will work
- preparedness to do overtime (usually paid time and a half)
- considered to be reliable and trustworthy (check references)
- average compensation if petrol expenses are not taken into account (at the time of the crisis was around $600 per month - see also Chapter 5 - Getting around)
- rules regarding smoking
- use of the telephone
- absence due to sickness or other problems
- vacation requirements
- transportation to and from work if the car he is to drive is not parked at his home
- days off
- method of payment
- willingness to do errands
- willingness to work with children, also experience in this field.

49

Expat guide: Moscow   **4/Finding accommodation**

Checking references

To improve your chances of finding an asset rather than a liability, always rely on word-of-mouth to find your domestic staff. Always ask for references and do a thorough interview.

Check references for authenticity and ask respondents to rate honesty, reliability, work habits and attitudes of the potential employee.

Ask for full personal details and take copies of original passports to see whether they tally. Passports should be checked for date of birth, number, full names, nationality, place of registration and validity. Follow up on references and check that the person who wrote the references, really worked for a particular company at a particular time.

It follows that you shouldn't employ someone without this information, nor entrust keys of an empty apartment to them, even for a short length of time, as they may be copied.

Tell your employee upon hiring what security measures you expect them to use including who should be admitted to the apartment (such as maintenance workers) and how to contact you in an emergency.

Instead of informing a telephone caller that no one is at home, they should be expected to let them know that the occupant is unable to respond to the call at that moment, but will do so if the caller leaves telephone number and name.

If you are unsure of a person's purpose in visiting you, or their identity, there is no need to admit them to your home, and police are required to have a search warrant.

5/Getting around

With some 10 - 14 million people, Moscow is the largest city in Europe. Unless you come from another equally large city and given the language problem, the chances are you'll find getting around by whatever means to be one of your first and biggest challenges. As with other information in this book, it is subject to change and you will need to confirm what the latest regulations in force are. Also expect legislation not to be uniformly applied.

Geography
Street numbers
These are usually listed clearly on most buildings on a sign with white letters on a blue background. They may be illuminated at night. Apart from learning the Cyrillic alphabet in order to be able to decipher just where you are, it's worth learning numbers in Russian as a priority because if you use taxis, for instance, you'll need to be able to quote the number of the street you wish to go to, unless, of course you write it down.

If numbers are separated by an oblique as in 41/46 then this indicates a corner address with the second number indicating the address on the smaller of the two streets. Sometimes an address will be 10/12 which indicates that the place you are looking for is at two addresses on the same street. This will usually be the case if the numbers are either both odd or even and if there is no great disparity between them.

Street names
Street names are usually well displayed and are usually listed in an address before the number.You'll come across the following nomenclature for roads:

alleya	lane
bulvar	boulevard
most	bridge
naberezhnaya (abb. nab.)	embankment
pereulok (abb. per.)	side-street, alley, lane
ploshchad (abb. pl.)	square
prospekt (abb. pr.)	road
sad	garden
shosse	highway
ulitsa (abb: ul.)	street

Expat guide: Moscow   **5/Getting around**

What to do if you get lost

Getting lost, especially in your first few weeks in Moscow, can be daunting, as you truly will feel lost and will not be able to recognise your whereabouts nor identify them. It's always best to return to your starting point and try again from a different perspective.

Always carry a map around with you, if not of the city, then of the metro. Also carry around a list of telephone numbers, preferably numbers of people whom you can contact if you are lost. Remember you will have to be able to describe where you are, for if you don't know, you won't be able to tell them.

The majority of children can speak some English as they are taught it at school, whereas the older generation is less likely to be able to speak English. So your best bet is to ask a child for help.

Maps

Try to locate maps that have transliterations of names on for obvious reasons. A very detailed map that comes in the form of a full-colour book is the Moscow Atlas which shows detail down to apartment block numbers.

If you use another map, make sure it has a key on it which will help with deciphering Cyrillic, if necessary. Ask other expats which maps they recommend.

Walking

This is probably the best way to discover Moscow and get a taste of the city, especially in summer. Be careful of uneven surfaces, bits of metal sticking out of pavements, unguarded open manholes, and in winter, falling icicles and icy surfaces.

Crossing roads

Many roads need to be crossed by underground subway crossover *(perexhod)* as they are so wide (some are 16 lanes wide). Walking across large intersections that don't have underpasses nearby can always be life-threatening, and the best bet is to join a group of jogging pedestrians (you have to jog to get across in time before the lights change) to assure safe passage. However, the fact that the crossing zone is actually there does not ensure any safety, but is instead an invitation to try your luck.

Whatever you do, do not assume that you can expect cars to stop if you are crossing on a zebra-crossing. Cars do not stop for pedestrians at zebra-crossing! You could also be on the sidewalk and be at risk, especially when obstructions or slow moving traffic impede impatient drivers who need to get somewhere in a hurry. Note that it is illegal to cross a road which has a corresponding subway that can be used.

There is no reason to assume that simply because a traffic light is red for oncoming traffic that vehicles will stop at the light. Always check to make sure that traffic has stopped and remember not to leave it too late to cross the road, given the early starts some drivers like to make.

Expat guide: Moscow   **5/Getting around**

Driving
The GAI (first things first)

The Moscow traffic police are part of an urban legend. Most foreigners will get to know who the GAI (pronounced 'gayi' and standing for *Gosudarstvenaya Avtomobilnaya Inspektsia*, are before anything else, as they are everywhere on the roads. The GAI or State Auto Inspectorate, has been renamed the DPS, though it will take a while for expats to call them by another moniker. The name change is intended to signal a public relations move that should make them being perceived as friendlier to drivers. Unless unusual security threats need to be responded to, officers are now supposed to stop vehicles for document checks only at special permanent posts, instead of simply randomly.

GAI uniforms are easily recognised, but if you miss the uniform, you will instantly recognise them by the peremptory twirling and pointing of their batons, one of which has even been auctioned at a charity gala evening. When a GAI officer points his baton at you, you will have no doubt as to the fact that he wants you to pull over. If you are ever foolhardy enough to ignore him, he will radio on ahead to the next GAI officer who will be very angry when he finally gets the message across to you that you should stop.

Despite the fact that their official salary is only some $125 a month, they have a huge presence in Moscow. However, according to local hearsay, they have turned to other means of supplementing their income, which is not condonable, but understandable. Part of the rationale behind the name change is a renewed effort to cut down on bribery.

Talking to the GAI

Do not attempt to speak Russian unless you are confident in it. Otherwise keep on speaking English or whatever language you speak. Generally they just give up. However if you do engage in conversation, things could get complicated.

Make sure you have 100% of the required paperwork. One expat has been stopped 65 times in a year, while another has been stopped only once. One couple's registration plates were missing and they had to abandon their car then and there and walk home with five large bags of shopping.

What the GAI will ask to see

You need to have all your documents handy for a GAI check:

- *tekhpasport*: a document which displays your name and the registration number of your vehicle
- *tekhosmotr* certificate: a document which indicates that your car is roadworthy
- *doverennost*: a power-of-attorney document containing the owner's signature and confirmation that you are permitted to drive the car (if you are not the owner)
- your Russian visa
- the Russian page of your International driver's licence or a certified translation of your home driving licence

53

Expat guide: Moscow   5/Getting around

If you are driving a foreign vehicle, you may also be asked to show documents proving that you have been allowed to import a foreign vehicle.

It is not obligatory to get out of the car when stopped by the GAI, but it is always regarded as being more polite to do so. You may also be asked to go and sit in the officer's car to discuss the issue if money is involved.

Paying fines

As it is illegal for the GAI to accept money in public, you will be invited into the officer's car to pay the fine. You should not pay more than $10 depending on the offence (see 'Alcohol' below). Some expats say you should refuse point blank to pay anything and instead ask to be taken to the militsia. Always ask for a receipt.

The correct procedure for paying fines, however, involves the officer writing out a ticket and taking your driver's licence. You will then have to go to a bank (usually Sberbank) with a temporary driving licence issued by the officer, to pay your fine and then visit a GAI office specified on the report *(protokol)* with proof of payment, before you will be able to reclaim your licence.

When he takes your licence, the officer should issue you with a temporary driving permit which you are allowed to use for a month only, before you will be deemed to be driving illegally.

If you believe you have been wrongly fined, you can appeal the officer's decision. In this instance, he will have to draw up a report which you will have to sign, indicating whether you agree with his assessment or not. Your licence will still be confiscated, but you will have to visit GAI Foreigners' Department at 8 Stary Tolmachevsky Pereulok to see if your side of the story has prevailed over his side of the story. If it has, your licence will be handed back to you without you having to pay a fine.

What you need before you can drive a car

A licence and registration are mandatory if you are in Moscow for longer than six months and these are often checked on the road.
To obtain a licence legitimately you need:
* your passport and a Russian visa registered at UVIR
* a medical certificate: Ministry of Health form 083/U-89
* An international drivers licence and a photocopy with a translation into Russian
* Two 3.5 x 4.5 cm photographs.
* about $40

These should be taken to GlavUPDK Spetsavtotsentr; *(tel: 240-2092; 8 Ulitsa Kievskaya).* With a valid driver's licence you can obtain a Russian driver's licence by taking a written test. However, if your licence has expired you will need to take a full driving test.

Without a licence at all, you will need to attend driving school and pass both the written and driving tests. Schools should be approved by the GAI otherwise test results will be invalid. It is possible to take the test without going through a driving school, but your sponsoring organisation should submit a request asking the GAI for a waiver.

Expat guide: Moscow   **5/Getting around**

It may be possible to get away with showing your national drivers licence but as many are in English and may not contain a photograph of you, they might not accept it as a legal licence.

Power-of-attorney

Not just anybody can drive a car. If you are driving somebody else's car, you will need a legal document known as a 'power-of-attorney' empowering you to drive the car, this is particularly applicable to spouses, company drivers and colleagues using company cars. In addition, you will need a valid driver's licence, a car registration. The power-of-attorney must be notarized by a Russian notary public, or certified by a representative of the organisation that owns the vehicle. Notarised documents are preferable as they are easier to validate. Under Russian law, the driver bears full responsibility for all accidents he causes. The owner only has liability to the point that damage to the vehicle has been caused. In the event of a serious accident, criminal charges can only be brought against the driver.

International driver's licences

These are valid for six months from the date of your arrival, although many expats simply submit IDL's throughout their stay. When they expire, you need to take an oral test in Russian which will determine how well you know your traffic rules. The best way to avoid this is by occasional visits home where you obtain a new international licence which will extend your remit for another six months.

Alternatively, if you are from the US you can look up IDL or International Driver's Licence on the Internet, print out an application form and mail it to the US with a cheque and photographs, and a copy of your current valid US driver's licence. Some suggested sites are: *www.20thcenturyinsurance.com/polsvcs/Intldriv.htm* (issues licences valid for one, three and five years) and *www.sterling-offshore.com/idapp.html*. Otherwise you can obtain an application form by post by writing to : Attn: International Driving Permit, AAA, 1000 AAA Drive, Heathrow, FL 32746-5063.

If you are British, the UK AA will send you a International Driving Permit through the post for £4. You will then have to post the completed application together with a copy of your licence, photograph and cheque. Visit *www.theaaa.co.uk/membership/offers/idp.html* for the application.

How to obtain a Russian driver's licence

As mentioned above, you will need to take an oral test in Russian to determine how well you know traffic rules. Unless you are a diplomat, you will also have to undergo a medical examination.

The GAI department dealing with foreigners *(tel: 951-0864/3262)* is located at 8 Stary Tolmachevsky Pereulok *(metro: Novokuznetskaya)*.

Expat guide: Moscow   **5/Getting around**

Redeeming International Driver's Licences for a local Russian licence

This must be obtained within six months after arriving in Moscow at the Central GAI station for Foreigners, located on 8 Stary Tolmachyevsky Pereulok, office 15. The cost of processing used to be around $40 and an examination is not required. You will need your home country's driving licence and a health certificate.

The (unofficial) rules of the road

- The first rule of the road you should learn is that pedestrians must at all times give way to cars, despite what you may have learned in the West.
- The second is that if you wait half a microsecond too long at the lights when they turn green for you, you are likely to be hooted at. There's no point in getting upset.
- The third rule is that the GAI rule, and you do not ignore a GAI officer (see below).
- Don't insult anybody.
- The biggest vehicle always has priority
- Remember to switch on lights in tunnels
- Flashing your lights at another vehicle is regarded as rude
- Constant amber traffic light means proceed with care
- Expect frustration galore if you have to make a left turn. Nine times out of ten you will have to travel a few kilometres extra before you can find a place to do a u-turn, or you will have to devise ingenious methods of reaching your destination on the left by turning right.
- Watch out for people swerving unexpectedly to avoid potholes.
- The best time to get acquainted with Moscow's streets as a novice are in the evenings and on weekends when the streets are less congested, however, you will then increase your chances of being stopped by a *GAIishnik.*
- Don't be surprised if cars travel against the flow of traffic in reverse or mount pavements with impunity.
- Although passing on the right is illegal, you are still very likely to encounter this practice, so don't discount it.

Buying your own car

Since the devaluation, new Russian cars (Lada Zhiguli, Lada Niva and Volga) are far better priced than they were prior to the 1998 devaluation, with Volgas selling at some $4,000 and the others for less. It's been suggested though that if a car is so new as to have been built in a climate of financial constraint, it is likely to be a worse bet than a slightly older car. Before buying a Russian car, find out the procedures required for having it 'checked and fixed'.

If you buy Russian, you will get a car that is inexpensive to purchase and inexpensive to repair, as most Russians know how to service them. Some who've tracked the repair and service history of the Nivas say that its possible to end up paying an amount equal to the purchase price for repairs over three years. It's also said that it takes two years of repairs from the time you buy a new Russian

56

Expat guide: Moscow   5/Getting around

car, to iron out all the faults inherited from the factory. The worst disadvantage of Russian cars is said to be their lack of safety - they do not give much resistance in a collision, and brakes need to be replaced regularly. In addition, the inconvenience factor is heightened with the possibility/probability that the car may have to be jump-started more than once in the winter. Volgas, in particular, have a reputation for being slower to start than Ladas.

If the car is second-hand, ask if it has:

- anti-corrosion treatment
- alarm
- stereo
- winter and summer tires

If you are buying a new car, you will have to pay an extra $500 for these features on top of the basic model.

If you want to buy second-hand, your best and most cost-effective bet is to buy a departing expat's car. However, you could also visit Moscow's largest car market which is off Ryazansky Prospekt, or ask your company driver to recommend a good market. Also visit the website: *www.auto.ru* (Russian).

If you do visit a market with the objective of buying a car, you will need to take a reliable Russian person with you (or your company driver) who can check basic car functions, determine whether the odometer has been tampered with and negotiate a price for you. The most popular Russian car is currently the Niva (like a Russian jeep). The most luxurious Zhiguli model is supposedly the ninth model which is the most comfortable, but which for this reason is also the one that is stolen most regularly. If you are not fussy about colour, select a white car, which tends to be unpopular among car thieves and therefore is the least commonly stolen car. If you prefer dark blue or red, it might cost you an extra $200 for these 'fashionable' colours.

You can only buy a car from the market if you arrange for your Russian friend to register the documents in his/her own name. He would have to supply you with a power-of-attorney which would allow you to drive the car for three years. The power-of-attorney should be notarized by one of the many notary offices around.

Some expats wax lyrical about Skodas (made in the Czech Republic) saying that now their manufacture is overseen by Volkswagen, they have become excellent cars. The only proviso is that you should check your guarantee carefully and book your service through 'Spartak' on Volgagradsky Prospekt. Other issues to watch for if you are buying a foreign car is that BMWs or 4x4's are attractive to car thieves, expensive to service, and they may have low clearance, making them problematic over pot-holed roads.

Registering a car after local purchase

You will need to visit the DPS office at Tsaritsino, which is a fair way out of town, so make sure you go early in order to be there between 09:00 and 11:00. Ask a Russian friend to phone ahead and find out what times and days they are open. Take your passport, visa and work permit/accreditation documents (depending on what is in force at the time). It's recommended that you show a polite but forceful attitude to make sure things keep moving. The car will be

57

Expat guide: Moscow   5/Getting around

technically inspected. Expect to have to return a second and sometimes a third time.

If you wish to avoid the extra legwork, one solution would be to issue a power-of-attorney to a Russian speaking friend/employee (eg your driver) to obtain the necessary approvals on your behalf. You will have to make a visit to the licensing office, however, to collect your number-plates. If you have a reliable Russian friend or employee, you can likewise get them to register the car in their name, and then give you power-of-attorney to drive and then later, sell the car. This option may be considered a little risky, but will cost a lot less than registering the car yourself. You have to pay a registration fee based on the value of the car... and of course, foreigners pay a higher percentage fee than do Russians.

Registering an imported car

Up until April 1999, companies were permitted to bring cars into the country on a duty-free basis, however new legislation required the payment of duty according to the vehicle's original value. A number of creative solutions to the problem of sometimes having to pay almost the entire value of the car in duty were mooted.

One idea was that the vehicle should be registered in the individual's name and that this could be achieved by driving across a border and then returning to Russia. You could then, apparently, obtain a six-month duty-free period of grace, after which you would apply for an extension. If this did not work, you could simply repeat the process of driving over the border again.

Parking your car overnight

Security depends on the area in which you live. If you park in the open, plan to be on the safe side, especially if you have a Western car, by using an anti-theft device of some kind. Many cars have alarms, some highly annoying in the variety of fancy tunes they produce.

Other options include parking in a fenced parking lot, or using the small portable metal garages (*rakushki* or seashells) that act as an eyesore and take up valuable space all over the city.

Buying a garage *(rakushka)*

Keeping your car in a garage will provide you with security and avoid the time-consuming need and bother of having to clear the snow off your car before work every morning.

These cost between $5,000 and $9,000 to buy. Alternatively you may be able to rent one. They are very small and only big enough to squeeze a car into, but it's what most people use, as buildings were not built with car owners in mind.

Because of the unsightliness of the *rakushki* and the waste of space their use involves, the Moscow City Government has embarked on a programme of building parking garages in residential districts. Each parking spot will be sold for about $8,500 and for that you will get a parking stall with metal doors and 24-hour security. Another option is available in the form of individual concrete enclosures which are sold for about $15,000 each.

Expat guide: Moscow   **5/Getting around**

Insurance

When looking for an insurance company you will firstly, need to ascertain that you are dealing with a reputable company that won't be blown away by the next crisis.

Liability insurance in Russia pays out comparatively low compensation if you hit a foreign car (and therefore more expensive to repair) or kill or injure a person. **Ingosstrakh,** *(12 Piatnitskaya Ulitsa)* a previously state-owned international insurer, is the largest insurer, and they tend to be more expensive than most insurers. **Kontinent Polis** *(tel: 926-0303)* ask for Svetlana Filipenkova who is a recommended agent, is said to be fast and efficient when it comes to paying claims.

Speed limits

Limits are 80km/hr on highways, 60km/hr on major roads, and less on side roads. However, on routes outside Moscow, the limit seems to drop to exceedingly low speeds such as 30km/h. Be very careful driving out of Moscow as the road is crawling with GAI. They're not that easy to miss as friendly drivers approaching from the other direction will usually flash their lights to warn you of their presence. Both in and out of town, the GAI aim a radar detector at your car and can determine whether you are over the speed limit. Fines are not huge as in the West.

Keeping in lanes

People change lanes recklessly, and often without using an indicator, so don't be too trusting.

Potholes

Watch out as some can cause major damage to your wheels and undercarriage, especially if you are travelling at speed and your car hugs the ground. Look out for other motorists swerving unexpectedly to avoid potholes.

Winter driving

Between October and March your car must have snow tires (though not if it is 4 x 4 vehicle). You need to indicate by means of a sticker on the back of your car showing what looks like an upside down 'M' whether you have snow-tires or not, as you will brake more sharply with them. You can be fined for not having the correct tires on your car.

De-icing windows

In winter, car windows tend to ice up easily. There are a number of de-icing fluids which you can use either by inserting into the spray tank in your engine, or by wiping with a rag. The cheaper types are not likely to work as well as the more expensive types of liquid. Vodka is always a good standby.

Expat guide: Moscow   **5/Getting around**

Parking

You can park where you like within reason. This is not as easy as it sounds, as it is estimated that there are three cars for every parking spot. Most buildings were built during the Soviet era when it was not envisaged that the number of cars would far bypass expectations. However, Moscow City Government is now obliging developers of all new buildings to include parking garages in their plans, which, it is hoped, will boost current capacity by about one third.

Many shops and offices have municipal parking attendants (identified by a badge) stationed outside, who give you a ticket and ask you to pay for a certain amount of time. Parking is relatively cheap, usually varying between $1 - 3.00 for up to 30 minutes. Parking fines are about $14. The sites are administered by the Moscow City Government and are identified by a large 'P' painted in white on a blue background, under which are what seems to be three coins with the length of time that you can park. You will need to rub off the date and time on the paper ticket given to you by the attendant, and display the card until your return, so that the cost can be tallied. If you do not comply, your car could be towed away.

There are only some six multi-level car parks as yet in Moscow although Mayor Luzhkov has plans of introducing dozens of new car parks in the next few years.

Drinking-and-driving

You are not permitted to drive after drinking. Don't chance it. You may be stopped and asked to take a breath-test. If you do not agree with the positive result of this test, you can ask to take a test at a specialist clinic. Fines vary between $100- $200.

There has recently been discussion in the Duma this year concerning the possibility of introducing a law which allows drivers one or two drinks only, so keep your ears open for any change in the law.

Security

Try not to make eye-contact with passengers in other cars. Try to drive with your doors locked. Use a device to lock the steering wheel in addition to a separate, portable locking device. Although others might pick up hitchhikers, avoid doing so yourself. Keep your car in good working order so that you minimise the risk of being stranded.

Number of passengers

You should not carry more than five people in your car unless your car is specially built to carry greater numbers.

Seatbelts

You can be fined for not wearing seatbelts in the front and if the rear of the car has seatbelts, these must also be used.

Expat guide: Moscow　　　　　　　　　　　**5/Getting around**

Children in front

Children are not allowed to sit either on the front passenger seat, or on a front passenger's lap.

Buying petrol/gasoline

In most petrol stations you pay for the amount you wish to put in your tank (price March 1999: around 18c/litre) at the cashier's window. After receiving a receipt, you then return to your car, fill it up to the desired amount (regulated electronically from the cashier's desk), replace the nozzle and drive off.

As the price of oil rose in 1999, there were occasional shortages of petrol at some petrol stations accompanied by increases in the price of petrol at the pump.

Some car owners have experienced the need to change spark plugs every three months or so to avoid jerky performance. This has been put down to the quality of the petrol. Most foreign cars should use 95-octane to obtain the best performance.

Accidents

Try to find a GAI (not difficult) if you require a police report (for insurance purposes), or if the accident has resulted in injury or death. If those involved agree that there were no damages or that the damages can be settled out of court, they are free to do so. If a GAI does need to be involved, you should then not move the vehicle from the site of the accident. To report an accident, dial the general police number at 02 or the GAI duty officer at *tel: 924-3117 or 923-5373.*

Carry bilingual accident information cards and forms in your car (ask your embassy). GAI should fill out an accident report and give you a copy of this. You need these for insurance claims. If you can't speak Russian and you have a mobile phone, try to get hold of someone who can interpret for you. Try and memorise the GAI officer's badge number for future reference. You will probably also have to visit an office in the district where your car is registered with all relevant paperwork (licence, insurance and registration) to fill out accident report forms. It's recommended that you take a translator.

Using your hooter/horn

Try to limit use of this to emergency situations.

Flicking of lights

This is not appreciated if intended to indicate displeasure.

U-turns and left-turns

Left turns are generally not allowed in Moscow (although they are allowed at some intersections). In order to reach your destination you will have to continue driving some distance past your intended left turning place and look out for a U-

61

Expat guide: Moscow   **5/Getting around**

turn sign suspended from wires hanging above the road. It is not permitted to do a U-turn in other circumstances.

Traffic lights

Many people do not observe them when they turn red and try to slip through while they can. If you are coming from the opposite direction, make sure you give some leeway to accommodate stragglers/rebels.

Signs on the backs of vehicles

Upside down M indicates a snow tires, whereas a teapot indicates a learner driver *(chainik)*.

What to carry in your car

In case you get stuck in a traffic jam, you should carry blankets (especially in winter) reading material, and drinking water. It's also recommended that you carry a set of triangles in case of breakdown, a small fire-extinguisher, first-aid kit and torch.

Car wash

Winter is the worst time for keeping a car clean. Within a few days of having your car washed it will be caked with soot and mud. The GAI insist that your number-plate should be visible and not caked with mud and they can pull you over and fine you if it is illegible. If the car is excessively dirty, they can also fine you. Therefore finding a car wash that's reasonably priced and reliable is imperative. Neither should you travel without clearing the snow off your car.

In early 1999, people were paying from the equivalent of $4 to between $6 - 12 for the car washes at service stations. BP is said to offer a service at about $8. If you have a Ford, the US IMPEX auto dealership will wash your car for about $3.

If you drive down Leninsky Prospekt (towards the centre) at evening rush hour, you can have your car washed by unemployed 15-year olds (or younger) while you wait in the traffic jam.

Car breakdown

Expats say the best form of help are passing motorists. If your car won't start in the morning, simply stand there with the bonnet open and pair of crocodile clips while scratching your head and a passing driver should soon stop to 'give you a light'. A small tip is usually appreciated. If there is something else wrong, they will also probably be able to help, as the engines of Russian cars are familiar to most drivers. There is no AA as such but road recovery firms such as 'Angel', may be of use if all else fails.

Expat guide: Moscow　　　　　　　　　　　　**5/Getting around**

Hiring your own driver

(see Chapter 4 - Finding Accommodation: Employing a driver)
The concept of having your own driver might be alien to you, though you should consider the following issues before you decide against having one.

You may come from a country where you are accustomed to driving on the left-hand side of the road, and you may not want to risk your life by changing your habits.

You may not mind changing your habits, but you may find the sheer size of Moscow intimidating, as well as the effort required to decipher the road signs.

You might simply need a driver who can ferry your non-working spouse and children from A to B which can be extremely useful.

Whatever your need, having your own personal driver in Moscow is no big deal as it might be in Western countries. The profession of driver is well-known in Moscow and many highly qualified people (physicists, rocket scientists) spend the rest of their working days ferrying people around. The bottom-line is that having a driver in Moscow can save you an enormous amount of hassle unless you are single and have no children, don't mind catching trolley buses or the metro which is very efficient, and have no great need to travel long distances every day.

After the crisis in 1998, the going rate for drivers was around $600 per month. This rate is negotiable depending on whether you supply the driver with your own car and petrol or whether he drives you around in his car using his own petrol. If he uses his own car, you will need to be able to compensate him for wear-and-tear repairs. Any overtime work should be compensated for.

Of course, it is always preferable to have a driver who can speak a little English. English-language ability, depending on proficiency, is compensated for about $100 - 300 per month.

Most drivers know the city like the back of their hand, and it will generally suffice to cite the address you want to visit and know how to explain whether they should wait for you or when to return. It's also a good idea to keep a copy of the Moscow Atlas map book in your car as it is extremely detailed and has some English maps in it.

When you spend a lot of time in the car every day, it can become lonely and boring if you can't chat with your driver, or even share comments on the latest car crash or traffic jam.

Drivers can simply be drivers, or they can become a very important part of your life. They will act as tourist guides, never missing an opportunity to point out a building of historical significance, or explaining the background to a street-name.

Many drivers are excellent with children, and often buy them sweets and small toys, picking them up and cuddling them when they had fallen and grazed their knees and drying their tears when they felt life has been unjust to them.

Of course, it's possible you will get a driver who is not all of the above. Do not stick with him but rather keep looking. Many drivers have years of experience with expatriates, which helps to smooth the way for the newcomer. They understand our foibles, and our vulnerabilities, and they know what to expect.

Expat guide: Moscow   **5/Getting around**

You could choose to hire a driver on a short-term contract, which should work out less than the monthly cost for a similar car in the West, taking into account the cost of buying the car, insurance, depreciation, petrol, maintenance.

Getting around without your own car

Car hire

A cheaper alternative to hiring cars from companies such as Hertz and Avis, is to use **Taxi Blues** *(tel: 214-6409, 212-4703)* which charges about $6 per hour for the first hour and less per hour thereafter. Their dispatchers call you at home when the car has arrived, supplying licence plate number and colour for easy identification. Trips to/from Sheremetyevo cost $14.

Almaz *(tel: 494-4019)* is another taxi company that is said to be reliable and reasonably priced. If you have a regular schedule, you could arrange for them to collect you for work at a certain time every morning and return you home or wherever in the evening. Almaz's fleet is a combination of Russian and foreign cars. They are also especially useful for airport runs.

Another company, **Taim-lug** *(tel: 151-1996; 151-5753)* offers Ladas, Volgas and foreign cars for rent starting from about $10 per hour

Taking lifts/hitch-hiking

Stand out on the shoulder of the road and make as if you are flagging down a car. Eventually (usually not more than a couple of minutes) someone will stop and ask you where you want to go. You will have to be able to convey your destination and ask them how much they would like you to pay them, generally in Russian. This is where it also comes in handy to know your numbers. In March 1999, informal rates were between $1.50 - 3.00 within the Garden Ring during the day.

We have had no problems with this form of transport, even with a family of five. Most drivers are chatty, kind and friendly. The later at night it gets, the riskier, especially if you are on your own and even more so if you are female. If you can't avoid this situation, try to memorise the car's number for possible future reference. Never enter or travel in a car with more than one person in it. It's wise to have your anticipated fare ready away from any other wad of cash, so you do not have to wave this in his face when paying.

Always agree the fare before departure. If you don't like what is quoted, (ask *skolka?* just say *nyet* and close the door) another car will soon be along. To indicate your destination, either have it written in Russian, or say the name of the street, followed by the number as in: *Prechistenka Ulitsa, dom 2.* You could also quote the name of the nearest metro, or a known building in order to indicate your destination. Only enter empty cabs, do not travel late at night. Some of them have meters. The tariff generally increases, the later it gets.

If you are in doubt about the driver, don't get in. If, after the ride has started, you feel something is wrong, do not hesitate to get out at the next opportune moment. It's best to sit in the back on the opposite side to the driver. It may also be wise to not give your exact destination, but rather one that is close by, if you are returning home

Expat guide: Moscow   **5/Getting around**

It is possible to book some taxis for an evening where you pay an hourly rate plus a booking fee.

Taxi stands are marked 'T' but taxis can also be hailed on the street. You'll also find them outside major hotels, railways stations and airports (watch out for exorbitant rates from Sheremetyevo Airport).

Lingua *(tel: 290-6324)* has English-peaking operators who will ask you for your name, address and phone number and will phone back with details of driver's name, car model registration number and expected time of arrival.

Taxi tariffs (official and unofficial)

After the crisis, taxi fares in gypsy cabs (i.e. anyone who stops for you) ranged from $1.50 - $4/5 within the Garden ring, depending on the time of day. Zhiguli owners seem to be readier to accept a lower fare than Volga owners. If you don't mind paying more, but want extra reliability, select the yellow cabs with the advertisement on the car's roof. They might cost more then the others do with a blanket fee, because they keep the meter running even through traffic jams.

Taxis from the airport

Although you might think you can flag down any car leaving the arrivals area of the airport on the upper level, in the logical assumption that it would be heading back to town, empty, you will find that the local taxi Mafia actually stop such cars and ask the driver to let you out so that you use them instead. Understandably, and because he does not want to get into trouble, the driver usually obliges. When you negotiate the fare, let them know (if you speak Russian) that you can take the mini-bus for a fraction of their rate. In 1998, the going rate was between $10 - 50 into town.

Some rate the green minibuses (route taxis) as very good in both directions. They do not stop at intermediate stops, with time taken depending on traffic from 50 minutes (light traffic) to 90 minutes (heavy traffic). You can catch them from the bottom of the departure ramp leading to the airport. Examine the route which is marked with prices and metro stop destinations on a notice to the side or back of the minibus. Luggage may be a problem if it doesn't fit under the seat, or on your lap or behind the last row of seats. You could get round the problem by paying extra to hire a seat for your luggage. Once you reach the metro, simply catch that to your destination.

Never accept an offer from the taxi touts standing at the exit gate to the departure area unless you want to pay $50 or more.

If you want to drive yourself into town, you can contact **Eurodollar** which has a kiosk at the airport prior to your arrival and arrange to have a car waiting for you. The tariff is about $50.

If you don't mind the walk to the Novotel hotel (about 10 - 15 minutes) you can catch its shuttle for free.

The company **Almaz** *(tel: 494-4019, Russian only)* charge some $13 for an outbound trip to the airport and $15 into town. If you call them in advance they can come to your apartment to collect you and also be there to meet you when you return to Moscow. You could also try **Taxi Blues** *(tel: 214-6409; 128-5957)*.

Expat guide: Moscow   5/Getting around

Avtoline shuttles run from Rechnoi Vokhzal metro to both Sheremetyvo I and II for about 50c one-way.

Public transport

The various forms of public transport are very affordable and generally reliable, especially the metro.

Trams and trolleybuses

These all cost the same (7c if you purchase tickets in advance or 10c if you buy them on the bus) and fares are payable for those aged over seven. The final trip of the day finishes at 01:00.

Fares are for a single trip regardless of the distance. You may not transfer tickets. It is normally possible to buy them from the tram drivers but check that you have not bought a fake. When you buy at the little kiosks outside the metro station, buy a long strip of ten for the sake of convenience.

You have to punch your ticket yourself in the strange contraptions situated at a number of places on the vehicle and then keep it available for rare inspection by an inspector who may fine you on the spot if your ticket is out of date or unavailable. Inspectors should show you ID when asking to see your ticket. You will probably be one of very few persons on the tram who punches a ticket. Others are either riding free or have monthly passes which can also be purchased at the small kiosks near the metro.

Tickets are issued per quarter (denoted by different coloured print) and are not considered valid outside of the dates shown. You can buy a monthly travel pass for about $3.50.

Tram stops are identified by a sign painted with a large 'T' hanging over the road from an over-head wire. If you are driving, you are not allowed to overtake trams when passengers are alighting. Instead, you must wait behind the tram until it is moving again.

A sign with the letter 'A' (to denote autobus) indicates the location of a bus-stop. Certain kiosks sell maps of the transport grid.

Moscow plans to phase out trams and trolleybuses and replace them with mini-buses in order to eliminate traffic jams and excessive exhaust fumes. The minibuses will be designed to hold 22 passengers. The plan will boost current routes from some 200 to about 500 or 700 as the mini-buses will be able to travel on routes that are now inaccessible to trams and trolleybuses.

Metro

The traditional green plastic token was replaced in early 1999 by magnetic cards. Cards are available for single journeys (about 15c) to 60 journeys ($5.50). Children under seven years of age ride for free.

The card must be inserted in the slot of the entry gates on the right-hand side. Wait until a red light shows before inserting. Once you have inserted it a white or green light will show and the gates will open to let you pass. Don't attempt to get through without a valid card as a light detector will automatically slam the gate shut, resulting in some very sore legs.

66

Expat guide: Moscow   5/Getting around

Currently, a card will allow you to travel any number of stops as long as you do not exit. In winter, some tramps board the circle line and stay on it all day for warmth.

You may change lines without paying extra. Unfortunately for the linguistically challenged, all the signs are in Russian only. Carry an up-to-date metro map in both Russian and English. Don't loiter and gawk as if obviously a tourist. Get on the metro as soon as you can, as the doors close very quickly.

On the metro each station is announced as you arrive, and the name of the next station is announced before the doors are closed. The metro system is highly efficient, with a new train usually arriving every two minutes never any longer than five minutes even in the slowest period. Besides, riding on the metro is a cultural experience, for the murals and carvings as well as for the people-watching factor.

Metros run from 06.00 - 01.00 and to 02.00 on public holidays. Make sure you get to your destination well before then as you would otherwise have to disembark at whatever station you are at.

If you can read Cyrillic, you will be able to find your way round the metro system. There are no signs in English, but otherwise it's reasonably easy to negotiate. Make sure you know which exit to use out of some metro exits, as exits allow you to emerge in disparate places which may not match up with directions that you might be following. Also be aware that a different coloured line might run on the opposite platform rather than the same line simply going in the opposite direction. Be very careful of pickpockets targeting commuters leaving and entering metro stations.

It might be worth taking the Patriarshy Dom tour of the metro system soon after you arrive. Apart from it being a cultural experience, you will also get some idea of the size and orientation of the system.

Train (*elektrichka*)

Outbound suburban trains caught from the main train stations can be slow and crowded, especially on Friday afternoons and weekends. Seats are uncomfortable and there are few amenities. If you anticipate problems buying a ticket, ask a Russian friend to write your destination in Cyrillic for you to show at the ticket window.

River boat

The official return of spring is marked by the return of the passenger/tourist boats to the Moscow River. Run by Capital Shipping Co, the boats are released from winter docking only when the river is free of all ice and snow and is safe to navigate without the threat of fresh snowfall. There is an annual flushing out of the river when dams are opened upstream, and the river level rises noticeably. This often depends on the level of these dams and in some cases, the flushing out process has been postponed for several years until the dam levels were satisfactory. The boats are usually working by mid-April, but this is dependent on weather and the flushing-out operation.

You pay a single fare, regardless of how many stops you travel, as long as you travel only in one direction. In summer, boats usually come at intervals of about 20 minutes or so, though there may be fewer boats and longer intervals between boats at the beginning and end of the summer season. The furthest points at which you can start your journey is Novospassky Monastery in the east and Kievsky Vokhzal in the west. The trips take approximately 1h 20/30 minutes from north to south or vice-versa.

Depending on demand, usually about eight boats are on duty during the week and 12 during the weekend. The service, which has been running since 1994, offers several stops, some near important landmarks and tourist destinations such as Park Kultury (Gorky Park) and the Kremlin.

Take a map with you, so you can identify the various landmarks along the route.

It is possible to take a picnic if you are going for a scenic ride, and you shouldn't expect any food of note on board other than crisps, sweets and ice-creams. Drinks are usually warm. *(See Chapter 9 - Keeping busy).*

Buying tickets

You pay the same for one stage along the journey as you would to travel to the terminus going in one direction only. Once you reach the terminus, you will have to pay the same amount to return. In 1999, adults paid $2 and children $1 each over weekends, and half that price during the week.

Longer trips

It is possible to take a boat or hydrofoil from Rechnoi Vokhzal to a pleasant out-of-town destination where you can have a picnic or barbecue *(See Chapter 9 - Keeping busy)*

6/Eating and drinking

Eating and drinking both at home and out of the home in Moscow is bound to be a markedly different experience compared with where you come from. For many it will be part of the delicious and revealing discovery of Moscow, particularly from the cultural point of view. For others, different cultural expectations in terms of service, cleanliness, pricing and ingredients will make them hanker after home. Nevertheless, it's all part of the heady mix of Moscow.

Restaurants

There's not much point in listing all the restaurants in Moscow in this section. The *Moscow Times*, in particular, has a page on its website (*www.moscowtimes.ru/mtout/restaurants.htm*) dedicated to restaurants and also carries information in its hardcopy. The *eXile* weekly newspaper prides itself as a discerning reviewer of restaurants, and the *Moscow Tribune* (when published) occasionally mentions restaurants as well. *Where Moscow* usually has good restaurant listings. Consulting these sources will help to keep you up to date on the constantly changing restaurant scene.

The following list (not comprehensive) includes restaurants which have been recommended by expats.

Expat hangouts

- **Chesterfield's** Owned by the former owner of the deceased and once famous 'Hungry Duck', Chesterfield's is a large, roomy place which serves a variety of Western foods (of varying quality) and which often shows overseas sporting events.
- **Moosehead Canadian Bar** The favourite meeting venue of the Canadian Businessman's association.
- **Planet Hollywood** Planet Hollywood offers a variety of events during the week, ranging from ladies night to Sunday brunches. Check the press for details.
- **Silver's**
- **Starlite Diner** There are two of these and they are both imported complete from the US. Hamburgers, fries, milkshakes and other similar fast foods are available.
- **T.G.I. Friday's** two branches 18 Ulitsa Tverskaya, and Okhotny Ryad Mall at Manezh Square.
- **John Bull Pubs**
- **The Great Canadian Bagel** Two branches recently opened to great acclaim, in view of the lamented demise of Dunkin' Donuts. The Great

Expat guide: Moscow 6/Eating and drinking

Canadian Bagel has received mixed reviews. It remains to be seen whether it will price itself out of the market. Thirteen bagels sell for about $6.

- **The Zoo Bar** *(tel: 255 4144/4108; 1 Kudrinskaya Square on the side of one of Stalin's Seven Sisters just near the zoo)* used to host a monthly get-together for the British Isles Club. Contact the Zoo Bar to find out if the event may be held again, or the British Embassy to find out details of other possible venues *(see Chapter 8 - Getting to know others)*.

Fast food

- **McDonalds** There are currently 25 dotted around town, a further nine in the Moscow region and a total of 45 in Russia. The company is planning to double the number of outlets in the next few years. The first to be built in Moscow was at Pushkinskaya in 1990 and is the largest McDonald's in the world, serving more customers per hour than any other McDonalds. It set the world record for most customers at a McDonalds when on one particular day it recorded 40,000 visitors. Should the interest grab you, take the opportunity to visit McDonalds' factory (McComplex) just outside Moscow, which apparently is the only McDonalds factory in the world, and which produces up to 1,500 burgers an hour. Tours can be arranged through Patriarshy Dom.
- **Subway** A Russian-owned independent franchise is situated towards the end of Leningradsky Prospekt, and another (joint-venture franchise) has been recently opened in a closed military academic institution, meaning it is out-of-bounds for expats.
- **Mir Pizza** (Pizza World) diagonally opposite from Smolensky Passage serves good pizzas and has a reasonable salad bar. Check out the free weekend entertainment for children.
- **Pizza Express** is situated inside the first floor of Smolensky Passage. Pizzas are relatively pricey.
- **Patio Pizza**
- **Sbarro's Pizza** *(Manezh; metro: Okhotny Ryad; and also Ramstore Plaza foodhall)* is highly recommended for authentic NY menu and reasonable prices.
- **Russkoe Bistro** (several branches) serves Russian fast food.

Hotel restaurants

Several hotels offer a Sunday brunch from 12.00 noon to 16.00 or thereabouts with entertainment for the children by clowns and magicians in many cases.

These are particularly worthwhile in winter when you want to get out of your apartment and pass the hours with some friends over a bottomless glass of champagne, wine or vodka. You will usually be able to eat all you want of caviar and salmon, cheeses, desserts, paellas, chilli con carne, seafood ragout, roast beef and Yorkshire puddings and assorted confectioneries. Prices in 1999 ranged around the $40 mark for adults and half-price for children over 3, with under 3s free.

- **Rennaissance**
- **Baltschug-Kempinski**

Expat guide: Moscow   6/Eating and drinking

- Palace
- Metropol
- Radisson-Slavjanskaya
- Marriott

Argentinian restaurants

- El Gaucho

Cuban/Spanish restaurants

- Taverna Marazul

Mexican restaurants

Moscow expats seem to have a craving for Mexican food. Some dispute that it is impossible to find 'authentic' Mexican food in Moscow, though they still seem to be prepared to settle for second-best. If you're satisfied with simply having spicy foods, try some of the many Georgian restaurants all over Moscow.

- Aruba
- Azteca
- Hola Mexico
- La Cantina
- Santa Fe

Italian restaurants

- Angelico's
- Il Pomodoro
- Italian Garden
- Rossini's recommended as serving decent helpings, reasonable prices, Euromix cuisine.
- Patio Pasta
- Figaro's

Pizza restaurants/take-aways

- Jack's *(tel: 956-6196)* open 09:00 - 10:00. Only delivery. Jack@Jacks.ru charges $20 to deliver a 16" pizza. They also have restaurant-style meals and Thai chicken is recommended.
- Tulios *(tel: 251-3338; e-mail: tulios@matrix.ru)* delivers everywhere and anywhere in Moscow. It offers two sizes of pizza, small and large, 11" and 16". Prices start at $9.95 and 20% discounts are offered on weekends. Tulios boasts that it offers real American pepperoni and real mozzarella.
- The **pizza boat** moored in the Moscow River off Frunzenskaya Naberezhnaya (opposite #18 and opposite the rides section of Gorky Park) does an excellent pizza (about $5 and delivery extra) and some pasta dishes. You need to get there very early (say 18:00) if you are going on a weekend evening as it gets very crowded. Otherwise make a reservation. The

Expat guide: Moscow   **6/Eating and drinking**

restaurant is open from 12:00 - 24:00 and has an outside deck which is great for sitting on in summer during the long evenings.

Georgian restaurants

Georgian restaurants are worth visiting for their very tasty food and often very reasonable prices.
Some terms you should know are:

lavash - a thin pancake like unleavened bread, delicious with hot sauce

kinza - a kind of parsley or cilantro, widely used in Georgian cooking

khachapuri - a wheat pancake layered with salty Georgian cheese (a meal on its own with a good bottle of Georgian wine)

lobio - a thick spicy red bean stew, white beans as well often served in a clay pot as a hot appetizer or *zakusk*

suluguni - fried salty cheese

kuch-machi - beef or chicken giblets with onion

kharcho - delicious and hearty spicy beef soup

tkemali - red or green sieved sour plums

lulya kebab - minced meat kebab

satsivi - a cold chicken dish in sauce

nadugi - home made cottage cheese with mint

pkhali - vegetable paste with spinach, walnuts and cabbage, looks awful, sounds awful, but tastes great

- **Aragvy**
- **Dioskuria** - just off the New Arbat, reached through the archway in the building opposite the Praga restaurant complex. Food is as good as Guriya's and the band are well worth listening to.
- **Elegance**
- **Guriya** very popular with expats, situated between Frunzenskaya Naberezhnaya and Komsomolsky Prospekt.
- **Iberia** (opposite Kuznetsky Most station on Rozhdestvenka) - The food is said to be good, reasonably priced (as is the wine) costing around $30 per person.
- **Mama Zoya's**
- **Suliko**
- **U Pirosmani's** - a more upmarket version of a Georgian restaurant with patrician diners and with superb view of Novodevichy Convent. Famous/notorious for hosting Bill Clinton during his visit to Russia in 1998.
- **Kabanchick**
- **Knight club** (Rytsarsky Club*)*
- **Shinok**

Bulgarian restaurant
- **Mekhana Bansko**

Russian restaurants
- **Shury Mury** (Hanky Panky) Café on Petrovka Ulitsa. Decor designed to make it look like the interior of a Swiss Chalet but serving Russian food such as stewed veal with vegetables in a pot. It's extremely popular and

Expat guide: Moscow   6/Eating and drinking

people often have to wait to be seated. Prices are not as reasonable as you might expect given its rustic decor. Shury Mury, which is the upmarket arm of the Yolki Polki chain, are very popular with Russian diners.

- One **Yolki-Polki** *(Tverskaya Ulitsa; metro:Pushkinskaya)* is said to offer a reasonable alternative to Tamerlane's Mongolian barbecue at a much better price of about $6.
- **1 Red Square** The address makes it sound more exciting than it is. The restaurant is situated off the lobby of the Historical Museum on Red Square. Unfortunately it is in the bowels of the museum and there is no view onto the square. However, it's faithfully historical, *ancien regime* type menu is worth exploring if you wish to see what nobility of old used to eat.
- **House of Artists** near the zoo just off the Garden Ring on Ulitsa Povarskaya the former meeting place of Soviet-sanctioned artists during Stalin's reign. There is a magnificent chandelier (donated by Stalin) and attractive decor. Atmosphere is subdued and elegant. Pricey.
- **Bochka**
- **Dve telezhki**
- **Ruski Grebok**
- **Grot (Grotto)**
- **Sedmoje Nebo** (Ostankhino Tower)
- **Restaurant Stanislavskaya 2** *(tel: 291 8689; 2 Leontievsky Pereulok; open from 18:00 - 02:00)* is rated as having excellent service, food and atmosphere, Slavic/European menu.
- **Shishka** *(tel: 921-0370; 21 Ulitsa Petrovka)* a recently opened restaurant, offers a mix of Russian and European cuisine. Try their business lunch and ask for *Cirny shishky*, delicious battered and deep-fried cheese balls.
- **Sudar** expect plenty of beef dishes, among them *Gusarskaya pechen* (Hussar's liver), Beef Stroganoff

Russian food terminology
It's worth knowing the generic names of certain ingredients:

Beef - *govyadina*
Pork - *svinina*
Lamb/mutton - *varanina*
Chicken - *kuritsa*
Fish - *riba*
Sturgeon - *assyetrina*
Rice - *ris*
Potatoes - *kartochka*
Salad - *salat*
Bread - *glebe*
Butter - *masla*
Milk - *moloko*
Tea - *chai*
Coffee - *koffi*
Sugar - *zakar*

Expat guide: Moscow   6/Eating and drinking

Chinese restaurants and take-aways

- **Chinese Dragon**
- **Chinese takeaway** at the start of Kutozovsky Prospekt on the same side of the road as the Ukraine Hotel. A great favourite with expats.
- **Chopsticks**
- **Dynasty**
- **Five Spices**
- **Junk Boat**
- **Mei Hua**
- **Ostrov Formosa**
- **WanFu**
- **Fanza**

Japanese restaurant

- **Tokyo**
- **Angara**
- **Yakitoria** (next to Beloruskaya railway station, on Gruzinsky prospekt) is highly rated for good food and service and very reasonable prices.

Indian restaurants

- **Darbar** at the Sputnik Hotel on Leninsky Prospekt.
- **Maharaja**
- **Talk of the Town** in the Park Place complex at 113/1 Leninsky Prospekt.

Uzbek restaurant

- **Beloe Solntse Pustyni** (White Sun of the Desert)
- **Bakhor** five different kinds of *plov* (rice and meat or fish dish) served, also a few horse-meat dishes for those who like it.
- **Nabruz** with intriguing Dastarkhan room designed for a small party of people and a variety of *plov* dishes, a wide selection of lamb dishes and kebabs.

Jewish restaurant

Carmel is said to be the only completely kosher restaurant in Moscow serves Russian-Jewish specialities as well as a separate section with a very wide variety of *shashlyks* (meat or fish on a kebab).

Mongolian restaurant

Tamerlaine *(tel: 202-564930 Prechistenka Ulitsa)* offers a novel way of selecting and preparing your food. Costs $40 per head (half price for children). Complimentary bread and salad.

Tibetan restaurant

- **Tibet Himalaya** *(tel: 917-3985; Kamergersky Pereulok, between Tverskaya and Bolshaya Dmitrovka)* is recommended, though service can be obsequious. Prices are mid-range ranging from about $30 - 70.
- **Tibet Kitchen**

Menus

You will rarely find a menu printed with the English equivalent. Consequently, you will need to become acquainted with some culinary terms so that you can order what you desire. Neither will you find many serving staff fluent in English. Never mind, it's quite fun seeing whether what eventually arrives is the same as what you ordered. It's also quite an incentive to learn Russian, and you'll probably find (depending on how often you eat out) that your grasp of Russian culinary terms is far superior when compared with other subjects.

Tipping

Tipping is not widely expected, but always gratefully received. However, be prepared to pay much more than in the U.S. In some restaurants, a 10 - 15% service charge will be added to the bill.

Service

Service can vary, but in the last few years competition has seen it improve in leaps and bounds. Loud complaining in public is not regarded as usual practice. By law, every establishment serving food and drink has to have a complaints (or nowadays a comments and suggestions) book (*kniga zhaloby*) displayed prominently for use by customers and subsequent inspection by the authorities. Likewise, if you are pleased with service, you are also welcome to inscribe your positive comments.

Prices

Prices vary widely with Moscow having a reputation for high prices, although cheap and reasonable prices are available in many places, especially the smaller, ethnic restaurants which have a large Russian clientele. Those that attract New Russians are likely to be pricey.

Credit cards

Not all restaurants accept credit cards, so either confirm beforehand or make sure you take enough rubles.

Exchange-rate

During the crisis much confusion reigned while the exchange-rate yo-yo'ed. Prices were quoted in y.e.'s (the unit typically signifies dollars), and exchange-rates were sometimes posted for viewing. It was often the case that diners paid for their meals at much higher rates compared with that day's official exchange-

Expat guide: Moscow　　　　　　　　　**6/Eating and drinking**

rate. If such a situation develops again, always check the restaurant's exchange-rate before ordering food so that you avoid a nasty surprise at the end of the meal.

Many restaurants started offering 'anti-crisis' menus with a group of certain items listed at lower ruble rates.

Shopping at the market *(rynok)*

There are a number of markets which are a revelation in terms of what they actually sell. It's well worth visiting them - don't be put off by the fact that you are one expat among many Russians. Try to take a Russian-speaking friend or your driver with you if you can't cope in Russian. If you are on your own and worry about understanding prices or even about shifting prices, use a small notepad to write down the sum you agree on with the vendor, and obtain mutual confirmation before paying.

Some expats joke about needing a Geiger counter before buying food at the market, while other long-term expats say it's not necessary, as the food is safe and actually tastier than imports, which are full of preservatives and additives.

When shopping for produce/meat at the *rynok* or on the street, beware of being ripped-off in terms of correct weight, i.e. is the 500g you are buying, really 500g? Some spot checks have revealed that a *rynok*/street 'kilo' can weigh as little as 480g. Watch when your produce is being weighed, and never accept any pre-bagged goods without having them re-weighed. Remember to take your own bags to the market. It goes without saying that once you reveal you're a foreigner, then it could be open season.

If you are worried about BSE or Mad Cow Disease, stay away from *rynok* beef, as it is not tested for BSE.

Watch date stamps carefully, as many expired products are sold as bargains. Some expats vouch for the safety of the markets, saying that the quality is excellent and if you know how to shop, the cuts of meat are an exceptional value. The meat is fresh (not frozen and re-frozen) and hormone-free.

It's also possible to sample any of the dairy, honey, pickled delights as well as the vegetables and fruit before you buy, and you can haggle on the price for as much as a 50% discount if you can speak Russian.

Fish market

Try **Palashevsky Fish** market near metro Pushkinskaya. To get there walk past the Pushkinskaya McDonald's, away from Tverskaya, and take the first right, then about 100 metres on your left you will see a sign for a fish market at the corner of a street going left. It's small, and also sells fresh vegetables and meat.

There are some reliable fresh fish vendors in certain food markets such as **Dorogomilovsky** market.

Thai food/SE Asian markets

- **Sadko Foodland** on Dorogomilovskaya sells coconut milk and lemongrass in a jar.
- **Vietnamskii dom** (market at corner of Ogorodny and Dobrolubova) at metro Timiryazevskaya.

Expat guide: Moscow   **6/Eating and drinking**

French food products

These are found in several supermarkets, but it's worth trying Progress and Sam (CAM) which is a chain of supermarkets (the biggest on Leninsky Prospekt) which even sometimes stocks fresh produce from Brittany and Alsace. Those seeking Orangina may be disappointed.

Japanese food products

A Japanese products store **Dzhapro (Sapporo)**, is located at the beginning of Prospekt Mira underneath a Japanese restaurant. If you cross the ring road and head up Prospekt Mira, on the right side, look out for it just after the cigar store. Several shelves of products such as soy sauce, tofu, sesame oils, noodles and dried fish and shrimp crackers can also be found in the front reception area of Tokyo restaurant. The products are not cheap, but at least available.

Indian food products

Indian Spice Store *(tel 232-2724; 207-1621; 36/2 Ulitsa Sretenka) and another branch (tel: 2080174) on the Garden ring between metros: Sukharevskaya and Krasniye Vorota.* Both shops only open at 11:00 and sell some Chinese products as well as well as all kinds of spices, chutneys, dried legumes (good chickpeas), in addition to regular foodstuffs.

Turkish titbits

Both Ramstores carry quite a wide variety of Turkish delicacies such as Turkish delights, seeds, nuts, crystallised fruit, halva and spices.

German beergarden

In early May, once the weather improves, **Art Hotel** *(tel: 432-7827; 41 Vernadskovo Prospekt)* opens a beergarden with wooden benches, birch trees, sausages, beer and schnapps and German-speaking-clientele.

Living a champagne and caviar lifestyle on a budget

It's quite possible to live a 'Champagne and caviar' lifestyle in Moscow, even on a small budget. However, remember that the source of caviar can be suspect, and you never know whether it comes from contaminated areas. Some wouldn't recommend caviar *(ikra)* from a *rynok* as you may get jars produced at 'underground' factories, which may endanger your health. Instead, you should consider buying it at a large, reputed food store. Beluga caviar is, of course, on the endangered list and it's up to your own morals whether you will choose to buy it or not. Try the *rynok* near **Belloruskaya Subway Station**.

Caviar can be purchased from:
- **Alla Ivanovna** *(tel: 590-9642)* (mainly sevriuga, about $40 for a (900g can) does deliveries.
- **Leningradskoie Rynok**, off Sokol in the fish pavilion, the best supplier is located in the left corner facing the entrance opposite the meat stalls.

77

Expat guide: Moscow — 6/Eating and drinking

(Beluga, costs about $10 per 100g). Always try before you buy, but only if it looks acceptable.

The Volga region (Astrakhan, in particular) is a large supplier of caviar.

There are three basic types of black caviar: beluga, sevriuga and osetra.

- Beluga has the biggest eggs and is grayish in colour. considered to be the most delicious and expensive as the fish is rare, endangered and only caught in winter.
- Sevriuga is smaller and darker, sevriuga fish is not big and usually carries about a kilo of caviar.
- Osetra is the smallest and the blackest in colour and possesses a more distinctive taste. This caviar is from a large fish which can be up to three metres in length and which can supply up to a bucketful of caviar.

Caviar is prepared either hot or cold, though the cold method is far more popular. Prepared hot, the raw caviar is put into boiling, salty water and cooked for 5-10 minutes. This is risky as the caviar can end up as hard little balls if overcooked, quality is lost though it increases in volume.

Prepared the cold way, caviar is first cleaned and sieved after which salt is added (about a matchbox for each kilogram). It is said that only a master caviar preparer can judge the perfect amount of salt as either under- or over-salted can result in an inferior product.

A third method involves 'hard-squeezing' caviar resulting in a hard block that can be cut with a knife, like cheese. This is said to provide the real taste of caviar, though this might be open to debate.

Note that *rynok* caviar sellers often add more salt into caviar on sale as it prolongs shelf-life and also helps to increase volume, thus boosting profitability.

To ensure you are buying good caviar, you should be able to detect a mild and not a strong smell, all eggs should be whole and liquid should be absent, otherwise its presence would indicate that the caviar has been frozen and unfrozen. Also determine whether salt content is to your liking.

Caviar bought in large quantities can safely be stored in your freezer if first separated into smaller containers. Allow to defrost for 24 hours in the fridge. Never refreeze and always eat within three or four days.

For those whose budget does not run to Veuve Clicquot, Russian champagne is a palatable alternative. Costing around $3 a bottle, you can find it in most markets, but if you're after dry champagne, you'll find it a struggle to obtain a bottle of 'brut', as most Russians like the demi-sec or sweet varieties. Your best bet is to contact the **Moscow Champagne Winery** and buy a case at a time.

Look in the shops for the international award-winning Russian brand Abrau-Durso brut from the Anapa region which is recommended as being the best Russian champagne.

Thanksgiving

- **Turkeys** have been available at Tischinka Supermarket in the past. Also try Stockmann, Ramstore, Progress, Seven Continents at the Old Arbat. The Diplomat Store on Bolshaya Gruzinskaya (not far from the Palace Hotel) has stocked butterball turkeys in the past. Turkeys are generally very expensive.
- **Cranberry sauce**: try Stockmann. Eldorado always has cranberry sauce although it is not called cranberry sauce. Alternatively try *pohlamoos*.

Expat guide: Moscow   **6/Eating and drinking**

Pohlad are red berries smaller than cranberries and grow in Finland and Estonia. Jelly and jam made from *pohlad* has been sold in the Leningradsky market.

- **Pecans** for making Pecan Nut Pie are available at Sadko on Kutuzovsky Prospekt.
- **Sweet potatoes/yams** are a non-traditional food product - Russians do not like mixing sweet tastes with savoury tastes. These have been sold at Stockmann.

If you don't want to go to the trouble of celebrating at home, the **American Chamber of Commerce** in Russia holds an annual Thanksgiving celebration with an old- fashioned, all-you-can-eat feast featuring favorites such as roast turkey breast and legs, giblet gravy, mashed potatoes, savoury bread stuffing, and for dessert, pecan pie, custard pie, apple pie, mincemeat pie, pumpkin pie, and ice-cream This takes place in November usually at a large hotel. Tickets can be obtained in advance only directly from the Chamber at Riverside Towers, Kosmodamianskaya Nab. 52/ 1B, 8th floor, near metro Paveletskaya.

Other places offering Thanksgiving feasts are Papa John's; Starlite diner; TGI Friday's; American Bar & Grill; Uncle Guilly's: Planet Hollywood; Le Gastronome; Samobranka in the Marriott Grand Hotel; Hotel Tverskaya; Aerostar Hotel; Lomonosov Restaurant in the Palace Hotel and the Radisson Slavjanskaya Hotel.

Christmas

Most of the ingredients listed for Thanksgiving (see above) apply for Christmas. Most of these are available, though always try Stockmann's for the more unusual products first. Several of the hotels put on Christmas lunches on 25 December, so if you're lusting after a Western-style Christmas feast, you don't need to be disappointed.

Miscellaneous comfort foods

Cyber-grocery *(www.cyber-grocery.ru;* was set up in 1999 to offer a seven-day-week, grocery shopping and delivery service to those who preferred not to do their shopping themselves. Cyber-grocery offers to locate those hard-to-find items and deliver to your door in ultra-quick time for a very reasonable fee.

- **Bagels** are sold at the newly opened **Great Canadian Bagel** shops (two branches)
- **Baklava** and other mid-Eastern type food at Ramstore
- **Brown sugar** at Stockmann
- **Breakfast cereal**: A small variety of imported cereals is to be found at most Western supermarkets but it's worth trying the Russian-made cereal which is very cheap and can be tasty, especially the chocolate-filled little squares.
- **Chickpeas** (dried) at Ramstore.
- **Cordial drinks** (concentrate diluted with water). Stockmann has a limited range imported from the UK.
- **Coriander (cilantro)** (fresh) is widely sold as 'kinza' from markets
- **Couscous** is sold at Progress or Stockmann

79

Expat guide: Moscow   **6/Eating and drinking**

- **English mustard** is sold at Stockmann
- **Godiva Chocolates** are sold in Petrovsky Passage
- **Halva** and other middle-Eastern food at Ramstore. Also try Russian halva which is widely available.
- **Maple syrup** from Eldorado and Global USA. You can also make it by mixing two cups of sugar, one cup of water and one teaspoon maple flavoring. Bring it to a hard boil while stirring.
- **Marmite/Vegemite.** This British/Australian delight is not to be found anywhere in Moscow. Perhaps some enterprising retailer will consider importing them in the not too distant future?
- **Picallili** is available from Stockmann.
- **Popcorn kernels** are for sale at Global USA on Tverskaya; the Gastronom Dorogomilovo, across Bolshaya Dorogomilovskaya Street from Kievsky Vokhzal.
- **Ricotta cheese**: Mega Center Italia occasionally sells real Italian Ricotta cheese; Global USA has American ricotta (White Rose); Stockmann's has ricotta cheese and fresh mozzarella.
- **Soy milk** at Stockmann's and Maria at 80 Leninsky Prospekt.
- **Sushi** is sold at a place in the Radisson Slavyanskaya right inside the entrance and Tokyo (in the hotel Rossiya, in the south-west corner of the building, although it is very expensive. Angara is said to have once had a decent sushi bar until they started putting mayonnaise into almost all their maki sushi. There is a cosy sushi restaurant directly to the right of the main entrance to Petrovsky Passage on Neglinnaya Ulitsa, directly across from the Central Bank building. They don't take credit cards, but it's cheaper than the Radisson.
- **Tahini** at Ramstore
- **Tofu**: the Japanese shop (see above) on Prospekt Mira often has tofu called *dzhapr.*
- **Whole wheat flour** sold at the **Indian Spices store** *(36/2 Ulitsa Sretenka (metro: Sukharevskaya).*

Cooking conversions:

If you are accustomed to using imperial measures (lbs/oz) only, consult the Internet for conversion data or consult your diary.

Buying Mexican ingredients to cook at home

- **Tortilla chips**: Stockmann has stocked big bags of real tortilla chips, although they were expensive.
- **Taco kits**, plus tortilla chips, refried beans, at Stockmann.
- **Corn flour** *(krakhmal)* is usually available at all major *rynki* such as Ryzsky, Leningradsky, or Kievsky. If cornmeal is hard to find, polenta is suggested as an alternative.
- Fresh **jalapeno** is hard to find except at *rynki*, but you might find bottled jalapeno. Alternatively, substitute with hot peppers.
- **Flour and corn tortillas**. Try thin Georgian *lavash* as an alternative to flour tortillas. Otherwise try Stockmann.

Expat guide: Moscow   **6/Eating and drinking**

Russian food

There's a belief that Russians don't have a strong culinary tradition apart from *bortsch* (beetroot soup which is supposedly Ukrainian in origin), *shchi* (cabbage soup) and *pelmyeny* (like ravioli). The dominant thread that runs through Russian cuisine is provided by Georgian cooking. However, look out for *blini* with caviar and sour cream, sturgeon (simply delicious), Chicken Kiev (also Ukrainian in origin); and don't turn your nose up at *kasha* (various kinds of porridge) cooked with butter. The down-side is that Russians believe in cooking with fat and oil a-plenty and sweet or sour cream is no stranger to the menu either. The Russians are also keen on cabbage in any form, as well as salads swimming in mayonnaise.

Traditionally the meal starts with cold appetizers (*zakuska*) such as smoked meats and fish and salads followed by soup and a hot dish, and finished with pastries or desserts containing fruit.

Some specialities to look out for include:

- *Shchi* - a soup generally made with salted cabbage, meat broth, spices and onion, often combined with cream. It sounds awful but can be delicious.
- *Solyanka* - a type of thick soup made with either meat, mushroom or fish (e.g. sturgeon or trout) with a bouillon base, can be fatty and rich
- *Bortsch* - a beetroot soup with cabbage, and other vegetables with pieces of meat and with a dollop of sour cream. Authentically, it is served with *(pampushki)* on the side.
- *Pampushki* are small, steamed and baked dumplings often served as an accompaniment to *bortsch* and with a garlic sauce.
- *Gleb* is bread, widely served as an accompaniment to any meal. Try the dark Russian bread which may be an acquired taste for some, but once acquired, is delicious.
- *Kasha* (literally porridge) can be made with a variety of grains such as buckwheat and millet with milk and butter and with either sugar or salt added depending on if you want a sweet or savoury kasha.
- *Ukha* is a fish bouillon soup varying in consistency and ingredients.
- *Rasstegai* is a stuffed bun with varying ingredients depending on the soup it is served with
- *Blini* are pancakes typically stuffed with red, beluga or sturgeon caviar and sour cream.
- *Blinchiki* are thin pancakes stuffed with fish, meat, ham, onion, eggs or pate.
- *Tkemali* sauce (Georgian in origin) is either red or green in colour and is a piquant sauce made from sour plums.
- *Pelmyeni* - a type of Russian ravioli made from noodle dough and usually stuffed with minced pork, veal or beef either individually or combined together with parsley, onion and meat broth. The *pelmyeni* are cooked in boiling water and sometimes accompanied by a sauce such as sour cream white sauce, mushroom sauce, soy sauce, chili sauce, vinegar or tomato sauce. Some restaurants also offer fish or chicken *pelmyeni*. Look out for frozen *pelmyeni* in the supermarkets.
- *Piroshki* are hot meat pies
- Baked sturgeon or sturgeon kebab on a skewer is especially worth trying while *Kulebyaka* is a multi-layered puff pastry pie containing a stuffing of

81

Expat guide: Moscow   **6/Eating and drinking**

salmon, sturgeon, hard-boiled eggs and mushrooms. Grilled salmon is also recommended.

- Game dishes are popular, with rabbit and venison widely available. Unless you like eating horse meat, be wary when you visit a Caucasian restaurant where you are likely to find delights such as colt's fillet on the menu.
- *Shashlyk* is widely available and you can select beef, veal, lamb, pork, fish or chicken. Best made on an open fire on a grill *(mangal)*.
- *Salat* - many salads make use of mayonnaise, with vegetables bathed in the sauce.

For those interested in Russian cooking, two new books in English are:
- a paperback edition of Joyce Toomre's annotated translation of Elena Molokhovets *A Gift to Young Housewives: Classic Russian Cooking*, from Indiana University Press;
- *The Russian Heritage Cookbook* by Lynn Visson from Casa Dana Books, a new imprint of Ardis Publishers, features a collection of favourite recipes of classic Russian cuisine from aristocratic emigre families and from elderly ladies living in Russia. For further information contact: lvisson@aol.com.

Also consult **Kulinar** *(www.cooking.ru/)* for more information about Russian food.

Shashlyk

Properly cooked *shashlyk* (meat or fish on a skewer cooked over an open fire) is particularly memorable. *Shashlyk* is originally from the Caucasus. In the summer, you can buy *shashlyk* virtually everywhere - try the numerous *shashlyk* bars in Gorky Park, Victory Park, VDNKh. Some expats believe that stray dogs often end up as *shashlyk* while others warn against dodgy hygiene practices by outdoor vendors. In winter try some of the numerous small cafes on the Old Arbat.

It's possible to buy a *mangal* or grill from hardware stores and markets. Look out for a particularly nifty version which folds up into a neat zip-up bag and selling for only $18 at Sokolniki open air market.

Recipe: *Shashlyk*

1kg meat or fish (young lamb is said to be the best meat for *shashlyk*, while sturgeon, being a firm-fleshed fish, is the best fish choice)
300ml water
3 medium onions
2 big spoonfuls salt
1 teaspoon sugar
½ lemon including juice and grated peel
3 tablespoons 9% vinegar or ½ glass sour dry red or white wine (wine is said to give a better taste)
½ teaspoon black pepper
½ teaspoon red pepper
1 bunch of dill
1 tablespoon oil
3 bay leaves

Expat guide: Moscow   **6/Eating and drinking**

Method:
Submerge meat or fish cut into 3sqcm cubes in this mixture and allow to marinate overnight. Thread onto skewers and cook, using a technique which is more akin to smoking, rather than direct grilling over hot coals. Do not allow meat to blacken.

Drinking water

It's strongly advised that you do not drink tap water. One source of pollutants comes from the leakage of cow manure into the water reservoirs during the spring thaw. Other concerns are ageing lead pipes and excessive chlorine in the water and heaven knows what else.

Many expats drink bottled water which is widely available. Rather go for familiar brands. You have no comeback on local brands which could be providing you with bottled tap water for all you know, especially those that purport to raise funds for church organisations.

You can also order 20-litre containers of purified water from **Kingwater** *(tel: 937-5015)* or **ClearWater** *(tel: 956-1161)* who both deliver. Prices are about $8 per container.

Alternatively you could choose to filter your own water, though you should check to see just what your filtering agent promises to filter out.

As a last resort you could boil tap water for 15 minutes at a rolling boil and let it stand overnight to allow the chlorine to evaporate.

Vodka

The national drink is probably too widely available, as illegal distilling is widespread. Be very careful which brand you buy, as you could land up with major headaches. Rather stick with the most expensive Stolichnaya vodka, which can be bought in most Western supermarkets. Some recommend authentic Smirnov vodka.

You will find that vodka is used for a wide variety of ailments, including de-icing of windscreens and paint-thinners! Russians also believe that 'pepper vodka' is a cure for sore throats, as it helps to 'burn away' the infection.

Beer

Just a few years before the 'beer explosion' hit Moscow, locally-made beer was described as 'water taken from the Moscow river with a lump of yeast added to it'. Now, brewers are setting up shop all over Russia. Baltika makes a range of beers, some less suited to Western tastes (No. 3 with the blue label is recommended as very pleasant tasting) and is cheap, selling at about 50c a bottle. A wide range of foreign beers sell in kiosks and in pubs. Don't be surprised at the Russian predilection for warm beer, nor should you be surprised to see Russians drinking beer on the way to work in the morning at outdoor kiosks.

It's possible to buy Baltika and other beers by the case at a cheaper price than at most kiosks from the new Stockmann store in the basement at Smolensky Passage.

Expat guide: Moscow   **6/Eating and drinking**

One wholesaler *(tel: 145-6018; 148-7373; 5, Beregovoi Proezd, metro: Fili)* offers good prices and adds a small charge per bottle for delivery for a minimum order of about 15 cases.

Another recommended place is the Yarmarka behind Dinamo Stadium. It is slightly tricky to get to, but prices generally run 10-25% less than kiosk prices. Large quantities can be purchased at most markets such as Kuzminki and Techstilshiki (both south-east Moscow).

It always makes good sense to wipe clean the neck of a bottle of beer before drinking.

Wine

While in Russia, try Georgian wine: Sedmoi Kontinent has a good selection. The Kinsmarauli is a good semi-sweet or semi-dry wine. The dry red Mukuzani with red label is recommended. The wineries sometimes omit to put a year of vintage on the label sometimes resulting in a wine that is over-aged. White Georgian wines are not rated as being as good as red Georgian wines. Many cheaper Georgian wines are available in kiosks and sell at about $2 a bottle. These are quite palatable, though, some might say, risky.

- Wine connoisseurs who prefer personal choice and home delivery of their wines should contact Robert Schenk *(e-mail:wines@glasnet.ru)*.
- **Beloe & Krasnoye** at Myasnitskaya
- **U Yara** *(33 Leningradsky Prospekt opposite Dinamo Stadium)* has a wide selection of foreign wines as well as champagne, ports, and spirits.
- **The Expo cash-and-carry** *(Krasnopresnenskaya Ulitsa)* has a large selection at every price range and from many different countries.

Fruit cordial

This does not seem to be widely available as in the West, but can be replaced with pure fruit juice in cartons. Recently Stockmann has started importing lime juice and orange cordial from Tesco in the UK.

Tea

Chai, as it is known in Russian, is a particular favourite and is most traditionally with water boiled in a *samovar* (large ornate kettle). Certain Russian and international companies are beginning to make endless varieties of fruit-flavoured tea (see Ramstore). You are able to enjoy iced tea, or a hot tea cocktail at many restaurants. Milk is not taken with these teas. It's also possible to obtain green tea and Ginseng tea at almost any *rynok*.

Coffee (beans and ground)

- **Chai-Kofe** on Myasnitskaya has good variety, at reasonable prices near the Central Post Office (metro: Turgenevskaya or Chisty Prudy)
- **Doutor** on Novy Arbat (in front of the Deli France)
- **Coffee Bean** in the Kuznetsky Most metro arch, look out for sign.

Expat guide: Moscow   **6/Eating and drinking**

- **Coffee Bean** at 18/3 Pokrovka is said to have great coffee, good cakes and very friendly staff. Every tenth coffee is on the house.

Cooking classes

A variety are available through the IWC (International Women's Club).

7/Getting to know others

If you come to Moscow with the intention of keeping to yourself, you will lose out on enormously beneficial friendships, relationships and insights that can be obtained in Moscow simply by getting to know others, whether these be other expats or Russians. Many seasoned expats are vehement that you will not get to understand Russia, unless you make the effort to get to know the Russians. If you make the effort, you will be very pleasantly surprised.

Those of a more active inclination can turn to the chapter 'Keeping busy', which lists many of the sports that can be enjoyed in Moscow. However, this particular chapter will focus on other, less energetic ways of integrating, including becoming involved in clubs and societies, your particular religion (if any), learning other languages, particularly Russian, and attempting to understand the Russian soul, which is an enduring and enriching, if somewhat baffling occupation for many expats.

Clubs and societies

Meeting others who are in the same boat as you, or who have been in the same situation, can help to put things in perspective. One expat was feeling sorry for herself until she met a young newly-arrived woman from Syria who had been married just before leaving Syria. She spoke neither French nor English, but only Syrian. She did not work, nor did she have children, so her means of escape from isolation, especially during the dark days of winter, were extremely limited, given that there were no other Syrian women in Moscow known to her at the time.

In joining a club you place yourself in a good position to focus on one thing that will bond you with others, such as a sport or hobby. A common interest, or simply the novelty of being in Russia, will ensure that the normal barriers of shyness and reticence one might find in one's own country are done away with.

The down-side is that you could make a good friend only to discover that as expats, they might be leaving in a few months, and this puts some people off from making the effort. However, it is precisely through such encounters that lifelong friendships are forged.

Asian Women's Group

Expatriate women from the Asia-Pacific region are invited to join this group which is designed to meet the particular needs of Asian women in the Moscow context. The group has been organised primarily for women from Asian countries, but also welcomes women from African nations. It aims to foster better cultural and even commercial ties while continuing to support the International

Expat guide: Moscow   **7/Getting to know others**

Women's Club to which many of its 1,000 members belong. Another aim of the Asian Women's Group is to give Russians a taste of the cultural diversity of Asia.

The group's activities include charity fairs, food festivals, sports events, cultural shows, lectures and other activities. Contact any Asian embassy to find out further details.

The British Women's Club of Moscow

The group invites all women British passport holders and spouses of British passport holders to a variety of functions. The group's aim is to provide these women with a focal point for sharing interests, supporting one another and generally being sociable. Functions include a monthly coffee morning held on the second Tuesday of the month at the **Brit Club** *(7 Kutuzovsky Prospekt)* from 10:00 - 12:00. The club (about 50 members) asks for a nominal contribution to cover the cost of refreshment. There is usually some kind of craft work display with items available to buy, and/or guest speakers. The meetings are a good port of call if you are new in town, as you can join on the spot. Children are welcome to the coffee morning.

The group also holds pot luck lunches, usually once a month. Guests bring along one contribution. pot luck dinners are sometimes organised in the evenings, to which partners are also invited. Once a month the group has lunch at a restaurant, and a Sunday brunch is held once a month at a large hotel. There is also interest in organising the occasional night-out-with-the-girls. For those who are struggling with their weight, the club has established a Fat-but-Fighting Club, where you meet on a weekly basis in order to share your weight-reducing expertise, support each other and record your progress, or simply commiserate with each other. A toddler's group is held every Monday morning from 10:00 - 12:00 for coffee, chat and play for pre-school children and, weather permitting, the group goes for a walk on Fridays to a local park.

The club is also involved in charity, where members are welcome to contribute their time or expertise, and once a year it organises a Christmas Carol concert.

Contact the British Embassy for further information

CWIM (Canadian Women in Moscow)

A group of French- and English-speaking Canadian women meet monthly at the Canadian Club in the Canadian Embassy *(333 Starokonyushenny Pereulok metro: Kropotkinskaya)* for a couple of hours, occasionally with a view to helping each other keep their head above water in Moscow. Contact the Canadian Embassy for further information.

American Women's Organisation of Moscow

The American Women's Organisation of Moscow (call the US embassy for contact details or *e-mail: awo@hotmail.com*) helps its 250 members adapt to living in Moscow. It provides social and cultural contacts in Moscow's American community, and informs its members about issues which may affect them as U.S. citizens living abroad. Whether you are a newcomer or a long-time resident, the AWO offers a variety of activities which will enrich your life in Moscow.

Expat guide: Moscow   **7/Getting to know others**

Members are women of all ages, married and single, empty-nesters, mothers and grandmothers, professionals, diplomats, working women and corporate spouses. Membership is open to women living in Moscow who are U.S. citizens or who are married to U.S. citizens. Non-voting Associate Membership may be offered to women who are not eligible for regular membership. Your $40 annual membership fee gives you access to free or subsidized social activities and educational events such as movies, parties, lectures about political and social issues in Russia, cultural events and holiday celebrations, bi-weekly coffees in members' homes for networking, companionship, and the latest information about what's available in Moscow, the 'Moscow Mentor' program, which pairs recently arrived American women with those who have already mastered the city, special interest group meetings, the AWO Newsletter, the AWO Directory and much more. Membership applications are accepted at all times.

The group is also involved in environmental clean-up projects, a speakers' series and several interest groups.

Both Russian and expatriate speakers regularly discuss culture, religion, business and other issues related to living in Moscow. The interest groups include a group that visits Moscow's museums, one that dines out at restaurants and another that meets for a happy hour at members' homes.

The organisation also seeks to focus on providing help to Russia's needy. Activities are planned for members' children, such as a Halloween party and a hockey game followed by indoor ice-skating. Contact Christy Ramos *(tel: 241-4988)* for further information.

The American Women's Organization publishes an annual telephone directory which lists the names and telephone numbers and e-mail addresses of its members.

Moskva Acceuil French Club

Moskva Acceuil is a French club with well over 100 members. It holds regular meetings with a cultural focus and publishes a very informative newsletter. Contact the French Embassy or **Centre Culturel Francais** *(tel: 915-7974; fax: 915-7684; open Monday to Friday 13:00 - 18:30 and Saturday 12:00 - 17:30. Closed from mid-July to mid-August and also on Russian public holidays).* Interest groups include: needlepoint; patchwork, egg-painting; porcelain painting; framing; bridge, mah-jhong; Russian literature; aerobics and charity.

Le Club France

Le Club France is a society for French-speaking business men and women who live and work in Moscow. A monthly dinner/debate is usually organised focussing on a general-interest theme. Contact Tatiana Choubina *(tel: 925-8978; fax: 937 19 11)* for further information.

Expat guide: Moscow   **7/Getting to know others**

The Spanish Centre

All Spanish-speaking expats are invited to the meetings at The Spanish Centre *(7 Rozhdestvenka; metro: Kuznetsky Most)* held every Saturday from 11:00 - 13:00.

The Navigator Mentor Program for Russian/expatriate women

The programme discusses cultural differences in English so that Russian/expatriate women can find out on a one-to-one basis what makes the other culture tick. Contact Olga Dougina, the Project Director *(tel: 932-3716 from 09:00 - 23:00; e-mail: dougina@glasnet.ru)* or contact Irina Gourouleva *(tel: 146-3739 from 19:00 - 22:00 or e-mail: irinagur@hotmail.com).*

The Professional Women's Organization

The PWO welcomes all professional women who wish to meet and network in an informal and relaxed environment. For more information contact Molly Boudreau *(sales@ponyexpress.ru).*

St Andrew's Society

Invites all interested in Scotland and Scottish dancing, to join. Contact Katrina Broadhurst *(tel: 243-3789)* for further information.

St George's Society

Aimed at English expats and their partners, the society organises several entertaining get-togethers and outings in the course of the year. These have included river-boat cruises and picnics; Wimbledon final; annual ball and pre-Christmas fun in the snow. Contact the British Embassy for further details.

Australia and New Zealand women's support group

The group meets on the first Friday of every month for a friendly coffee morning at an informal venue where those of similar origin can socialise and swap practical tips. For further details contact Janne Kelly, *(tel: 291-2432)* or Vicki O'Neill *(tel: 135-8758)* or contact the Australian embassy.

Moscow Irish Community

Among other get-togethers, the group organises the very well attended St Patrick's Day Celebrations and Emerald Ball in March every year (with the exception of 1999). Contact the Irish Embassy.

Moscow Rotary Club

The club regularly meets on Wednesdays at 19:00 at the Russian Business Centre of Trade, *(5/10 Chistoprudny Bulvar tel: 280-3138; 921-7773; 956-5555).*

Expat guide: Moscow **7/Getting to know others**

The Moscow Oratorio Society

For information contact Cy *(tel: 120-4185)* or Neil *(tel: 420-5181)* or Linda at *(tel: 956-1019)* or Bonnie *(tel: 122-3010)*.The society comprises a choir open to all those who love to sing. All nationalities welcome. No auditions!

Moscow Expat's Bridge Club

Contact Paul Holland *(tel: 152-6588)* or Marie-Lou Portgies *(tel: 238-7551)*. The club meets at the Aerostar Hotel on the first and third Saturday of the month and are always looking for new blood (intermediate and advanced).

Johns Hopkins Alumni

Johns Hopkins University School of advanced international studies alumni
For details call Eva Pregon *(tel: 937-3232)*.

Society of US Service Academy graduates

Members include graduates from West Point, Annapolis, the Air Force and the Coast Guard and meet regularly. Contact David Saunders *(tel/fax: 229-0287)*.

Moscow Mensa

Mensans seeking to join Moscow Mensa contact *e-mail*: *brent.cutler@eu.effem.ru*.

The German-speaking women's club

Meets informally and conducts cultural programmes. Contact the German embassy.

The IWC (International Women's Club)

(tel: 147-224; Office hours Monday 14:00 - 16:00; Wednesdays 10:00 - noon.)
The club holds general meetings once a month except over the holiday summer season. Annual membership fees are $50, with no discounts for pro-rata membership.

Newcomers' coffee mornings are held once a month, often at an ambassador's residence so that foreign women new to Moscow can meet current members as well as other new arrivals. These coffee mornings are an opportunity to start adjusting to life in a new city. Reservations must be made 24 hours in advance.

Members of the steering committee are available to explain the Club's activities. You can decide then if you want to join, or you can join at one of the general meetings. On joining you receive a welcome-pack that cites essential information, as well as a member's directory.

The club has a monthly newsletter packed with all sorts of interesting items relevant to life in Moscow. Its biggest drawcard is the availability of some 80 hobby/interest groups, which is a further opportunity for house-bound women to meet others and socialise.

Expat guide: Moscow   **7/Getting to know others**

The IWC begins its new season each September usually with a meeting held at the US Ambassador's residence, Spaso House, on a date announced in the Community Bulletin page of the *Moscow Times*, from 10:00 - 12:00. Membership is open to expat women and up to 5% of its membership may come from the Russian community. The working language of the club is English, so a good command of the English language is a necessity.

IWC membership fees support charitable causes within the Moscow region. Additional fees may be required to support interest group activities such as cooking, language, and architectural classes (see list below). Monthly general meetings are held the 3rd Thursday of each month at different embassy locations except December, when the Winter Bazaar is held instead, and June, when the annual picnic takes place, and during the summer months of July and August when most people are away.

The Charities Interest Group conducts many projects/programs and activities throughout the year. Volunteers are needed at all different levels of involvement, from fundraising to donations collection and distributions to soup kitchen support to development of educational programs for orphans and/or handicapped children. The group can also provide corporations with information regarding planned giving. If this type of work interests you, contact the Charities group at the September meeting.

Groups include:
- Architecture
- Art history
- Ballet interest group
- Ballroom dancing
- Bible study
- Bowling
- Brazilian and Latino dancing
- Bridge
- Ceramics
- Cinema
- Computing
- Cooking
- English conversation
- First Aid
- Flowers
- Handicrafts
- IWC charities
- Italian conversation
- Jazzercise
- Library club
- Mah-jong
- Moscow art group
- Musical society
- Museums
- Picture framing

Expat guide: Moscow   <u>7/Getting to know others</u>

- Photography
- Painting
- Russian painting
- Russian contemporary art
- Russian conversation
- Russian history and culture
- Sculpture
- Spanish conversation
- Swimming
- Tennis
- Theatre
- Toddlers
- Toddler's gym
- Turkish conversation
- Wine tasting
- Yoga

IWC women receive a membership directory thrice-yearly filled with names, numbers and nationalities of members.

The club holds gala evenings, and a winter and summer carnival, all in aid of fund-raising for charities.

The International After Work Meeting Point

A weekly get-together at 19:00 on Wednesdays at various venues. for expats and friends. Entrance is free. Contact Janina Prim *(e-mail: meetingpoint@expat.ru)*.

Japanese interests

Those interested in Japanese cultural issues can take advantage of the following opportunities by contacting the Japanese Embassy:

- Japanese martial arts centres for Aikido, Kendo, Karate and Shotokan
- Bonsai club
- Japanese classical music ensemble
- Origami centres
- The Moscow Ikebana Club

The British Isles Business club

The club used to meet at the Zoo Bar *(1 Kudrinskaya Ploschad; metro: Barrikadnaya)* on the third Wednesday of every month at 18:00. The club is essentially for anyone who is either from Britain or Ireland or works for a British or Irish company. People are welcome to simply socialise and are not obliged to talk business. Contact the Zoo Bar or British Embassy for meeting details.

93

Expat guide: Moscow　　　　　　**7/Getting to know others**

European Business Club

The club holds regular 'Euro drinks' and is open to all registered representatives of EBC companies and their EU guests. For more details, contact the club *(tel: 721-1760, fax 721-1761 or e-mail ebc@online.ru)*.

Canadian Business Association

The association holds regular functions at which both members and non-members are welcome *(tel: 931-9905 or e-mail cbar@matrix.ru)*.

English-language Alcoholics Anonymous *(see Chapter 10 - Staying healthy)*

The Juggling Club

Aspiring jugglers should contact James *(tel: 425-7069)* or Laura *(tel: 150-7053)*.

New Muscovite programme

The Aerostar Hotel *(tel: 213-9000 ext 2209, Irina, or fax: 213-9001)* holds a New Muscovite programme once a month, at which you are able to meet other newcomers to Moscow and pick up useful information. Contact the hotel to find out dates of meetings.

Charity

There are many charities in Moscow which could do with donations (particularly in winter-time when clothes and food donations are sorely needed). Donating your time is also very welcome and a good way to get to meet both Russians and expats who are also involved in charity work. If you're a good organiser, there is plenty of work involving other expats when it comes to helping organise fund-raising events.

- **The women's prison with children** The Center for Prison Reform will collect donations. Contact Liuda Alpern *(tel: 206-8658 or 206-8684)*.
- **The Center for Humanitarian Assistance** The center helps the homeless in Moscow and in the past has organised an American style rummage sale and auction in early December.
- **The Moscow Protestant Chaplaincy** The Chaplaincy *(Hungarian Cultural Center, 36 Prospekt Mira)*, runs three *stolovayas* or soup kitchens:
  - 38 Ulitsa Ostozhenka (from 09:30 - 12:00);
  - Stolenikov Pereulok (serves from 10:00 -11:00);
  - 17/25 Ulitsa Mosfilmovskaya (serves from 11:00 - 13:00).

Volunteers can, and do show up at any time to help. Any server will be glad to show you the ropes.

Helping at the soup kitchens on a once-a-week basis can be rewarding, not only because you're fulfilling a very valuable function, but also because you'll be able to meet other expatriates, meet Russians, and improve your Russian. If you speak some Russian to the people you're serving, they usually appreciate it, as do

Expat guide: Moscow   **7/Getting to know others**

those helping in the kitchen. For further information, contact *(tel: 143-3562, e-mail: mpc@cityline.ru).*

- **Alumni of the FSAFLEX** (Freedom Support Act Future Leaders Exchange Program) The alumni collect warm winter clothes in good condition for donation to an orphanage. Donations can be brought to the ACTR/ACCELS office Monday - Friday, 09:30-18:00 *(3 Leninsky Prospekt, Room 502, metro Oktyabrskaya).*

- **The IWC Charities group** The group accepts canned food /toiletries /clothes /other donations (but not medicines) for redistribution to the needy (soup kitchens, orphanages, Humanitarian Center for Aid, Mother Teresa's street clinic and children's home, single moms, etc.). Items may be dropped off on Mondays between 12:00- 3:00 at 3 Dmitry Ulyanova, (just off Leninsky Prospekt). The office is above the *biblioteka*, room #210.Collections of donations can be organised, but you should allow a few days so that donated driver services may be coordinated.

- **The Moscow Centre for Prison Reform** The centre *(4 Luchnikov Pereulok, Room 24, between Liubyanka and Kitai Gorod metros)* is always seeking basic food items, vitamins and clothes for 80 babies aged between one and three years. The children whose mothers are serving sentences at the Mozhaiskaya Women's Colony, 100 km southwest of Moscow, are currently living in a children's home located at the colony. The babies are in urgent need of dried milk; butter; cream of wheat/semolina; vitamins; juice (non-citric); baby clothes. If you would prefer to make a financial donation, that would also be gratefully received. Contact Liuda Alpern for more details *(tel: 206-8658; 206-8684; e-mail: mcprinf@glasnet.ru).*

- **The Russian Orphanage Association** can be contacted through Michael Vassiliev; c/o Novgorod Baby Orphanage, *(7 Ulitsa Sushanskaya Borovichi (tel: (816-64) 3-45-05; fax: 3-41-12; e-mail: orphan@novgorod.net or www.geocities.com/~rusor)*

- For those interested in charities: lists, procedures, legislation, contact the Charities Aid Foundation *(tel: 928-0557or e-mail* lenay@glasnet.ru*)*.

- Other charities to look out for are: The Red Cross; the Salvation Army; Medecins sans Frontieres; Downside Up and the Irish Orphan Association.

Religious groups

Many expats rely on meeting others through religious organisations. Consult Chapter 10: Staying healthy, for details of religious groups operating in Moscow.

Russian customs, traditions and courtesies

It does no harm to be aware of some of these customs:
- Spitting three times over your left shoulder will prevent bad luck.
- Never refuse a drink or toast.
- Don't be offended at the much closer body contact Russians will have with you. They are simply less reserved than many Westerners are. They may stand far closer to you than you are accustomed, or touch your arm when making a point, for instance.
- If you sit in the corner of a spare table you will not marry for seven years.

Expat guide: Moscow　　　　　　　　**7/Getting to know others**

- Do not return home if you forget something as it will bring bad luck. If you must return, first look in the mirror.
- Don't kiss or shake hands over a doorstep as this will lead to quarrels.
- Don't give an even number of flowers unless you are going to a funeral.
- Never ever whistle indoors, nor in a taxi as this guarantees that all your money will soon desert you. (A friend was nearly thrown out of a taxi by a very disgruntled taxi-driver when he started whistling).
- Always take a gift of flowers or chocolates when visiting a Russian hostess.
- Before you leave for a trip, always sit down with all your bags and coats before you leave for at least two minutes to obtain good luck and also think of the things you might have forgotten.
- When visiting a Russian home, all stops will be pulled out to make sure that you have an enjoyable time. Hostesses will go to a lot of trouble (however humbly) to ensure that you eat (and drink!) well and sufficiently.
- Don't express a liking for anything belonging to your host/ess as you might very well find that this is given to you in a spirit of overwhelming generosity (this might stop short at daughters, though!)
- Take your shoes off when visiting a Russian home. You may either walk around in your socks or be handed slippers to wear, or bring your own slippers.

It also helps to remember the following courtesies:
- Respect the intelligence and learnedness of Russians, you might very well find out that your driver is a university professor, or your nanny a pediatric surgeon.
- Never criticise Russia even though Russians may do so themselves. If you have to criticise, limit your criticisms to politicians and the weather.
- It's better not to express an academic interest in their misfortunes, nor to take delight in being in Russia at such a momentous time in their history (which seems to be all the time).
- Do not boast about the West.
- Remember that Russians have their own opinions regarding the conflicts in Kosovo and Chechnya. Be sensitive to the fact that they probably have been exposed to propaganda different from the propaganda to which you have been exposed. It's probably better all round to avoid the subject of the war, even if people try and draw you into it.

Cultural holidays/celebrations

Because expats tend to rub shoulders with people from diverse cultures, it's worth knowing a little about some of these cultures and the way they celebrate their important holidays. There is no way that this book can cover all the cultures you are likely to meet in Moscow, however, a few of the more prominent cultural celebrations are described here.

96

Expat guide: Moscow　　　　　　　　**7/Getting to know others**

Halloween

This essentially North American tradition is growing in popularity, and not a year goes by without a large party being organised at some venue or other. You will need to keep your ear to the ground in early October find out which venue has been chosen for the party which takes place on the last Saturday of October. In the past up to 1,000 revellers have joined in the fun, which requires that you dress as ghoulishly as you can.

The American Women's Organisation has organised Halloween parties at Planet Hollywood and the Starlite Diner in the past. Make sure you book early, as you will be turned away from the door if you arrive without a reservation. Try the shop on Nikolskaya Ulitsa near metro Teatralnaya for ghoulish accessories.

Diwali

Snowing or not, Moscow's Indian community celebrate Diwali, or the Festival of Lights every October. Said to be the time for spring-cleaning or looking for a new house, giving out sweets and, for individual homes, lighting fireworks.

Fourth of July

Big on food, big on celebration, big on people (unless it's washed out by rain) - the Fourth of July American Independence Day celebration which is organised annually by the American Chamber of Commerce, promises all this.

Depending on the weather, it's not unusual for up to 7,000 people to pay about $5 to have the opportunity to savour such delicacies as corn on the cob, chicken and ribs, fajitas and cold beer. The celebration usually takes place at the huge Kuskovo Estate in south-eastern Moscow.

Tickets prior to the event can be booked at the American Chamber of Commerce at a slight discount on production of a passport. Entry can also be gained at the gates on the day, but there are long queues for those who don't arrive with a ticket. There are fireworks displays later in the day which starts at 14:00 and lasts till 23:00. Side events include soccer and volley-ball friendly matches, coupled with big name entertainment including jazz, pop and classical, children's amusements such as bouncy castles and clowns.

Much patriotism is in evidence, so come prepared to join in. Children under 12 are free. Apart from beer, no alcohol is permitted. Passport identification may be required. Take the metro to Ryazansky Prospekt and then board either a chamber shuttle bus or city bus #208 or 133

Canada Day

The Canada Day celebration has taken place in past years at the Canadian Moosehead Bar. Contact the Canadian Embassy.

Bastille Day 14th July

In the past, Moscow's French community has been out in force at the Hermitage Theatre and neighbouring night-club Parizhskaya Zhizn to celebrate the anniversary of the storming of the Bastille in Paris.

97

Expat guide: Moscow   **7/Getting to know others**

Delicious food, a choir, a catwalk show and an impressive fireworks display with a party lasting till dawn are some of the major features of this celebration. Contact the French Embassy if you wish to attend, though you may need to prove French citizenship).

American Thanksgiving Day

Thanksgiving celebrates the first 'dinner' held by the Pilgrim settlers in America, supposedly with peaceful native Indians who had helped them learn to plant crops and husband domestic livestock. The tradition grew to encompass a celebration of the harvest in years to come and to give thanks for the welfare of those present.

Turkey is traditionally served on Thanksgiving Day for Thanksgiving dinner and this is accompanied by sweet potato casserole, mushroom or oyster stuffing or cornbread dressing, peas or beans or mashed potatoes, giblet gravy, home-made rolls with butter, salad, cranberry sauce. Dessert might include ambrosia (fresh orange slices or fruit with coconut flakes and sugar), pumpkin pie with whipped cream, mincemeat pie, pecan pie, or any other favourite. The traditions vary depending on which state you come from. Watch the press for details of Thanksgiving dinners offered at many hotels and restaurants in Moscow.

Western Christmas

Westerners will not miss the pleasure of Christmas in Moscow, as Mayor Luzhkov has decreed that the season starts on 1 December meaning that all shops have to display Christmas decorations, and the streets are lit up with Christmas lights from that date.

For those who enjoy Christmas but are tired of the lengthy Western Christmases where shops capitalise on shoppers' need to prepare for the big day from as early as September, this official 'setting' of the Christmas season can bring much relief.

Most businesses continue to work on Christmas day (25 December) as it is not an official holiday, though the Russian Christmas celebrated on 7 January, is.

Nevertheless, many hotels and restaurants put on Christmas spreads with traditional foodstuffs, meaning that you won't have to forego your traditional celebrations.

Some of the Western supermarkets sell turkey and most of the trimmings, though you should bring what you can in the form of sauces and stuffings from home to avoid disappointment. Stockmann was selling 8kg turkeys for some $60 in December 1998.

Those who want to buy Christmas trees *(yolki)* ($3/m) will find them available at stalls on the side of the road from about the 15th December becoming more widespread from the 20th December. You can also sometimes buy the far more expensive Danish spruce ($50 per metre). Traditional Christmas tree adornments are widely available in the shops.

Ask your Russian friends for contacts who deliver trees (available in different metre lengths). One supplier *(tel: 457-1420)* sells trees at 1.5m - $15; 1.5 - 2m - $18; 2 - 2.5m - $22; 2.5 - 3m - $26.

Expat guide: Moscow　　　　　**7/Getting to know others**

Christmas carol services take place before Western Christmas at a number of venues, one being St. Andrew's Anglican Church *(8 Voznesensky Pereulok, e-mail: st-andrews@unforgettable.com; www.bspark.demon.co.uk/st-andrew).*

New Year's Eve/New Year (31 December/1 January)

This is a widely celebrated event though many Russians will also be found at home around the Christmas tree, where they will be opening their gifts and celebrating with champagne and a large dinner. There are a host of functions arranged around town for those who wish to celebrate in the company of others. Visiting Red Square for the countdown to midnight is an unforgettable experience and not to be missed. Crowds are well-behaved and cheerful. However, note that fireworks are much in evidence (and to good effect) though the fact that empty champagne bottles are used as rocket launchers might give you the idea of the amount of risk you could face from wayward fireworks.

Expect to receive cards wishing you *C Novim Godom* (Happy New Year) printed on them. The tradition of celebrating New Year developed only some 50 years ago when the Communist government decided to replace Christmas.

It is not unusual for *Ded Moroz* (or the Russian equivalent of Father Christmas) to visit restaurants with *Snegorushka* (his snowgirl helper) to help spread some Christmas cheer.

Russian holidays
New year (1 January)

This coincides with Western New Year (see above) but has a different significance for Russians.

Orthodox Christmas (7 January)

The Orthodox Church celebrates Christmas on 7 January according to the Old Julian calendar which was in use until 1917. With presents opened on New Year's Eve, Russian Christmas is focussed on attending church services. Throughout the Christmas season emphasis is placed more on Father Christmas (*Ded Moroz*) and his helper *Snegorushka* (snow girl) rather than the Christian depiction of the Christ Child.

Old New Year (13 January)

This is not a public holiday and by now, although most are weary of celebration, this day is still celebrated. It falls later than Western New Year's Eve because of the difference between the Julian and Gregorian calendars.

Pancake week (21 February to 1 March) *(Maslenitsa)*

Pancake or *blini* week is a pagan feast also celebrated by Russian Orthodox Christians in preparation for Lent. Folklore tradition celebrates the bidding of farewell to winter and a welcome to the return of the sun. However, you would do well to ask 'what sun'? at this stage of the winter which still seems firmly entrenched. You may come across street-shows and sleigh or *troika* rides in the

99

Expat guide: Moscow   **7/Getting to know others**

parks and in some streets, also the ritual burning of a straw man symbolising winter whose ashes are spread on fields as fertiliser for the spring planting.

Traditionally butter, eggs, sour cream, *blini* and caviar are eaten, allowing people to store up enough fat through the seven weeks of Lent before Easter.

Watch the press for restaurant promotions and events such as a procession to St Saviour's Cathedral and festivities at Kolomenskoe Estate and the Poklonnaya Gora war memorial. This festival is not celebrated as a public holiday.

Defenders' Day (23 February)

Men are honoured for their contribution to Russia, with firework displays and gatherings in Gorky Park, although this is not regarded as a public holiday.

International Women's Day (8 March)

This is the day when Russian women get to be lauded for all their hard work (you'd think it should be an everyday festival) and their ability to run a household.

Both under Soviet rule and 1991 following the fall of communism, International Women's day is celebrated as the second most important day of the year after New Year's day. Flowers, chocolates and perfume are heaped on wives and girlfriends, and even female employees.

Orthodox Christian Easter

This is usually celebrated a week after non-Orthodox Easter although sometimes the time lag is longer. Holidays are not taken. It is regarded as far more important than Christmas.

May day/Labour day (1 May)

This celebration coincides with the unofficial start of spring, and usually good weather brings many people out of doors to take part in unofficial political parades. You can expect firework displays in the evening all over town. Gorky Park is particularly crowded. Be careful of heading down a main thoroughfare and heading into the back or front of a streetwide procession. Old-timer communists claim the day as their own and use it as a political platform to hark back to the days when 'things were better'.

Expatriates, depending on their inclination and work load, often work on this day, although depending on company policy, may not.

Under Stalin, Red Square would be filled with obligatory huge demonstrations and celebrations. The holiday also marks the time when the snow should have melted and cars head out to the dacha loaded with plants carefully nurtured for weeks before in warm flats, and gardening implements.

Don't expect to get much work done during the first week of May as this is traditionally the week that Muscovites spend planting potatoes at their dachas.

Expat guide: Moscow   **7/Getting to know others**

Victory Day (9 May)

A traditional military march takes place on Red Square. In the recent past it has featured up to 5,000 servicemen and a 600-member band, but don't expect tanks or armoured vehicles.

The day celebrates the end of the war in 1945 with Russia's victory over Nazi Germany and commemorates the 27 million Soviet citizens who died in the war. The 50th anniversary was celebrated in 1995 with huge parades, mammoth fireworks displays and cloud-free weather guaranteed by the mayor, Yuri Luzhkov.

Victory *(Pobedy)* day draws out old communists, some bearing posters of Stalin, trades-unionists, skinheads and other opposition groups who use the day to demonstrate their dislike of the government. You'll see diminishing ranks of medal-clad veterans gathering in Gorky Park and in the square fronting the Bolshoi Theatre. Victory Day is one celebration that appeals to Russians across the political spectrum regardless of differences. All feel the debt owed to their countrymen who died during the war to stop Hitler in his aim of conquering Russia.

Independence day (12 June)

It is not clear why this holiday is celebrated.

Moscow day (1st Sunday in September)

This is Moscow Mayor Yuri Luzhkov's opportunity to splash out and make Muscovites feel proud of their city. Prior to the crisis, no expense was spared to the extent that even the clouds were seeded on Moscow's 850th anniversary in 1997. Facades of buildings were painted and cleaned and no less than three days of festivities celebrated its founding. Top acts were hired from all over the world, including Pavarotti who was to sing in Red Square, and Jean Michel Jarre who conducted a son-et-lumiere spectacle. Unfortunately the event was relegated to second place by the death of Diana, Princess of Wales on 31 August.

In 1998, just as the economic crisis was breaking, Luzhkov still went ahead but with a drastically cut program of celebrations.

Be wary of crowds of drunken youth, blocked off roads, overcrowded metro stations and a large militsia presence.

Revolution day (7 November)

Also known as the Day of Reconciliation and Accord, this used to be held on 25th October to celebrate Red October and Revolution day, but since the change in calendar, the celebration is now on 7th November. This day is generally used by demonstrators to air grievances in public.

Constitution day (12 December)

The infant Russian constitution is celebrated on this day.

Expat guide: Moscow   **7/Getting to know others**

Annual events

These are just a few of the annual events that take place in Moscow. Bring your tuxedos and ballgowns as there will be plenty of opportunity to wear them. Tickets usually cost from about $75 to $150 per person and functions take place at Moscow's five-star hotels.

The St Patrick's annual ball

Watch the Press for details in March or contact the Irish Embassy.

The St Andrew' Society annual ball

Usually takes place in late October or November. Watch the press for details.

Moscow Dragons Rugby Club charity ball

This usually takes place in aid of charity in December. Entertainment includes a champagne and jazz reception, magician, live music, DJ, and full open bar and buffet. Contact committee members.

The Moscow Oratorio Society's Annual Christmas Concert

This is usually held in early December. The choir sings selections from classical composers such as Handel, Bach and Vivaldi, as well as many popular Christmas carols. It's billed as the concert of the season and proceeds are donated to charity. Check the Community Bulletin in the *Moscow Times*.

The IWC annual charity ball

The International Women's Club event usually takes place in February.

The Anglo-American School charity auction ball

The Charity Ball which attracts up to 350 guests, takes place in early March every year.

Feminism

Though Russian women might not have quite managed to crack the Russian glass ceiling, you'll see them supervising road crews, shovelling tar, wearing raincoats in the rain while they plant flowers in street gardens, dressed in workmanlike clothes, sweeping up the streets at 06.30 in the morning, summer or winter.

Although Soviet 'feminism' saw to it that women had an equal 'right' to work in the coal mines, or break up the streets, it still did not do much to help the hardworking and 'liberated' woman where her hardest work lay, in the home.

Today some 8% of Russian women choose to stay at home to look after the children. Despite Perestroika, the consistent and relative dearth of men depleted by the wars and Stalin's terror and by the downward trend in their longevity (around 57 years), the situation is such that there is an estimated three women to one man. This has led to men becoming highly prized simply for being male.

102

Expat guide: Moscow　　　　　　　　**7/Getting to know others**

Consequently, women have found that in order to find a mate, they generally have to be guarded when it comes to demanding equality, though this tendency is said to be more confined to the lower class, middle-aged sector of Russian womanhood.

As a result, feminism as found in the West has not had much opportunity to get a foot in the door. However, research suggests that the typical profile of a 25-year old in the year 2000 would be an ambitious, independent, educated woman who works and earns enough money to remain independent.

The old stereotypes persist in Russia, where men stand back for women to go through doorways or open doors for them, or insist on carrying their bags. This can be perceived as charming by some Western women. Russian men are derided for being emotional infants, while their counterparts in the West are seen to be emotionally castrated. Others say that the Russian man is 'unambiguously male' which would imply that the Western male is 'ambiguously male'. Which would you rather have?

While not expecting to reach the heights of political power as has occurred in other male-dominated societies such as Pakistan and Turkey, the new Russian woman now chooses 'businesswoman' as her preferred choice of career title over 'hard-currency prostitute' which was said to be an aspiration in the early 1990s.

When inaugurating the Woman's Day holiday, the Soviet leadership wanted to highlight the equality of the sexes which it claimed was absent in capitalist societies. Even though they have benefited from improvements in benefits and health care, the notion of equal rights is still very far away from being realised by Russian women.

The Russian soul

Many philosophically-inclined Westerners visit Russia intent on discovering the secrets of 'the Russian soul'. This notion, and even its existence, is debated endlessly, in attempts to solve the tormenting and romantic mystery of a concept which some say doesn't even exist, or at the very most, is exaggerated.

In an effort to define it, some propose that it is embodied by a deeper spirituality than is found in the West, part of which can be attributed to the Soviet legacy.

Because Soviet oppression empowered the personal and the cultural, human relationships gained currency and became precious in the face of the very few other distractions available to the populace. Psychologists have said that the West represents the individual while Russia represents the collective. It would follow then that capitalism tends to subvert the human spirit, and its emergence in Russia since 1991 could have led to the decline of the Russian soul as people increasingly adopt the more individualistic, and thus more selfish, approach of the West. Lapeyrouse, an American philosopher studying the Russian soul says: You can't understand Russia, you can only believe in it.

Yet others describe Russia as being like an onion and point at the onion-shaped domes all over the land, determined to find a significant link with its endless layers.

Part of the attempts to demystify the Russian soul can be found in the efforts by Western political and economic theorists to define just why Russia can't

103

Expat guide: Moscow   **7/Getting to know others**

simply become a clone of a Western country such as the United States. Perhaps Russia's mystery stems from its unpredictability.

Many factors are cited as being the cause of why the Russians allowed the collapse of their society. Apart from the emergence of widespread corruption, as well as blame being laid at the door of the US and the IMF for allowing this to happen to their society, these factors are easy to understand. There is, firstly, no historical tradition or gene-pool memory of democracy or of the market economy. There is also Russia's geographical isolation from the west; its lack of a viable coastal economy; indirect and costly transport links with Western Europe; the fact that Russia lacks a civil society with most of the intelligentsia being killed off by Lenin, Stalin and those who succeeded them; the lack of independent power centres such as a religious or trade-union movement which might constrain the actions of the government, and finally the continuing authority and presence of the Communist party, whatever its form.

Many expats are mystified at the complacency of Russians in the face of their various crises over the years. Many Russians, when asked, will say stoically: 'We're used to this sort of setback. We've had it so many times before. We've coped before and we'll cope again'. Others explain it by saying that as Russia has never been a democratic society, the majority of Russians do not know what democracy and human rights are all about. They have become accustomed to the fact that their opinion is meaningless and that their leaders are all-decisive and all-powerful. Indeed, many Russians prefer a strong tsar-like figure as a leader, rather than one who seeks compromise. This is a form of learned helplessness where any initiative or individual action is regarded as worthless and pointless. Because of the power and comfort of the group as opposed to the individual, this approach is self-perpetuating.

Yet another explanation alludes to the fact that Russian children have not been (especially during the Soviet years) taught to question, but instead are taught to accept whatever is passed on to them. This would inculcate the climate of acceptance and help to stamp out individual and possibly dissenting thought, as would the memory of what happened to dissenters in communist times.

No doubt, Russia and its soul will continue to haunt those who wish to get to the bottom of the mystery for many generations to come. Whatever happens, it would be a great loss to have Russia lose its soul to the West.

The dating scene in Moscow

Many single male expatriates are attracted to Russia because of the excellent reputation of its 'Slavic beauties'. Not only are the women more beautiful than their Western counterparts on a per capita basis, their more feminine ways tend to attract Western men who are tired of what they see to be materialistic and aggressive (ambiguously female?) Western women. Easy access to Moscow's estimated 80,000 prostitutes has also been a factor in this demographic trend.

With equality becoming more and more evident in the West, a growing number of single expatriate women are appointed to responsible jobs and find themselves alone in Moscow, and, quite naturally, on the lookout for company. Feedback is divided on the issue of whether their male expat counterparts or indeed, Russian men, are worthwhile as a source of relationships, and many end up spending their free time alone with the television or a good book.

Expat guide: Moscow　　　　　　　**7/Getting to know others**

Long-term residents say that Moscow does not suffer from a shortage of suitable men, especially if you meet them in the course of pursuing your own interests instead of simply pursuing them as men. This is advice which would go down well anywhere.

Some ideas put forward include the formation of a singles' adventure club where members take turn planning some sort of mystery outing every week, the more unusual the better. People would be told where to meet and from there would continue to the planned event. Another suggests that each single woman invites a male acquaintance (whether or not chemistry is involved) to a party where they are free to mingle with others or not.

Others have found the expat dating scene for women to be less than ideal, with expat males being perceived as having more opportunities in the dating game and therefore being less 'available'. The cultural differences between Russian males and expat males are said to make the former more interesting relationships, though fraught with difficulty as the result of different expectations on both sides and the inevitable language problem. The most difficult situation occurs when the woman is independent, and liberated and work-orientated.

According to anecdote, expatriate men seem to fall in one of three categories: they are only interested in short-term relationships; they have a wife or girlfriend back home but will quite happily cheat on them while in Moscow; or they have Russian girlfriends or wives.

Others say there is plenty of opportunity to be found at the Hash *(www.orc.ru/~force10)* if you are sporty, or at the concert halls or ballet theatres if you are culturally-inclined. Chesterfields' bar is said to be a last-ditch resort for those who are really desperate.

Communication with others

You may be part of the group that groans inwardly when they contemplate having to learn Russian, but it truly is the best way to get a lot more out of life in Moscow. In fact, the number of expats that can speak a bit of Russian is enough to make non-learners hang their heads in shame.

There are myriad opportunities to learn Russian, some professional, some freelance. Whichever route you choose, bear in mind that many Russian teachers tend to be of the old pedantic school, meaning that they enjoy drilling their students to the point of boredom and exasperation. In a way, this is similar to the old-style way of learning the piano where you have to practise scales endlessly compared with the modern way where you end up playing bars of a popular tune by the end of your first lesson, thus motivating you to learn more. Try to determine which method your prospective Russian teacher prefers before you embark on a course of lessons.

If you really don't want to go all the way, at least make an attempt to decipher the Cyrillic alphabet, which will mean you will be able to read a word and possibly identify it (for instance in the metro).

Some Russian teachers who have been recommended are:

- **Elena** *(tel: 256-1370).* has enthusiasm and patience in abundance. She can come to your office for lessons.
- **Katya** *(tel: 954-6730 or e-mail katya@varga.pvt.msu.su)* Experienced English-speaking Russian teacher. Flexible schedule, low price.

Expat guide: Moscow   **7/Getting to know others**

- **Kira** *(tel: 163-0539)* is said to be an excellent Russian teacher used by companies to teach expatriate employees. She speaks English and Spanish, is a graduate of Moscow State University in Foreign Languages, and is available for individual lessons at a rate of $15 per hour. She may consider small groups as well.
- **Yuri** *(yurii@edunet.ru)* eager to improve his level of speaking English can help any expat with his/her Russian.
- **Natalia** *(tel: 335 688)* Only $5 per hour, speaks good English.
- **Svetlana** *(tel: 205 7164)* Basic Russian lessons $7 per hour.
- **Irina** *(tel: 265 1241)* A good Russian teacher (also speaks English) available for private/group lessons.
- **Lyudmila** *(tel: 333-1801)* rated as 'fantastic: well-organized, flexible, and above all patient and encouraging'.
- **Yevgeni** *(tel: 135-2076; 135-8891 daytime or 129-1978 evenings)* professional Russian instructor who is able to work with anybody at any level and obtain quick results. *(e-mail: anatoly@sovam.com)*
- **Irina** *(tel:/fax: 930-1892)*
- **Larisa** *(tel: 180-6516)* charges $10 to $15 per hour.

Learning Russian and other languages

There are opportunities in Moscow to learn languages other than Russian as well. If your favoured language is not on this list, contact the embassy concerned and ask for further advice.

- **The International Center of Moscow State University** *(tel: 124-8011)* offers short- and long-term intensive Russian language courses for both individuals and groups.
- **BKC** *(tel: 737-5225; 737-3303; e-mail: bkc.ih@g23.relcom.ru; website: www.bkc.ru, office #8470 9/15/2 Ulitsa B. Nikitskaya)* supposedly the largest foreign language institute in Russia. Courses offered include Russian, English, German, French, Spanish, Italian, Greek and Japanese. It also provides preparation courses for TEFL/TOEFL and Cambridge/RSA CELTA.
- The **Dialect Centre** (Academy of Foreign Languages) near metro Academicheskaya caters for students between basic and intermediate level. Classes are held throughout the week and the monthly cost is $100 regardless of commitment.
- **Polyglot** *(tel: 426-3144; 426-1001; fax: 426-1122)* is a company that offers all kinds of language lessons.
- **The English Club of the Modern University for the Humanities** *(Ivan, tel: 235-1619; 235-9671; Monday - Friday 10:00 - 19:00; 34 Ulitsa Mikhailova; metro: Ryazanskiy Prospekt; e-mail: vanorus@yahoo.com)* offers an opportunity to meet informally with Russian students. The aim of the English Club is to allow students to practice their conversational skills and learn more about life in the world beyond Russia through meeting native speakers. They meet every Monday at 19:30.

Expat guide: Moscow	7/Getting to know others

- **Pericles ABLE Project** *(tel: 292-6463/292-5188; Room 319, 10 Ulitsa Tverskaya)* offers advanced and intermediate level in small courses and beginning levels in private lessons.
- German is taught at **The Goethe Institute** *(tel: 936-2457/6; fax: 936-2232; 95a Leninsky Prospekt)* Classes close for the summer but resume in September
- Spanish can be spoken in conversation in an informal group *(tel: 258-7943 office; 906-5896 home)* Those who speak Spanish and/or are interested in any aspects of Spanish and/or Latin-American culture meet once or twice a month to chat in Spanish, dance and have a couple of drinks.
- **Helen** *(tel: 488-3824 after 21:00)* is a graduate in English and Spanish and will swap English conversation for Spanish lessons or conversation.
- **Paloma** *(e-mail: seth@agmar.ru)* offers group or individual Spanish lessons according to your background and specific needs; both long term and crash courses offered. She charges $15 - 20 per hour, per person, depending on the number of students, the frequency of classes, and the type of instruction needed.
- Recommended as an excellent Spanish teacher: **Ramon Gomez** *(tel: 268-0733)*
- **Le Cref** *(tel: 784-6369)* is a French-language school and staffed by native speakers.

Teaching English

There are always openings for teachers of English as a second-language. It's preferable to have a TEFL/TOEFL or other language-tutoring qualification. Some offices like to have their staff coached in American English, or Business English.

There is also great demand for English speakers to have conversation sessions with Russians so that the latter can improve their English. They usually offer Russian-language tutoring in return. This can prove to be a very enjoyable and richly rewarding way of learning about Russia and its people.

8/Keeping in touch

It would seem that communication or keeping in touch with local expats and with the outside world is one of the most vexing topics for local expats. No wonder, for in a place like Moscow communication of all kinds is vital, simply because of the different culture, language and distance from most places people would call home.

It's always of benefit to be able to keep up with what's happening to family, friends and local events at home, whether it be through books and other forms of printed literature, or via the Internet and e-mail; via television and video or the postal system.

Printed matter
Books
Where to buy in Moscow

- **Shakespeare and Company** *(tel: 951-9360) 5/7 1st Novokuznetsky Pereulok)* Browse through new and second-hand books while sipping freshly brewed coffee.
- **The American Bookstore** *(tel: 241-4224; 8/10 Denezhny Pereulok)*. Smaller than Anglia and with a US slant, they are able to order any books for you. They also sell at list price, with no markup. Look next door in the Russian bookshop which also has English-language books and stationery, sometimes at better prices.
- **The Anglia British Bookshop** *(tel: 251-5985; 2/3 Khlebny Pereulok)* has a very good selection and can also order anything you need.
- **Dom Knigi** *(tel: 970-0090; Novy Arbat)* is a huge two-floor shop with numerous different sections, mostly Russian items, but also with a few English sections. It has an antiquarian and stamp section, as well as stationery.
- **Pangloss** *(tel:/fax: 299-5481; 9 Palashevsky Bolshaya Pereulok; e-mail: pangloss@aha.ru)* sells French/German/English/Italian books as well as literature, art and philosophy. They have a fast and reliable book-ordering service. Pangloss is also said to hold art exhibitions, show movies, hold debates and offer fresh croissants to Saturday morning shoppers.
- **Biblio-Globus** *(tel: 924-4680; 6 Ulitsa Myasnitskaya; e-mail: biblio.gl@g23.relcom.ru)* stocks English-language publication.

Expat guide: Moscow   **8/Keeping in touch**

Book-exchange

Starlite Diner *(tel: 290-9638; 16 Sadovaya Bolshaya Ulitsa;. metro: Mayakovskaya)* has a free book-exchange situated near the bar on the way to the bathroom. You bring a book to swap for any of theirs. You can either keep them or return them for others.

Libraries

Although libraries are fast made being made redundant by the Internet, bibliophile expats might wish to visit local libraries and see what is on offer.

The Foreign Literature library *(tel: 227-8810; 1 Bolshaya Nikoloyamskaya. metro: Kitai-Gorod, or Taganskaya)* the cost of a library card is very reasonable with a slight surcharge if you want it laminated.

Don't take reading matter with you, it might be confiscated. The American Centre *(tel: 956-3260)* and British Council are in this building. The American Centre Library is a free lending library, open to anyone but used primarily by Russians. It is supported by the US government in a small way and will gratefully accept donations of good quality fiction or non-fiction by American authors and/or about the United States.

Foreign newspapers and periodicals

The following companies can organise subscriptions of your favourite periodicals/newspapers:

- **Esprit** *(English tel/fax 151 5779;office hours 11-00 - 19-00; e-mail: esprit@orc.ru.* This very efficient service can deliver the UK Sunday Times to your door on the same day as publication! Run by Katrina Broadhurst, Esprit Newspapers & Periodicals strives to obtain ANY named publication of your choice for a reasonable fee.
- **Presse-Point International** *(tel: 154-5562; fax: 234-2999; e-mail: int@presspoint.rosmail.com)* delivers a wide variety of international press in Moscow.
- **Pangloss** *(tel:/fax: 299-5481; 9 Palashevsky Bolshaya Pereulok; e-mail: pangloss@aha.ru)* sells French/German/English books as well as literature, art, and philosophy. They have a fast and reliable book-ordering service.

Books by post

It is debatable whether you should ask for books to be posted to you in Russia, though many expats have reported success in this regard. You might instead consider having the books mailed to your home organisation and then hand-carried in by visiting staff. If you do order books to be posted to Russia, expats say you should have it sent as a gift to you to avoid extra Customs charges. Others say that if you send through a courier company you should ensure that the books do not weigh more than 20kg in order to avoid Customs examinations.

You can order books by catalogue:

- **The Good Book Guide** *(tel: 44 171-490-9900/fax: 490-9908)*
- **The Sunday Times Bookshop** *(tel: 44 990 134-459/fax: 44 1326 374- 888 e-mail: bookshop@sunday-times.co.uk)* or you can order them on-line:

110

Expat guide: Moscow   **8/Keeping in touch**

- Order books via the Internet from sites with search and browse features.
- **Amazon.com** *www.amazon.com* with more than three million books. Delivery from either the UK or US is said to be about two weeks if you use a postal service provider.
- **Barnes and Noble** *www.BarnesandNoble.com*
- **The Internet Bookshop Search** *www.Bookshop.co.uk*

Local English-language newspapers

A number of publications can be collected for free in hotels, restaurants and selected shops.

- *The eXile (www.exile.ru)*This foul-mouthed and highly controversial paper (not for the family) which occasionally runs articles that raise interesting issues, and occasionally scoops other Moscow press, is obtainable on-line or for free through offices of AlphaGraphics and CopyGeneral and a few other sites around town.
- *Moscow Business Telephone Guide (www.mbtg.net)* is the *de facto* telephone directory used by English speakers. It contains listings of phone, fax numbers and addresses of businesses, restaurants etc. Up until November 1998, it was printed in English, however, since then, the publishers have started publishing a version that first lists Russian names alphabetically followed by English names, making it much more difficult to find information in a hurry. You can purchase it at a number of supermarkets, or find it free at some hotels. You can also contact the MBTG offices and ask them to deliver for a fee. A new edition comes out several times a year. The on-line edition includes a map, company search feature, global business directory, photo-tour as well as the entire contents of the printed edition.
- *Moscow Times (tel: 937-3399; fax: 937-3393)* is published from Tuesday to Saturday and features local and international news with the occasional full colour supplement. It is by far the most respected and read of the English-language press in Moscow. Available for on-line *(www.moscowtimes.ru)* and distributed free at many outlets.
- *Russian Business Review* **(formerly Russia Review)** is a full colour, monthly magazine published by the same publishers as *Moscow Times* and available as an insert.
- *Moscow Tribune (tel: 135-1114; e-mail: tribune@glas.apc.org)* this is a much thinner and less regularly published newspaper than the *Moscow Times*, but still very much worth reading.
- *Estates News.* This full colour monthly tabloid features news of interest to the real estate and construction industry. It has sections devoted to different Eastern European countries. It is distributed free at many hotels and restaurants.
- *The Russia Journal (www.russiajournal.ru)* was launched in early 1999 and focuses on hard-core political and economic analytical-type articles with the occasional more general interest article as well. It is a published weekly on Mondays and is available on subscription, or free on the Internet. Some copies may be available at the larger hotels.

Expat guide: Moscow   8/Keeping in touch

- *Where Moscow* This monthly full colour magazine aimed at the tourist or visiting business person and loaded with advertising, contains information on shopping, dining, entertainment, tourist attractions, special events and features.
- *AmCham News* - Bi-monthly publication featuring current business issues in Russia. Available on-line *(www.amcham.ru)*.

Local French press

Look out for the free newspaper **'Les Nouvelles Francaises'** usually available at the Progress supermarket *(metro: Park Kultury)* or at the Radisson Hotel. French magazines are also sold at Progress, Pangloss (see earlier) and at the shop at the Hotel Mezhdunarodnaya.

Local German Press

'Moskauer Deutsche Zeitung' is in Russian and German and can be obtained from *tel: 937-6547; fax: 937-6545 or e-mail: mdz@cityline.ru*

Local Italian Press

The first issue of the free newspaper, **'Impresa Italia'** appeared in February 1999. For further information contact e-mail: *direcon@dol.ru* or *tel: 415-4034; fax: 415-2910.*

Audio

Radio

Unless you speak Russian, don't expect too much in the way of entertaining radio in Moscow. Of course, there are the local pop stations some of which are certainly worth listening to:

- **Radio Maximum** pop music   67/103 FM
- **Radio Classica** classical pop music   103 FM
- **Evropa Plus** pop music   106.2 FM
- **Radio Orpheus** classical music   72.14 FM
- light jazz   102 FM
- **Radio 101**   101FM
- **RDV** pop music   105.2 FM
- **Ekho Moskvy** music, news, talk-shows   91.2 FM
- **Radio Serebryany Dozhd** pop and oldies   100.1FM
- **Radio Rossiya Nostalgie** English, French and Russian   100.5FM
  oldies/pop
- **Nashe Radio** only Russian pop and rock   101.7FM
- **Radio 7** Russian oldies and classical music 104.6FM
- **Radio Stantsia** English and Russian pop music   106.8FM
- **Khit FM** (Hit Fm) English and Russian pop music 107.4FM

Expat guide: Moscow   **8/Keeping in touch**

- **Avto-Radio** Russian music   90.3FM

If you want to keep in touch with what's happening in the wider world in English try:

- **BBC** frequencies SW 6.195; 9.410; MW 648; 1260 MW (also reported as 1250 MW). Look up *www.bbc.co.uk/worldservice* which lists services and features publications as well as searchable database of World Service Radio frequencies.
- **Radio 4** frequencies after shut down FM 92.4 to 94.6
- **VOA** 918 MW 'Open Radio' - VOA at night or *consult www.voa.gov* lists frequencies, services and schedules.
- **NPR (National Public Radio)** can be listened to for free by visiting its web site *www.npr.org*.
- **Radio Free Europe** *www.rferl.org*

If what you are looking for is not listed above, consult the Internet or subscribe to:

- **BBC On Air magazine** *(tel: 44 171 257-2211;fax: 44 171 240-4899)* published by the BBC World Service every month, it lists worldwide frequencies.

Portable ham radio licensing/registration

Do not try to bring/register your own devices from abroad. This will only waste your time and money, and besides, you might run the risk of being accused of bringing in espionage equipment. Instead, you can obtain similar equipment in Moscow for the same price or cheaper, together with permits, licences and registration. Radio and computer kiosks sell them locally at VDNKh.

Do not try to get around the radio licence requirement for any radio transmitting equipment capable of transmitting above 15kHz. It is possible to obtain a reciprocal licence valid for one year if you have a non-Russian amateur radio licence. The reciprocal licence costs about $150 and takes about two months to process.

All radio transmitters must be declared when clearing Customs.

Compact discs

You can purchase pirate CDs at the local CD market at Fili or from many kiosks around Moscow for a fraction of the price you would pay normally (1999: about $3) however, you will be contravening the law though it's unlikely that you will be apprehended for doing so while in Russia. Secondly, you may buy defective CDs.

Even though the vendor might play them for your prior to purchase, you still run the risk of them going wrong at a later stage. Ask the vendor to write his name andstall number on the cover so that you can return them if defective. Mayor Luzhkov had announced plans to restrict the sales of videos to only three markets and ban their sale on the street though this was still to come into force at the time of writing.

If you want to purchase legal copies, many shops also sell these but at a much higher price.

113

Expat guide: Moscow   **8/Keeping in touch**

Compact disc player repair

The **M.Video** service center on Ulitsa Maroseika, across from McDonald's (metro: Kitai Gorod) is said to be reliable and cheap.

Audio cassettes

Likewise, you are able to purchase these at the CD market or at kiosks for about $1 a piece. Blank audio cassettes are widely available.

Television/video

Many apartments (depending on rental) come equipped with TVs and often video recorders; if not, these can be easily bought locally. It is not really worth your while to bring a TV/video system over from the US (unless it is multi-system) as the NTSC system is not compatible with the local PAL system. Prices of locally-bought equipment are not unreasonable and if they malfunction, you're more likely to be able to find someone who will be able to fix them quickly.

Remember that some VCRs are not 100 percent multi-system meaning that they will play either PAL/SECAM or NTSC, but record only in PAL/SECAM.

Television and VCR repair

There are plenty of TV and VCR repair shops, although some that are recommended are:

- **Singapore**, on the Ring road almost across from the zoo on the ring, not too far from the US Embassy.
- A small repair outfit in the Frunzenskaya area is reasonably priced and do speedily. At 2nd Frunzenskaya, drive behind the car part and supply shop, on the left side of the building. You should see a indicating the TV repair shop.
- **Vartan** *(tel: 232-2222; 232-0000 pager ID: 14941)* is said to be able to fix almost anything, from TVs to VCRs to video cams. He also speaks English and pricing is very reasonable.

If you prefer to deal with the manufacturing company/dealer repair, expect to pay twice or triple the amount.

Satellite television

There are basically two kinds available outside the US: a fixed dish system that focuses on one satellite, and a motorized dish system that allows a person to tune in many different satellites.

The motorized dish costs some US$600 - 750 but will allow you to watch programs on different satellites, while the fixed dish covers only one satellite, costs about $200-250. Recommended systems are supplied by Pace, Grundig and Uniden.

It would seem that for reception to be optimal your dish would need to be installed facing the south-south-west. Some apartments come pre-wired for satellite television.

Try:

114

Expat guide: Moscow   **8/Keeping in touch**

- **General Satellite** *(tel: 719-9191)* will install a dish tuned for the Hot Bird satellite. They require a moderate one-off payment and no monthly fee. Of course, the more you are prepared to pay, the more channels you will get. General Satellite offers 90cm dish with analog decoder costing around $200. Installation fee starts from about $90 depending on roof, floor, cable length will get 16 channels including Eurosport, Euronews and BBC as well as some Italian, Spanish, French and German channels.
- **Antenna Mir** *(tel: 125-0066)* offers various solutions/packages which contain CNN/movie channels/Cartoon Network etc.
- **Kosmos** *(tel: 210-7010; 210-9052; 210-9057;286-4125; 728-7028 www.ktv.ru)* is a local satellite television provider which offers a number of packages at different fees. The most basic package offers local Russian television stations (six at last count). If you wish to watch foreign channels such as CNN, Eurosport, BBC Prime and World which share only one channel, Cartoon Network, TNT, Hallmark, Animal Planet, Discovery etc, you will need to either take out a subscription with Kosmos or purchase and install your own satellite TV system. Kosmos charges a fee ($60) for the decoder and an installation fee ($18) in addition to the monthly charge for dual audio channels which are broadcast in English and Russian.
- If Kosmos can't get a signal from your roof (it happens) you will need to install satellite TV. However, some areas in Moscow such as Kutuzovsky or Frunzenskaya might have a cable station that latches onto other stations which you may obtain by default and get channels such as NBC, Eurosport, BBC, DW, RaiUno, MTV, Euronews, but no CNN. Up to January,1998 CNN was available anywhere in Moscow, but their contract ran out and their signal stopped. You can however get it on Kosmos TV. You can also speak to Kosmos about adding a low-cost, audio service.
- See if a new competitor **Telemos**, which was cited to be cheaper than Kosmos is up and running.
- **STM** *(tel: 535-9532)* install a 2.5m dish which allows you to view CNBC, Eurosport, Euronews, BBC Prime, CNN, SkyNews, TNT, Cartoon Network, TV1000, TV3 (three Scandinavian channels), National Geographic plus others including three English channels. Total cost is about $1,000 including installation and a one-year guarantee.
- **Sky Sat** *(tel: 215-9603)* offers Sky, BBC, USA and Scandinavian (in English) and European channels. You need to buy a 'non-unique' smart card every few months for about $30, which, after the initial cost, is the only expense. Sky channels are the same as Sky 1 and Sky 2 as seen in the UK. The full cost of dish and decoder is in the region of about $1,900.

Finding satellite frequencies

To find satellite frequencies consult:

- *www.satcodx.com* (charts, footprints, etc.)
- *www.tele-satellite.com* (European SATTV magazine)
- *www.sat.ru*

115

Expat guide: Moscow   8/Keeping in touch

Obtaining a Eurocrypt or stereo decoder/anti-dubbing device

- **Corbina** *(tel: 755-5648; www.corbina.ru)* charges $50 per month for unlimited service however, they restrict the number of new customers.
- As channels such as CNN and Discovery are voiced over in Russian, you can revert to English language by hiring a stereo-decoder from **Kosmos**, but these are not always in stock. At the time of writing the cost was $60. Technical support and installation costs an extra $18. The decoder works for some of programmes only depending on whether the dubbing is on a separate voice track than the English. This will include CNN, Discovery, Nickelodeon, Travel and Eurosport with options open for future channels. Check whether the device works on channel 30 (International movies dubbed into Russian) or whether it only works as a mute function.

Buying videos

It is possible to buy pirated English-language videos both at **Fili CD market** and at underground kiosks (best one in the underpass at Smolenskaya opposite Pizza World) or in the underpass at **metro Oktyabrskaya**. Underpasses near the Metropol Hotel and at Tverskaya/Pushkinskaya stations have kiosks which sell tapes. The tapes cost $7 or so each and occasionally one is defective in some way. If you ask for a receipt or ask the merchant to sign and date the product, you will normally be able to exchange it. The most commonly encountered recording standard is PAL.

The mayor was scheduled to ban street and underground sales and confine the sales of videos (with added tax) to two or three centres.

- There is a video shop at **18 Kutuzovsky Prospekt** *(open Tues-Sun from 10:00 - 20:00)* which is highly recommended, though it is difficult to find. Look for an unmarked door with a bell around the left side of the building towards the rear. Ring the bell for entry. It is said to offer a good selection of newer releases, classics, and concert videos. If you sign up for an account number you will get one free for every 10 movies you buy. Movies sell for about $6 - $7. Picture-quality and sound-track are guaranteed and exchanges are permitted for dissatisfied customers with a valid reason.
- Supposedly the best supplier of English-language movies is **American Video** *(tel: 229-8797)*. They are sometimes able to deliver from their 60-page-long list of movies, as long as you choose a minimum of five movies which you can keep for a week. If you take 12 you pay for 10 only and get to keep it for two weeks.
- **MGU (Moscow State University)** has an extensive catalog of movies available in English, English with subtitles, and with Russian translation running for about $3 - 5 per complete tape. The cost is roughly 25 percent less if you bring a blank. They are 'exempt' from piracy charges since they are a recognised educational institution. You can find them at the Humanities Building 1 (across the street from circus on Vernatsky Prospekt) between two main front entrances near room 7. There is no clear sign that would indicate their whereabouts but they are located near the photocopying

Expat guide: Moscow　　　　　　　　　　**8/Keeping in touch**

machines. The guards may stop you if you don't look like a teacher or student but you could suggest you are visiting the video centre.

- **Video Express** *(tel: 926-4508 or 926-4509; 16 Malaya Nikitskaya)* situated through the archway and across the courtyard. Video Express rents out both PAL and NTSC videos and delivers within the garden ring.

Converting films from NTSC to PAL or vice-versa

It is possible to convert films from one format to another at a cost of about $30 or more, but there is a big loss in quality. Try Gum in Red Square, and TsUM by the Bolshoi, also SIVMA on 34 Kutuzovsky Prospekt. APS is developed on a next-day basis.

US NTSC video system vs multi-system VCR

If you have an NTSC tape which you want to play on a VCR machine or vice-versa, you may need a 4-head multi-system VCR. Many VCR systems call themselves multi-system because they play some types of NTSC (many will play SP and LP, but not SLP. (SP-Standard Play, LP-Long Play, SLP- Super Long Play). Most movies are SP and these should not cause a problem. But if you have TV recordings sent from the US, they are probably being taped in SLP format. The only VCRs that can play these particular tapes are multi-system-four headed VCRs.

Your TV will also need to be NTSC-compatible although this should be simple to figure out.

Video cassette repair

Try **Varus Video** *(tel: 170-2210)* or any VCR repair centre.

DVDs

One expat recommended that if you buy a DVD player locally, find out if it has multi-zone capability to get around zone restrictions imposed by manufacturers. It's possible to order DVDs from *www.dvdexpress.com*.

Video-CD

These are not as good a quality as DVDs. These have been seen for sale at, among other places, the books section of Progress Supermarket on Zubovsky Bulvar, near Park Kultury.

Computers
Bringing computers in

It is not worth bringing computers or faxes and accessories as they are all available in Moscow, though remember that faxes will be likely to have their display in Russian unless you can locate one in English. Purchasing them locally would eliminate the need for converters; eliminate the need to clear them through

Expat guide: Moscow   **8/Keeping in touch**

Customs and problems of getting them out again. You could bring laptops, but first confirm worldwide guarantee options and locate Moscow agents.

Buying computers locally

Most are assembled locally. You should be certain that you can take the computer back within the first week if it doesn't work properly.

The enclosed Savyolovski market near the Savyolovskaya metro station is recommended for selection and prices which are generally 10% below shop prices. A simple desktop computer with Windows-95/98 for office tasks including monitor but no printer, would cost about $500 (January 1999).

TOK *(tel: 755-6525; Neopalimovsky Proezd; metro: Park Kultury)* is said to offer good prices and service.

Laptops can be purchased at **Nexus** *(www.nex.ru)* and they seemed to be cheaper than other places, with good service as well.

Technical support

Most dealers will be able to help you but at a price.

- **ARITA** *(tel: 202-4874)* is recommended as a computer support/services firm with reasonable rates and reliable, well-trained staff.

Freelance trouble-shooters

- **Pavel** *(tel: 188-1244 (home -leave msg) or via pager tel: 234-9696, pager #58338)* is a self-professed computer trouble-shooter.
- **Ruslan Trefilov** *(via cbarich@east.ru)* is a recommended trouble-shooter and can speak English.
- **Igor** *(tel: 732-5248)* is highly rated and can set up basic operating systems, e-mail, etc.
- **Stas** *(tel: 495-9870)* is recommended and can speak English. His rates are said to be reasonable.

Computer accessories

Although there are many outlets selling computer accessories, visit the following if you are looking for a reasonable price option:

- **Savyolovsky Electronics Rynok** (metro: Savyolovskaya) - follow the signs.
- **Mitino rynok** (market) is not recommended as outdoor storage is not good for cartridges., but there is no harm in visiting it to see what is available.

Software

Hundreds of programs are available illegally at Fili CD market at very low prices, but you run the risk of a variety of glitches, viruses and lack of documentation. If you choose to buy from the market, remember to ask the merchant to sign and date the program. There are also many shops in Moscow which will sell you legal copies at similar prices to the UK and US.

118

Expat guide: Moscow   **8/Keeping in touch**

Mac programs

You can buy legal Mac games at a Mac dealer such as MacCentre. Prices are high and you may even have to wait as they have to order the game for you in the US.
Illegal copies are available at Fili's CD market (Gorbushka) but some are said to be useless.
You could try the kiosks underground at metro: Pushkinskaya near the Tverskaya exit.

*   **MacCentre** *(tel: 956-6888;www.maccentre.ru;14 Nikoloyamskaya Ulitsa)*
*   **MacStudio** *(tel: 202-5052; 14, 2nd Obydenski Pereulok)*
*   **SoftUnion** *(tel: 956-6753; 974-7800; www.softunion.ru)*
*   **Terem** *(tel: 956-0404; www.terem.ru)*

Internet
Cyberspace a la Russky

In mid-1998,it was estimated that there were more than 20,000 Internet servers across Russia, some being commercial with others being linked with companies, academic or government institutions. At that time, the Moscow Business Telephone Guide listed over 40 Internet service providers and more than 400 computer merchants and services. A 1997 survey revealed that some 600,000 of 148 million Russians used the Internet while other sources estimate it to be as high as 1.7 million. At present, only a fraction of the 6.2 million people online in the US, Russia's Internet users were expected (pre-crisis) to double every year.

Sixty percent of all Russians using the Internet were in Moscow, and 80% of all users were female. From 1,000 Russian companies with their own web pages in 1997, a four-fold increase was expected in 1998. Disadvantages working against the widespread use of the Internet in Russia were considered to be that the low average salary prohibits the cost of a computer, modem and phone line connection, while on the other hand, the poor quality of local phone lines mitigates against reliable usage of the Internet, often limiting usage only to e-mail.

Widespread credit-card fraud dented the growth of the Internet in Russia, with providers such as Compuserve and America On-Line turning down the opportunity to work in Russia as a result of the problem.

In Moscow, the current cost of telephone line usage was free in 1998 if the server accessed a local number. The only cost payable was to the server. This might change if scaled billing for local calls is introduced by the government.

Internet service providers

When assessing ISPs look for speed of service, connection hit rate and tariff. Ask them to give you a test account (usually for 24 hours) so that you can assess if it works well for your needs. Some of the many ISPs are:

*   **Adicom** *(tel: 259-8641)* is said to be good with first-time connections and no busy signals but they are pricey They have several packages available on pricing. If you spend a lot of time on line (say over 100 hours per month) it becomes more expensive, but for less frequent users they have discounted

119

Expat guide: Moscow   **8/Keeping in touch**

rates of $1.70 per hour 08.00 to 01.00 and $0.90 per hour from 01.00 to 08.00.

- **Russia-On-Line** *(tel: 258-4170)* has, in the past, offered two different plans. One is 'No monthly fee, $1.45 per hour' the other is '$35 monthly fee for 20 hours, then $1.25 per hour thereafter'.
- **Glasnet** *(tel: 291-4343; www.glasnet.ru)* is said to be relatively cheap, helpful and good value for money. It has a 24-hour user's helpline in Russian and English. Free time is offered from 03:00 - 09:00 every day. They offer mailbox-only accounts for those who do not wish to surf the Internet.
- **Matrix Technologies** *(tel: 967-8152; www.matrix.ru)* reportedly reliable with good rates for unlimited time.
- **PTT Teleport** *(tel: 752-8282)* Users report that it takes a lot of time to get connected but once on-line, disconnections are rare even for long periods. Charges $40 per month for unlimited access.
- **Cityline** *(tel: 232-0389; www.cityline.ru)* offers discounts for volume .
- **Combellga** *(tel: 956-5021; e-mail: support@co.ru.)*
- **4unet** *(tel: 255-9282; www.4unet.ru)* sells by the hour and offers good connections, with little delay if lines are busy.

The following are issues you should examine when selecting an ISP:

- Do they have a single connection fee?
- What is their rate per Mb of input/output?
- What rate is charged per connection hour?
- What is the fixed rate per month?
- What Mb is allowed at the fixed rate?
- What is the rate per Mb over and above the allowance?
- What is the best connection rate in Kbps?
- What is the general connection rate in Kbps?
- What is the average number of dial-ups needed for connection?
- How would they rate their connection stability?
- Do they supply a free e-mail mailbox?
- Free web hosting allowed on server?
- Helpful or unhelpful technical support?
- English-speaking staff
- Web pages in English
- Account credit checkable on-line
- Number of e-mail account status warnings before cut-off

Regardless of what your connection software says, it is doubtful that true 33.6 access is available on regular Moscow lines. True speeds are probably somewhat less. It is not the ISP or the equipment that counts, but rather the amount of noise on the line which is related to the age of the line. Your best bet, if this is crucial, is to find accommodation in an area which is known to have good access speeds.

If you are convinced that your modem needs upgrading, rather than your telephone line, swap modems with someone who has good access speeds and see if that makes a difference.

Expat guide: Moscow   8/Keeping in touch

Some believe that the worse the line quality, the bigger the difference will be between a high-end and a low-end modem. The modems which are said to deliver the most reliable connections over poor telephone lines are the high-end models of MultiTech, Motorola and US-Robotics (3COM), although the low-end US-Robotics Sportster does not work well on low quality lines.

Others say that there's nothing wrong with the Sportster modems. Some suggest that there's no reason to skimp on a modem and that you should pay for the most advanced model your ISP supports in order to avoid headaches.

If you already have a dated modem, find out which 'error correction mode' works best with your quality of line. Your ISP of choice should be able to assist you with this.

Internet average hourly rate

The average charges for Internet connection in Moscow in terms of the hourly rate charged by the ISPs are in the region of $1.00 per hour, but can get cheaper with discount plans from ISPs which offers discounts for volume.

Logging on/staying on line/service interruptions

Again, the key to this problem, which is widely experienced, appears to be the relative newness of an exchange, particularly on wet days. If you're on a really old exchange, it would seem that no ISP provider would be able to help you. You could also try unplugging your phone once you are connected, as it may draw power from the line and slow it down. Also try downloading large files in the morning, when the rest of the Western world is asleep.

Some expats recommend using GetRight shareware (downloadable from the Internet) which enables you to pick up your connection from where it left off when it was disconnected. You could also try the light version of ReGet, which is a similar program.

Hacking

If you run Windows 95, use a remember password feature and also run pirated software from CDs from Fili/ Gorbushka, software jokes forwarded to you by an unknown source and software, downloaded from unverified sources, you apparently run a high risk of your account password being stolen. Any of your files can also be stolen.

One service provider's client account was hacked and over $100 in charges run up on the account resulting in the account being frozen and the service provider demanding to be paid before switching the account on again. This has been attributed to a malicious program called 'Black orifice'. Further information and a 'detect' program is available from

* *www.glasnet.ru/glasweb/help/security/* or directly from its author's page
* *www.spiritone.com/~cbenson/*

Another attributable culprit is something called 'Trojan horse' which has been used in attempts to steal users' passwords. These are self-extracting archives. Some 'Trojan' programs send the user information as soon as a connection is made to the Internet. Regular password changes are said to not be able to protect your account from abuse. If you have enabled the option to save your password in

121

Expat guide: Moscow   **8/Keeping in touch**

dial-up networking the situation can be exacerbated. To avoid this, disable the feature and manually enter your password every time you connect.

Sometimes the only option for a computer infected with a Trojan Horse virus is to reinstall Windows 95/98 from scratch on a newly formatted disk. You should not execute any attached binary file, unless the source is completely trustworthy. Files downloaded from .ftp archives may also contain these viruses. Always use up-to-date anti-viral software as a measure of protection.

Service providers say that protection of a password is the owner's responsibility and that the owner will be liable for every session opened using his login and password.

FSB monitoring of e-mails

Some say that the FSB is willing, anxious and quite possibly able to read any and all e-mail sent in Russia and warn you to be careful what you ask advice on in open forums.

Others say that two reasons why it is safe to discuss whatever you want:
1. it is technically NOT possible to monitor all the e-mail traffic.
2. FSB is not interested in minor violations, discussions and rumours.

For further information on this topical subject, visit the following site: *www.ice.ru/libertarium/eng/sorm/index.html*

E-mail lists

The Expat-list

By far the most interesting site for expats is the Expat-list which was launched in mid-1998. This grew (at the time of writing) to close on 1,500 subscribers and acted as a great network for expats (and English-speaking Russians) who pondered the crisis and famously, where to get kitty-litter during the crisis. There is plenty of straight-talking on the list as well as spats, and bouts of flaming. Some obstreperous individuals have even been banned from the list.

To subscribe, send a message to listserv@irex.ru. In message text, write: subscribe expat. The List Manager is Nicholas Pilugin (*nwpilugin@glasnet.ru*) The Expat-list is archived on irex.ru both in the form of hypermail accessible through the WWW: *www.irex.ru/lists/expat* and in the form of majordomo archive of digests (use INDEX EXPAT and then GET EXPAT with the appropriate file name). The latter way is for those with a good majordomo experience.

For a list of commands, including how to leave the list, send 'help' in the message to listserv@irex.ru. All messages for the list should be posted to expat@irex.ru.

The list is run along strict lines which generally restricts discussion to Moscow-related topics. The sheer volume of posting to the Expat-list (up to 80 or more messages a day) may make it a good alternative to switch to the Expat-digest which combines all the day's postings in a few mailings, leaving your mailbox less cluttered.

Nicholas has compiled the following list rules:
- No commercial messages. A commercial message is a message offering the products or services of a for-profit company posted by either the business or an individual who serves to profit from the posting of such a message.

122

Expat guide: Moscow   8/Keeping in touch

Companies may identify themselves as providing a specific product or service in response to a posting seeking such goods or services.

- Treat your fellow Expats with courtesy and respect: no profane or insulting language.
- Auto-reply: Do not to auto-reply from the list digest or you'll resend everything that appears in the copy of the digest to the entire list. Also, trim the previous message when using autoreply; a few lines are enough to let everyone know what it is you're referring to.
- The list is free, but list owner Nicholas maintains the right to cut off anyone who abuses the list and its subscribers. Messages are posted directly to the list without pre-screening or filters.

Johnson's Russia List

If you are interested in Russian politics and economy, then this daily or weekly service (free subscription, but voluntary subs welcome) is definitely worth a look. It's a compilation of the most relevant news stories from around the world concerning Russia. The list is managed by David Johnson (davidjohnson@erols.com) whom you need to contact to subscribe as it is not an automated list.

Johnson's Russia List began in May 1996 with the objective of monitoring the Russian presidential election, and soon developed into a vehicle for the provision of diverse information and analysis about contemporary Russia. A weekly edition (The Russia Weekly) contains additional content. Subscribers are able to receive the shorter version (or both). All materials distributed by JRL are strictly for purposes of education, criticism, and discussion. Most materials from newspapers and magazines are distributed only for the personal use of the recipients and are not to be used in any way outside of normal fair use practices. You do not need to be an expert (known or unknown) to contribute your views for circulation on JRL although many academics evidently subscribe to it.

Websites

Politics and Economics in Russia

- *www.russiajournal.ru The Russia Journal* is published weekly

Buying shares on the Internet

There is a large number of Internet Brokers today on the WWW. The first to establish this business was Lombard - *www.lombard.com*, but shop around.

- *www.dbc.com* Data Broadcasting Corporation
- *www.cnnfn.com www.quicken.com* have information about e-trade

Business News

- *www.rbc.ru* Statistical data supported by the Department of Statistics of Russian Federation
- *www.reuters.com*
- *www.bbc.co.uk*
- *www.rferl.org* (Radio Free Europe / Radio Liberty)
- *www.russiatoday.com*

Expat guide: Moscow   **8/Keeping in touch**

The above offer in depth coverage in English. Reuters and BBC are updated numerous times daily while RFERL and Russia Today tend to be updated only once a day.

- *www.cnn.com* but news coverage is not as good as Reuters and BBC.

Expat finance

- *www.expatworld.com* 'Expat Investor' A bi-monthly magazine aimed at helping expats to manage their finances, with additional on-line sections on leisure and property. Free subscription worldwide via their website.
- *www.expatfinancial.com/helpful.htm* Expat Financial gives advice on buying health insurance or a financial plan.

Corporate Expatriates Online Survival Guide

www.terracognita.com/World_Journey.html Arthur Andersen, The Economist Intelligence Unit (EIU), and Craigshead Publications have launched CountryNetTM, a comprehensive new online information service designed to give expatriates, international road warriors and global nomads all the information they need to relocate and operate knowledgeably, safely and effectively in new countries, cultures and business markets worldwide.

Expat spouses

- *www.egroups.com/subscribe?list=spouses-expat&verify=8418.* The site allows spouses around the world to share experiences. If, for some reason, you cannot access this location with your web browser, you can also subscribe to the group by sending a blank e-mail message to: *spouses-expat-subscribe@egroups.com*

Expat newsletter

- *www.expatexchange.com* or *mail@expatexchange.com* with a member network of over 3,000 offers links, articles and chatrooms.

Expat Overseas Digest

The free newsletter for Americans living abroad dispatched monthly from the Middle East by William Beaver *(editor@overseasdigest.com)* editor & publisher, Kuwait City, Kuwait).

Weather around the world.

- *www.wunderground.com*
- *www.usatoday.com/weather/basemaps/wworld1.htm* World Weather Index to weather around the world - five-day forecasts for temperatures and rain offered by USA Today.
- *www.weather.com/weather/int*

Free Web-based e-mail groups

- *www.eGroups.com* start your own e-list.
- *www.onelist.com*

Expat guide: Moscow   8/Keeping in touch

Free e-mail forwarding

If you change accounts and want mail sent to the old account forwarded to your new account try:

- *www.iName.com* which will forward to any POP3 account regardless of how many times you change. It will also hold mail if you are experiencing problems with your server.

Current exchange-rates

- *www.newman.ru/INTERLINE*
- *www.travel.com.hk/currency.htm* Foreign exchange-rates. Just enter the currencies required for an up-to-date exchange-rate.

Russia

- *www.moscow-guide.ru.*
- *www.russiatoday.com* carries current Russian general and business news.
- *www.amcham.ru* is the site for the American Chamber of Commerce in Russia. It displays an online calendar of events and committee meetings as well as an alternate-monthly magazine. Committee meetings provide a good insight into what members of the business community are talking about (non-members may attend a maximum of two meetings).
- *ruslife@rispubs.com* RusLife Online - an online publication of Russian Life magazine
- Boris Nemtsov's site
- Lenin's Mausoleum which takes you on a guided tour of his tomb.
- Sergei Kiriyenko's site
- Interfax News Agency The Web Site For News and Information on Russia, CIS and Baltic Countries. Contains daily news, special and industry reports on events in Russia an CIS countries.
- *www.kremlinkam.com* Kremlin Web-cam

Restaurants in St Petersburg

- *www.cityvision2000.com/restaura.htm*

Raising children in Moscow

- *www.onelist.com* subscribe to **Mothers in Moscow** list. The list was recently set up by two expat mothers and focusses on discussion about raising children in Moscow, a useful resource if you need to find entertainment venues, nannies, resolve medical issues and organise play groups or simply to make friends with others who have children. Dads are welcome to join too.

Expat issues

- *www.kit.nl* Relocation Tips and Resources
- UK cultural briefing and intensive language training Farnham Castle (The Centre for International Briefing) in Farnham, Surrey, UK; *(e-mail: cib.farnham@dial.pipex.com)*

Expat guide: Moscow   8/Keeping in touch

- *eca@ecaltd.com* ECA (Employment Conditions Abroad) is a subscription-only site. Based in London, it offers more than 800 member companies accommodation reports, country profiles and other advice. Your employer might be willing to subscribe.
- *www.branchor.com* Living Abroad Magazine publishes individual country extracts include useful summaries on culture, documentation, everyday life, housing, tax, banking, fast facts.
- *www.escapeartist.com* aimed at expats worldwide plus message board and links.
- *www.expatforum.com*
- *www.transition-dynamics.com/resources.htm* Transition Dynamics features articles of interest to global expats.
- *www.globalnomads.association.com/gniintro.htm* Global Nomads is a not-for-profit organisation focusing on the expat experience.
- *www.fawco.org/clubtabl.htm* Federation of American Women's Clubs Overseas (FAWCO) serves American women abroad
- *www.lonelyplanet.com* Lonely Planet Online Publishers of the Lonely Travel guide-books offer brief but pertinent information on the countries they cover, online.
- *www.relojournal.com/world.htm* Relocation Journal lists sources of information for many countries, plus articles on living and working abroad.
- *roughguides.com/travel/index.html* Rough Guides offers a site that is similar to the Lonely Planet guide concept.
- *www.odci.gov/cia/publications/factbook/index.htm* CIA World Factbook offers information about countries worldwide.
- World Electric Guide. Check here first to find out about electrical supplies and running your computer in foreign countries.
- *www.indo.com/distance/* How far is it? This site will tell you the distance from one city to another, worldwide.
- *www.wco.com/~doo/cgi-bin/time.cgi* tells you which time-zone is where.

Travel

- *www.itn.net/airlines* Airlines of the Web links to websites of almost every individual airline in the world. Go to Airlines (not Virtual Airlines), and then select the appropriate region to access individual airlines' home-pages.
- *www.easyjet.com* The EasyJet website offers online booking, flightmap and price information for its UK and European routes.
- *www.rnw.nl* **Transsupport Database** supplies information about driving conditions in other countries.

Health

- World Health Organisation: International Travel and Health Vaccination requirements
- *www.intmed.mcw.edu/travel.html* International Travelers Clinic is a US-based healthcare service for travellers planning trips abroad.

126

Expat guide: Moscow   8/Keeping in touch

- *www.tripprep.com/index.html* Shorelands'sTravel Healthline Travel health and safety guide, including country profiles, general health concerns, preventive medicines, etc. Includes regional security updates.
- *www.moon.com/staying_healthy* Staying Healthy in Asia, Africa and Latin America for those living as well as travelling off the beaten track.
- *www.burkebros.co.uk/kids.html* Moving with Children provides useful tips on how to involve your children in your move.

Languages

- *www.travlang.com/languages/* Useful introduction to many of the languages of the world.

Free on-line translation services

- *www.babelfish.altavista.digital.com/*
- *www.translate.ru/eng/its1.asp* PROMT offers an on-line English/Russian Internet translator
- *www.smartlinkcorp.com/f_news_08.htm* allows you to surf Russian web sites with WebTranSite 98.

Embassy resources

- *www.escapeartist.com/embassy1/embassy1.htm* Embassies and Consulates Worldwide
- *travel.state.gov/travel_warnings.html* US State Department Travel warnings and consular information.
- *www.fco.gov.uk/* UK Foreign Office British Foreign and Commonwealth Office advice for travellers. Includes 'do's-and-don'ts sections.

Foreign newspapers

- *www.webwombat.com.au/intercom/newsprs* - a comprehensive list of links to online newspapers on the net, listed alphabetically by country.

Education

- *www.mit.edu:8001/people/cdemello/geog.html* College and University Home Pages in over 3000 colleges and universities, in more than 80 countries worldwide.
- *www.henleymc.ac.uk/contents.htm* Henley College (UK) Master of Business Administration provides advice on studying MBA by distance learning.
- *www.dur.ac.uk/~dbr0www2/index.html* Durham University
- *www.open.ac.uk/OU/Intro/WhatIs.html* Open University (UK)
- *www-icdl.open.ac.uk/icdl/index.htm* International Centre for Distance Learning Database of institutions offering world-wide teaching at a distance, together with programmes and courses.
- *www.ibo.org/* International Baccalaureate Organisation gives details of IBO's programmes, aims and international schools directory (over 750 member schools in over 90 countries).

Expat guide: Moscow   **8/Keeping in touch**

- *www.ecis.org/directories/index.htm* European Council for International Schools On-line directory of international schools worldwide. Higher education directory includes information on applying to colleges and universities.

Moving

- *www.stevensworldwide.com/resident.html* Residential moving. Handy tips on moving pets, antiques, computers and more.

Buying flowers

- *www.floralshop.co.uk*
- or call 1-800-FLOWERS for the US for bouquets costing about $50.

Moscow on-line grocery service

Cyber-grocery *(www.cyber-grocery.ru)* was set up in 1999 to offer a seven-day-week, grocery shopping and delivery service to those who preferred not to do their shopping themselves. Cyber-grocery offers to locate those hard-to-find items

British food

British expats abroad will enjoy *www.3ex.com* which features a list of foodstuffs that can be shipped abroad. They sell everything from Digestive biscuits, Heinz baked beans and soups, Oxo cubes, Walkers crisps, IrnBru and Cadbury's chocolate, right down to the Christmassy stuff like Christmas pudding and cake. If there is something you want and it's not on the list, e-mail and ask if it can be ordered.

Recipes

If you've left your recipe books at home, consult the Internet, there are loads of sites to help you decide whether you want fat-free Banana Sundae or to determine just how much potassium goes into a banana. Just remember that many recipes might feature ready-made products which you might not be able to find in Russia. They will also often feature ingredients in Imperial measures rather than metric.

Travel in Russia

Travel - **Hotels and Travel in Russia** provides country wide hotel directories, local hotel directories and hotel web sites, maps, and tourist information.

Talking by computer

The ICQ program is said to be a means of talking to friends globally. It is a type of instant messaging system used to communicate with your friends in real time whenever they are online. Downloads are available for free at

- *www.cnet.com/Resources/Topdownloads/PC/Result/Download/0,162,51122, 00_html*
- *www.mirabilis.com (the original owner before AOL bought ICQ)*

| Expat guide: Moscow | 8/Keeping in touch |

- *www.icq.com*
- *AOL Instant Messenger*
- *Microsoft*
- *Yahoo!*

You can chat live while watching the letters being typed across your screen in almost real time as the other person types. You can also immediately send files and URL addresses.

A new program called QTalk works in conjunction with ICQ. If you have a microphone and speakers or headset you can talk to anybody on your ICQ list. Privacy features ensure that you won't be intruded upon by strangers.

Voice recognition software

A Dragon Systems product called 'Point and Speak' provides 'true continuous speech recognition'. You speak at your normal pace and basically 'tell' it what to write. It can work faster than many people's typing and results in minimal errors.

Wintel dictation packages are said to be reasonable while Mac dictation packages such as VoicePowerPro are not. It can take hours to 'train' it to recognise your voice.

Cybercafes

- **Chevignon Internet café** *(tel: 733-9203/5; 14 Stoleshnikov Pereulok; metro: Teatralnaya).* Always open. Centrally located; Expect to socialize and drink on the 2nd floor rubbing shoulders with video-playing teenagers while paying $5 for either half an hour on the Internet or for drinks. Both interchangeable.
- In the **Galereya Acter (Actor's Gallery)** on *Ploschad Pushkina; 12 Tverskya-Yamskaya.*
- Try Virtual World **(Partya)** computer and electronics store. Detailed information can be found on *www.partya.ru.*
- **The Foreign Literature library** *(tel: 227-8810; 1 Bolshaya Nikoloyamskaya metro: Kitai-Gorod, or Taganskaya. Open Monday to Friday 11.00 - 11:45 and 14.00 - 19:45 for e-mail and Internet (2nd floor) 10.00 to 5:45 on weekends for Internet only on 3rd floor)* The allotted time is half an hour but expect at least an hour's wait. Don't take reading matter, it might be confiscated.
- **Moscow Intercity and International Telephone** *(tel: 246-0427; 46 Stary Arbat; metro: Smolenskaya. Open 11.30 - 20:00)* Internet Café with drinks. Efficient service, Soviet roundabout payment system, atmosphere quiet, lowest rate in Moscow, three computers, no long lines.
- **Microage** *(tel: 258-7885; 53 Leningradsky Prospekt; Monday to Friday, open 10:00 - 20:00. Saturday: 10:00 - 18:00; metro: Aeroport.* Microage has only a few computers, service costs about $7 per hour. This is not a place for socializing, the atmosphere is business-like. Expect a queue.
- **Agmar Multimedia Internet-Salon** *(tel: 974-7484; 974-7458; Formerly VDNKh (The All-Russia Exhibition Centre) Pavilion 69 metro: VDNKh. Open 10:00 to 19:00 daily).* This is at an inconvenient though there are more

Expat guide: Moscow   **8/Keeping in touch**

than 10 computers; cost is approximately about $2.50 per hour plus extra if you need help. Drinks are available but not obligatory.

- **Agmar** *(tel 342-9900; 10 Brateyevskaya Ulitsa, korpus 1; metro: Kashirskaya (followed by bus #740 or #742)*
- **Agmar** *(tel: 245-8496; 28 Komsomolsky Prospekt (Moscow Youth Palace, containing metro) metro: Frunzenskaya)*
- **Agmar** (*tel: 255-9191; 23B Krasnaya Presnya)* situated in the basement of **Planet Hollywood**
- Inside the electronic store Partiya at the corner of Volgogradskii Prospekt and Abelmanovskaya street in Taganska. Open to 21:00 daily.

- **Internetovsky zal** in the mall behind the 1905 metro station. Open 24 hours. Costs $1-3 per hour depending on time of day. Discounts for students.
- **Compulink** *(tel: 131-4156; 85 Udaltsova Ulitsa)* also offers free access.
- The **Internet café** *(tel: 918-1117; 5A Energeticheskaya litsa)* charges just over $1 per hour.

Telephone

Reception

The crucial issue regarding quality of reception in Moscow is the age of the telephone system in a particular area. In the right areas (ask around), reception will be excellent, indeed international calls will have the person you are speaking to wondering if you are in the same town. However, when lines are bad, reception can be so poor that you will find yourself asking people to repeat themselves or shouting to them, while on other occasions echoes interfere with reception.

Dialling codes

Local and international dialling codes are in the Moscow Business Telephone Guide.

Telephone book/directory inquiries

The Moscow Business Telephone Guide is the telephone directory used by English speakers. It contains listings of phone, fax numbers and addresses of businesses, restaurants etc. Up until November 1998, it was printed in English, however, since then, the publishers have started publishing only a version which gives Russian priority. It is usually published several times a year.

If you cannot find a phone-number for any civic, legal, educational, municipal, or medical in the Moscow Business Telephone Guide or any other directory, you can call 09 for free. You will need to be able to speak Russian and also be quick as each call is limited to two minutes duration. Working hours are from 08:00 - 21:00) Monday to Friday. **Moskva Dlya Vas** (see below) can be accessed for emergency information outside these times.

If you require any other number you need to call 05, wait for a long beep and then dial 9. This will give you access to a paid service, Moskva Dlya Vas (Moscow for you) which can advise you on addresses, activities and even working hours of companies. If you have an individual's name and address you

130

Expat guide: Moscow   **8/Keeping in touch**

can also obtain their number from this service. Costs range from 7c to 60c depending on which advice you seek. These charges apply during weekday working hours 06:00 - 22:00. Outside these hours, information will cost twice as much.

These telephone service lines only operate in Russian.

- 007: telephone numbers of companies in cities other than Moscow
- 975-9122: programmes of Moscow theatres
- 927-0562: (free) locate pharmacies which stock the medicine you are seeking or call 05-0 for access to the paid service
- 05-3: advice on the best way to reach your destination in Moscow by public transport
- 222-2085: lost property for the Moscow metro (recent lost items found include a live crocodile and an urn of human ashes)
- 298-3241: lost property for other public transport services.

International calls

How to get through: You have to dial '8', then pause, and wait for a click, before proceeding, inserting '10' in front of the country code.

Interrupted calls

Some people have consistently had the experience that the phone goes dead on international phone calls after about 30 minutes. During Soviet times the KGB routinely recorded outgoing international calls on tapes that lasted about 30 minutes. If true, this may suggest that Russian authorities have started once again to monitor international calls.

Callback services

- **Rusnet Labs** *(tel: 330-6492)* recommended as good value for money. Contact the marketing department and ask about 'Direct Call' service.
- **Transatlantic Communications** *(www.t-atlantic.com; e-mail: inquiry@t-atlantic.com)* Charge 99c per minute from Moscow to the US and 49.9 cents from the US to Moscow.
- *www.kallback.com.*
- The program IDT Net2Phone can be downloaded from *www.net2phone.com* and use it to dial over the Internet. The free version allows you to dial toll-free numbers in the US for instance to obtain credit-card information. If you don't have a microphone, the audio output from the other end is said to be satisfactory. You can also use this program to call any number anywhere for a fee.

Telecom providers

MGTS (Rostelekom) or the Moscow City Telephone Network, is the city-run telephone service provider but commercial organisations such as Comstar, Combellga, DirectNet, MTU-Inform, Global One, Sovintel, TransTelecom; Telcom and West Call can supply you with a first and second line with various waiting times and at various prices. MGTS is cheaper in almost every instance,

Expat guide: Moscow   **8/Keeping in touch**

but the drawback is that you are likely to wait much longer than you would with a commercial service provider.

Collect calls

- Call the **AT&T USA Direct-dial-up** number in Moscow *(tel: 755-5042)* You will be immediately connected to an operator in the US who can place your collect call although the system which only works for non-800 numbers. Charges are at the standard tariff from Moscow to the US.
- **Sprint Global One** has a local access number *(tel: 747-3324)* recommended by users as not having a regularly occurring cut-out, and an improved sound quality of the connection.

Shared line

Sometimes an apartment will have a telephone line shared with a neighbour. It's possible to have a line installed from a private phone company such as Comstar, or Sovintel. In addition to installation costs, you will also have to pay a monthly fee.

Installing a second line

Comstar *(tel: 956-0000; www.comstar.ru)* supplies a line with an international satellite system number costing $250 for installation and first month's service. Comstar will supply you with a line without a Moscow city phone number (it has a number, but on a different city/country code). Without the Moscow number it costs around $250 to install.

The line is said to be equivalent to European/US standards - If you change residence the fee is not wasted if you move to a line-compatible building.

Paying your phone bill

Bills are sent out monthly although times vary. Check that long-distance calls listed tally with those you have made. If you do not pay by the date indicated on the bill you are likely to be cut off which can incur considerable hassle. Bills are paid in rubles at a special counter at your local Sberbank. Always ask for a receipt which you should keep in a safe place in case of later disputes.

Mobile phones: benefits, costs and providers

Apart from needing a mobile phone for business, they are especially beneficial if you are likely to be lost or involved in an accident.

There are numerous telecom providers. The main service providers are

- **MCC (Moscow Cellular Communications** *(tel: 744-4444; 18/20 Ulitsa Vorontsova)*
- **BeeLine (Vimpelcom)** *(tel: 755-0055; 10/2 Ulitsa Vosmovo Marta)*
- **Mobile TeleSystems (MTS)** *(tel: 928-4355; 2 Ulitsa Sadovaya-Karetnaya)* Ask friends and colleagues for recommendations. Apart from comparing connection fees, instrument charges and per-minute charges, find out:

132

Expat guide: Moscow   **8/Keeping in touch**

- whether your provider truly roams in cities other than St Petersburg as well as internationally
- how accounts are reconciled and how regularly
- if they have dual-standard (GSM - 900 and 1800) systems
- what procedures you should follow to inquire about bills
- charges for voice mail, and call forwarding
- what pre-paid card schemes are offered
- what extra services they offer or are likely to offer in the future.

If you carry a cell phone, you need to carry the licence (from your cellular operator) with you whether the phone is foreign or local as this may be required for a document check by the militsia. Failure to produce a licence might result in confiscation or a few hours detention.

Greetings cards

- **Stolitsa** on Pokrovka Ulitsa near to the junction with Zemlyanoy Val (Garden Ring)
- **Hallmark** store in both Ramstore complexes
- **Dom Knigi** on Tverskaya

On line greetings cards are available from *www.bluemountain.com*

The Russian post

The Russian postal system has a reputation for unreliability, though quite a number of expats report satisfactory and reasonably speedy service. Nevertheless, expatriate residents also rely on alternative, private express and non-express mail delivery services which are provided by a number of carriers and service companies.

However, now and again a word of praise is said in favour of the Russian postal system with expats reporting that their mail has arrived safely and on time.

Buying foreign stamps

American stamps can be ordered by post from Stamps etc. catalogue; US Postal Service, PO Box 57 Grand Rapids MN 55744-0057. Only diplomatic personnel can obtain stamps from the US Embassy Post Office.

Independent postal providers

It's worth considering the following issues when signing up to use the services of an independent postal company:

- ask whether junk mail, and catalogues addressed to you are removed without your approval
- ask what procedures are used to advise clients of service interruptions which might affect bill payments and cause needless hassle
- also ask who pays for late mail deliveries
- find out what happens when mail is stockpiled outside Russia as a result of strikes in other countries. Given that you have a weekly limit on the amount of mail you receive, stockpiling would mean that you receive no mail for

Expat guide: Moscow   **8/Keeping in touch**

some weeks and then amounts of mail that are way over your limit on other weeks.

- Find out whether you require membership for receipt of mail.
- Ask what the procedure is regarding the attachment of return addresses on out-going mail.

The two major services used by expats are:

- **Independent Postal Services (formerly Post International)** *(tel: 209-517; 250-4272; e-mail: post@win.pop.online.ru; 43, 2 Brestskaia Ulitsa; metro: Belorusskaya (ring entrance).* If you subscribe, you can receive up to 900g of mail per week for free, and send up to 450 g. Every additional ounce (30g) is 60c plus a stamp. Subscription costs about $60 per month.
- **PX Post** *(tel: 956-2230)* delivers and receives mail daily via the U.S. and U.K. PX Post also offers express mail service.

Couriers

Expats have had mixed experience using couriers. Ask around for personal recommendations.

- **DHL**: *(tel: 956-1001)*
- **UPS**: *(tel: 253-1937)*
- **Federal Express**: *(tel: 234-3636)*
- **TNT Express Worldwide**: *(tel: 156-5771)*

Posting books

Books can be mailed by surface or air at the international post office (*mezhdunarodny pochtampt)* at metro Nagatinskaya. Staff wrap the books in 3kg bundles for you in heavy manila paper with string. Simply bring your own plastic bags and ask them to wrap the books first in order to prevent any possible water damage en route. Surface mail to the US can take as long as three months. Be aware that you may still need permits to export dictionaries, books dealing with art or books published before WW2.

Receiving parcels by mail

Ordering by catalogue and giving your work address seems to increase the chances of demands for large duties and paperwork.

If you send items via DHL or TNT, ask for the facility to have the package insured, as it is rarely mentioned to the sender. Smallish items marked as 'documentation' have a higher chance of arriving unscathed.

Be careful when you declare the value of the goods not to overestimate value unnecessarily, as you could be charged half the declared value.

It's worth noting that legally, declared value for carriage cannot exceed the one for Customs.

Customs has the right to levy duties either by value or by weight.

There is no special Customs regulations for courier services, and Express Delivery is an unknown concept for Customs officials, though moves are afoot to speed up delivery.

Expat guide: Moscow   **8/Keeping in touch**

If you are thinking of sending small (2.5kg) packages from your home country via an airline that serves Moscow, call the local representative office and ask staff to explain their document service (as opposed to cargo).

Some expats say it's not worthwhile having clothing or toys sent via courier as reams of obscure documentation is required wasting time and effort. Whether you will still receive your package eventually is not assured.

Ensure that a complete packing list is enclosed.

Duty (30 - 50% on packages worth more than $100 including postage) may be charged and consequently it's not worth listing a higher value than what the goods are worth.

9/Keeping busy

Before you move to Moscow, you might wonder how you would fill your days. However, once you see what Moscow has to offer in terms of entertainment you will find that there really is much of interest to do. The tourist guide-books have written most of what there is to write concerning all the cultural gems you can visit and learn about; consequently, this book will not examine them but rather look at those aspects of Moscow life that are not normally written about in the guide-books.

The chapter is divided into:

- Cultural pursuits
- Indoor recreation (all year round)
- Outdoor recreation (summer)
- Outdoor recreation (all year round)
- Outdoor recreation (winter)

Cultural pursuits

• *Dancing*

The Moscow Beach Club *(tel: 299-7353; metro: Chekhovskaya)* gives Latin dance classes at various times in the evening throughout the week. The club is situated behind the Lenkom Theatre at 6 Ulitsa Malaya Dmitrovka. Season tickets for ten lessons each are supplied to non-members.

Club Hippopotam in the same building as Santa Fe restaurant *(metro: Ulitsa 1905 Goda)* has a Latin American dancing evening on Thursday nights.

The School of the Moscow State Classical Ballet *(6 Ulitsa Neglinnaya)* Classes for beginners are usually on Tuesday from 18:30 - 20:00. Classes for advanced students are held on Thursday at the same time. Contact 288-9393 to confirm. The studio was at one time run by expatriates with classes taught by professional Russian ballet instructors. One option available was Latin dance.

Moscow's General Headquarters of Internal Affairs (GUVD) House of Culture dance school *(tel: 978-8046 45/3 Ulitsa Novoslobodskaya; metro: Novoslobodskaya)* Monthly tickets can be purchased The club offers the amateur a range of options from traditional ballroom to foxtrot, rhumba, waltz, tango and Latin salsa. People from all age groups and backgrounds meet regularly at the club, which was originally intended for the entertainment and relaxation of Moscow militsia officers.

The Modern Ballroom Dance School *(tel: 275-1596; 4 Ulitsa Vostochnaya; metro: Avtozavodskaya)* is located in the Culture House of the ZiL truck manufacturing plant. Lessons in batches of 10 are offered to both children

Expat guide: Moscow   **9/Keeping busy**

and adults. It boasts a reputation as being one of the city's best dance schools. Several graduates have reached champion status.

The La Bamba club *(tel: 977-4266; Molodyozhnaya Hotel, 27 Dmitrovskoye Shosse; metro: Timiryazevskaya).* This is the place for salsa and merengue lovers on Friday and Saturday nights. If you are a salsa novice, or just want to brush up on your steps, classes are available free of charge in the club every Friday from 22:00 - 23:00. With the latest music played by South American DJs, the place is popular with Russians and Latin Americans.

Artistic pursuits
Drawing and painting

Khudozhestvenny Salon, *(tel 924-5793; Petrovsky Passazh shopping mall, 12 Ulitsa Petrovka, open 09:00 - 20:00 Mondays - Saturdays; metro: Kuznetsky Most)* This is said to be the best place for obtaining art supplies. Art books are to be found on the ground floor. Venture downstairs if you're looking for easels, art supplies, water colour paper, or large sheets that can be cut to size. White water-colour paper, sketch paper, paper for pastels, coloured tissue and tracing paper, coloured pastel paper are available, as are brushes, palate knives, imported paints, fabric and silk paint, paint for glass, metal and wood. Also available are plasticine and craft kits for children.

Central House of Artists *(opposite Gorky Park entrance at 10 Krymsky Val).* The Central House of Artists charges a small entrance fee and houses several small galleries. Visit the outdoor gallery (summer and winter) along the embankment and also at the Vernissage adjacent to the Central House of Artists and bordering the Garden of Fallen Heroes.

Art Service-Centre *(Central House of Artists, tel: 238-4356; 10 Krymsky Val, 10:00 - 19:00 daily; metro: Oktyabrskaya)* This shop sells paints for enamel and glass, brushes and educational books in different languages. There are also Italian acrylics, oils and coloured opaque glass for mosaics and a framing service. Also look at the selection of Russian artwork and posters which are reasonably priced.

Everything for the artist, *(tel: 230-1913; 10 Krymsky Val, open 11:00 - 19:00 daily; metro: Oktyabrskaya).* The shop situated in front of the petrol station in front of the House of Artists sells all types of paint, brushes, pre-stretched canvasses, metallic paint, Easter-egg-dyeing kit, flat easels and glitter craft paint and a small selection of frames, including very reasonably priced pine frames. There is also a framing service in a tiny office to the immediate right of the front door as you enter. Oleg does not work on Mondays.

Brushes and canvas are sold in the rear of the of the *Khudozhestvennyi Magazin* across from the Marriott Hotel on Tverskaya Ulitsa.

• *Appreciating Russian art*

Classes are offered in English on Russian art for expats. *Contact e-mail: alvarezkl@hotmail.com.* The International Women's Club also holds special interest groups in this field.

138

Expat guide: Moscow
9/Keeping busy

Buying art

Impoverished artists sell their art in a wide variety of places in Moscow. The old Arbat and the riverbank outside the Central House of Artists (opposite Gorky Park), and the underpass immediately in front of Gorky Park are your most obvious choices. You will also find a wide selection at Izmailova market.

Some private studios show artists' paintings and will organise to obtain all the permits necessary for exportation. If you find an artist whose work you like, see if you can commission him to do more work in that particular genre for you.

Museums

There are a large number of museums to visit, (best saved for the winter) some of which are very impressive. As most of the exhibits are identified in Russian, your best option, unless you are fluent in Russian, is to take a bilingual Russian friend along to interpret as this will make it all the more engrossing.

Be prepared to pay higher prices than locals, even though this practice is illegal, according to the Constitution.

Consult some of the many excellent guide-books on Moscow for listings of museums or look in the Moscow English-language Press for details of addresses, opening-times and exhibitions.

Opera, theatre, ballet, classical/modern music

There is a huge selection of venues and performances for these different genres which are advertised weekly in the Moscow English press.

Buying tickets for performances at the Bolshoi

Send an e-mail to *aaa@telemost.ru* which runs a private ticketing agency and will deliver tickets. If you send them a subscription request, they will send you updates on Moscow cultural life on a weekly basis.

You can also try:

- **OM Company** *(tel: 494-0145)* for Bolshoi tickets
- **Intourist** 11 Stolechnikov Pereulok *(tel: 924-2585)*
- *Teatr* kiosks at metros Arbatskaya and Pushkinskaya
- **Metropole Hotel** (very expensive)
- The *kacca* at the **Bolshoi** *(tel: 292-9986; or 292-0050 everyday except Monday from 12:00 - 19:00 with a break for lunch between 15:00 - 16:00)*
- You can also buy tickets from touts outside the Bolshoi just before the performance. However, you should always check the date printed on the ticket, before purchase and remember to bargain.

The Conservatory *(tel: 229-818; 229-0658; 229-9430; 229-7795)* and the **Rachmaninov Hall of the Conservatory** *(tel: 220-0294)* are said to be one of the best deals in Moscow with low prices and high quality performances.

Playing music

You can buy sheet music at **Dom Knigi** on Novy Arbat, where there is a small selection on the 2nd floor, although you will need service assistance. There are

139

Expat guide: Moscow   **9/Keeping busy**

also a couple of shops in the immediate vicinity of the Conservatory Grand Hall at Bolshaya Nikitskaya Ulitsa.

Singing

The **Moscow Oratorio Society** rehearses for concerts held throughout the year. All nationalities are welcome. Usually you are not required to attend an audition. The Society meets every Wednesday at 18:45 and also on Saturdays, closer to the date of the concert. Rehearsals last about two hours. Members are asked to pay a choir membership fee which covers the cost of music and salaries for the society's director and rehearsal pianist *(e-mail: Carolyn_Hovorka@notes.eycis.com)*.

Piano lessons

Natalia *(tel: 203-0432 from 10:00 - 12:00 or after 20:00)* is a professional pianist and experienced teacher who offers piano lessons for any age and level. She is said to be able to solve problems caused by incorrect teaching methods and remedy the results of overplaying and tired hands.

Cinema

The **American House of Cinema** *(Radisson Slavjanskaya Hotel; tel: 941-8747 www.domecinema.ru)*shows recently released films in English with Russian headphone translations from Wednesday to Sunday. Films change frequently. Prices are discounted for weekend matinee performances. Be prepared for a showing to not take place even though advertised, owing to lack of patrons.

The **Dome Theatre** *(tel: round the clock hotline: 941-8747 recorded information in English then in Russian; or tel: 941-8890; www.americancinema.ru) Renaissance Hotel, 18/1, Olimpiyskiy Prospekt, metro: Prospekt Mira)*. Latest Hollywood hits in English with Russian translation by headphone. Shows change twice a month. There is a half-price discount for schoolchildren, students and pensioners from Monday to Thursday only.

The following cinemas show films in Russian, some with sub-titles. Watch press for details:

Kodak Kinomir, *(tel: 209-4359; 200-3563; 2 Nastasinsky Pereulok, metro: Pushkinskaya/Tverskaya)* usually shows movies in English with Russian sub-titles. Call the theatre for showtimes.

Udarnik Cinema *(tel: 959-0856; 2 Ulitsa Serafimovicha; metro: Polyanka)*

Pushkinsky Cinema *(tel: 229-0111) Pushkinskaya Ploschad; metro: Chekhovskaya.*

Stamp-collecting

Try the **post office at Chisty Prudi** (just near the metro) as well as the Philatelic Centre on the 2nd floor of the General post office (26 Myasnitskaya).

Dom Knigi on Novy Arbat has a large collection of stamps for sale. Also look out for stamp-collectors on the side of the road on the clockwise flyover leading down to the canal south of metro Kurskaya.

140

Expat guide: Moscow   **9/Keeping busy**

Indoor recreation (all-year round)

• *Aikido*

An 8th Dan black belt holder, Dave Eayrs *(tel/fax: 237- 4747; 952-6374; e-mail: misogi@co.ru)*, teaches the Japanese art of Aikido. He usually runs group and individual classes on Wednesday evenings and Saturday and Sunday mornings. Depending on demand he runs a special ladies-only class which is very popular. **The Aikido Federation** *(tel: 160-9343, 353-5558 or 175-2223; e-mail aikiru@dol.ru)* and the **Tomiki Aikido Federation** *(e-mail: aikido@corbina.ru or www.corbina.net/~aikido.ru)* should be contacted for further information.

• *Banyas (bani)*

There are thousands of *bani* and saunas all over town, though one that is particularly popular and well-known is the **Sandunoff** *banya (tel: 925-4631; 14 Ulitsa Neglinnaya)* where you can undergo the entire *banya* experience including massage and flailing with birch twigs *(vyenik)*. Sexes are strictly segregated here and at other public *bani*, either in separate bathhouses or on separate days. Here, there is no class distinction and you can meet all types of Russians.

Bani are a traditional way of conducting business and have the effect of 'levelling the playing field' while helping to build trust and break down barriers. Without smart clothes, it is reasoned, people have to rely on communicating in ways which do not rely on outside superficiality. However, it's not obligatory that you do not wear a swimsuit and you are free to do so or not, though you might wish to be guided by fellow *banya*-goers. Be warned that some *bani* attract a marked prostitute presence. Several *bani* also offer haircuts and manicures.

It's best to go with a Russian friend so that you can have the drill explained. In case these are not provided, bring a towel, shampoo and plastic slippers *(tapochky)*. Bring a plastic bag for your outside boots during winter.

The procedure involves first showering, then sitting in the *banya* (five to seven minutes for the novice) then break for a drink after a dip in the cold splash-pool before returning to the *banya*. This is carried out several times. It's not advisable to visit a *banya* on a full stomach or if you are inebriated.

Many families have their own *banya* at home and may invite you to join this distinctly Russian experience which often involves all the family with food and drink being served.

Those listed below are all open from 08:00 - 22:00. Phone first to confirm whether they will be open for males or females on the day you wish to visit.

- **Astrakhanskiye Bani** *(tel: 280-3429; 5/9 Astrakhansky Pereulok; metro: Prospekt Mira)*
- **Bani na Presne** *(tel: 255-0115; 7 Stolyarny Pereulok, metro: Ulitsa 1905 Goda)*
- **Sandunovdkiye Bani** *(tel: 925-4631; 14 Ulitsa Neglinnaya; metro: Kuznetsky Most)*
- **Seleznevskiey Bani** *(tel: 978-8491; 15 Seleznevskaya Ulitsa; metro: Novoslobodskaya)*

141

Expat guide: Moscow   **9/Keeping busy**

- **Varshavskiye Bani** *(tel: 111-1545; 34 Varshavskoye Shosse; metro: Ngatinskaya)*

• Basket-ball

Basket-ball is very popular in Russia and many sports centres have basket-ball facilities.

Contact **Moscow Hoops Basket-ball** *(tel: 381-4401/8504/4517; 382-9218 or fax 382-8505)* or **Bison Basket-ball Club**, *(tel/fax: 582-9010; Kuznetsky Most; metro: Teatralnaya)* for further information.

• Billiards

Billiard and pool tables are often found in bars and sports clubs and bowling alleys.

• Bowling

Bowling is relatively new to Moscow, having been established only in the last few years. Russia is catching up fast though, and already the second Russian championship has been held and there are plans to develop a 40-lane centre at Olympiskiy Sports Complex in time for the Bowling World Cup in the year 2000. There are reportedly 300 bowling lanes in some 20 centres in Moscow, but quality varies. Prices are still relatively steep at about $15 - 30 per hour, though they have come down from the days before the crisis when only bankers could afford prices of around $50 per hour. Alleys are often open till the early hours of the morning and many provide play facilities for children. Billiard tables are often in evidence.

One cosmic bowling venue, **Zebra**, is situated in the same building as metro Frunzenskaya, at 28 Komsomolsky Prospekt, offering black-lit rolling with fluorescent balls, though the lanes are shorter than regulation length. It's open till 05:00 and prices are discounted in the afternoons.

Cosmic bowling is also available at Dinamo Stadium (see below) and at 18 Lev Tolstoga Ulitsa, *(tel: 246-3666; metro: Park Kultury)* a venue which is extremely popular and which bills itself as the biggest bowling alley in town. Prices are discounted by 50% before 17:00 and there is no limit to the number of people who play per lane. There are 16 lanes and pool tables are also available.

Try also **Bi-Ba-Bo** *(tel: 937-4337; 9 Karmannitsky Pereulok, near Smolenskaya metro)* (across from the entrance to the John Bull Pub, 3rd floor) which is said to have the best lanes in town; **Mezhdunarodnaya Hotel**, *(tel: 253-2382; 12 Krasnopresnenskaya Naberezhnaya)*; **Kegelbahn**, Kosmos Hotel *(tel: 217-8680, 150 Prospekt Mira; metro: VDNKh)*; **Dom Turista** *(tel: 434-9076; 146 Leninsky Prospekt)*, is said to be American-style with some nine lanes; **480 BC** *(tel: 939-8412; at Orlyonok hotel 15 Kosygina Prospekt; metro: Leninsky Prospekt)*; **B - 69** *(tel: 935-0504; 69 Ulitsa Vavilova; metro Profsoyuznaya)* even has a banya, swimming-pool and Jacuzzi as well as a restaurant.

Mini-bowling can be played at **Tsentr** (see below under 'multi-purpose') and **Sharovaya Molniya** *(tel: 212-0779; Dinamo Stadium 36 Leningradsky Prospekt; metro Dinamo)* which has two bowling facilities that are linked, the

142

Expat guide: Moscow   **9/Keeping busy**

first (five lanes) being not as modern as the second (six lanes cosmic bowling). The alley is at the back of the stadium which faces Leningradsky Prospekt.

• *Bridge*

The **Moscow Duplicate Bridge Club** invites intermediate or advanced bridge players to join an English-speaking group for bridge on the first and third Saturdays of the month. Play usually takes place at the Aerostar Hotel starting at 12:45 and finishing around 18:30. The fee to cover the cost of the room and coffee is approximately $8 per person, paid in rubles. Contact: Paul Holland *(tel: 198-6694)* or Steve Trowbridge *(tel: 124-0320)*. Both expats and Russians are welcome as long as they can understand play in English.

• *Broomball*

Broomball has been popular among the expat community for over 30 years. The American, Finnish, Canadian, British and German embassies may be able to give you fuller details. Broomball is said to be a good injury-free alternative to ice-hockey and despite its image as sporty housework, it is said to be loads of fun.

• *Chess*

Sokolniki, Izmailovsky Park, VDNKh and Gorky parks have chess corners where you can join a game. Otherwise try the **Central Chess Club** *(tel: 291-0641; 14 Gogolevsky Bulvar; metro: Arbatskaya)*.

• *Darts*

Although darts is still fairly new in Russia, you can enjoy a game at the recently opened **Dartmaster** *(tel: 362-6020/6011; 33 Ulitsa Povarskaya; metro: Krasnopresnenskaya* which welcomes new players and offers free lessons and advice for beginners. It has seven electronic darts machines as well as classic dartboards. It is open 24 hours a day. If you pay $20 you can join the league allowing you to take part in darts contests. The place also has pool tables. Dartmaster has a shop which sells boards, darts and accessories.

• *Fencing*

Contact the fencing club at Dinamo stadium *(tel: 213-7730)*. The entrance is up one flight of stairs next to the *trenazhurniy zal*.

• *Fitness*

The personal fitness craze has mushroomed in Moscow over the past few years. Most expats tend to go for the expensive and well-equipped handful of fitness centres which have a social aspect to them as well. Ask clubs what discount they offer for group membership and persuade colleagues to join you.

If you are seriously looking to simply train with weights and basic machines in small, unpretentious premises, there are hundreds of these hidden all over the city, and usually they cost far less than the flashier gyms.

Expat guide: Moscow　　　　　　　　　　　　　　　　**9/Keeping busy**

◊　**Park Place Sport Centre** *(tel: 956-5288; 113 Leninsky Prospekt; metro: Yugo Zapadnaya; open 07:00 - 10:30)* has a small gym with few machines. They offer aerobic classes twice a day. Other facilities include a tennis court (extra cost); dry sauna; solarium (at extra cost again) but no pool. Cost is about half the price of the bigger gyms.

◊　Izmailova Hotel complex (opposite from the Izmailovskaya metro exit) has a fitness centre (**Marcus Aurelius**) on the 2nd floor with state of the art machines and weight training equipment. The club is clean and modern, having been opened in 1998. Facilities include sauna, solariums, aerobics. Membership costs about $1500 annually with a discount for new members.

◊　**World Class:** The branch at Oktyabrskaya metro station (behind the French Embassy) has facilities which include: aerobics, bicycles, weights, Nautilus-type equip, sauna (Swedish and Turkish); swimming-pool; tennis court, squash, massage and a tanning salon. The second branch at Oil House *(metro: Yugo Zapadnaya),* has the same features as the first branch but lacks tennis and squash. Its swimming-pool is said to have a propelled slide.

◊　**Radisson Hotel** has a small gym but the equipment is modern and decent and it features a swimming-pool.

◊　**The Greenway Club** at TsSKA *(on Leningradsky Prospekt)* has a free-weight/machine/cardio set-up, with an Olympic-sized swimming-pool (supposedly the best in town out of all the fitness centres) and sauna. It costs about $240 per month.

◊　**The Zal Championov** gym at Dinamo Stadium is reportedly small, with mostly Olympic-style free-weights and home-made machines intended for serious body-builders only. You can either pay per workout (about $2.50) or per month (about $20). It's open from 09:00 - 22:00.

◊　**Fit & Fun** *(tel 924-4315; 924-1121; building 1, 12 Chistoprudny Bulvar, open Monday - Friday 07:00 - 23:00 and weekends from 09:00 - 22:00),* is supposedly a very upmarket club with a good variety of machines including those that can estimate your maximum resistance. Thirty types of aerobics classes as well as aqua-aerobics (in a small swimming-pool) are offered. Other facilities include saunas and steam rooms, beauty salon, massage and tanning beds, restaurant, café, vitamin bars and a kid's club. Annual membership prices were about $3,000 (basic), and $2,100 for a second family member but confirm latest prices. The club offers computerised tests which determine output/fitness level ratios. Machines are then correlated to work accordingly when you are using them.

◊　**Petrovka Sports** *(tel: 299-5262; 4 Pervy Kolobovsky Pereulok; metro: Pushkinskaya)* offers a package ($150) for ten aerobic classes plus sauna. Regular packages cost $1,500 for six months, $2,400 for one year, phone to confirm latest costs. The club has good facilities but no swimming-pool. Facilities include: aerobics, massage, solarium, saunas, steamrooms, beauty centre, vitamin bar, kid's club, personal training and boutique.

◊　**Planet Fitness Clubs:** *(tel: 203-1999; fax 203-1919);* **Beach club** *(tel: 299-7353; 209-3892; 6 Malaya Dmitrovka; metro: Pushkinskaya.)* is said to be small and with no pool. It costs some $1,200 per year and offers weights, cardio-vascular equipment and sauna; **Vertical Planet Fitness** *(tel: 964-2405; 8, building 1, Ulitsa Korolenko);* **Golden Keys** *(tel: 723-7326; 1a*

144

Expat guide: Moscow   9/Keeping busy

Ulitsa Minskaya) has an approximately 20m swimming-pool and Nautilus free-weight facilities including tanning, saunas, a steambath, massages, hair salon, shop, and health bar. Cost is about $2,700 per family per year. This is said to be the best branch of the chain.

◊ A Russian gym *(tel: 369-3733; 27, Ulitsa Mironovskaya)* that charges only $320 per year is clean and offers a combination of Russian and German free-weights, weight machines, exercycles.

◊ **US embassy fitness club** open only to US passport holders. Application for membership which entails a security clearance procedure that can take a few months, depending on demand.

◊ **Le Meridien Moscow Country Club** *(tel: 926-5924),* is an exclusive and expensive sport and recreation club which offers a full range of indoor and outdoor facilities all year round including squash, tennis, swimming, interactive golf activities and more. During 1998 prices were quoted as being $1,900 for a couple and $ 1,100 or so per single (confirm latest prices). It has all the standard free weights, some different brand of machines and a range of bicycles, stairs and assisted pull-up devices. This is not an expat hangout but more for the serious fitness devotee.

◊ **Gold's Gym** *(tel: 931 -9616; fax: 931-9625Stadium of Young Pioneers, 31 Leningradsky prospekt, Building 30, metro: Dinamo.)* is billed as having top-class equipment and with a price-tag to match, the gym offers aerobics, tennis, squash, basket-ball, solariums. Membership is offered at full or off-peak. It is possible to transfer membership if you have to leave or you decide you are fit enough, though a transfer fee is charged. During holidays or illness you can freeze the membership for a maximum period of 10 weeks (minimum one week at a time). In addition to all the usual exercise equipment they offer free: sauna /Jacuzzi/aerobics/yoga/basket-ball/soccer. Squash is $5 for 45 minutes and tennis is $30 an hour.

◊ **Chaika** (Seagull) Sports Complex *(tel: 246-1344; Ulitsa Ostozhenka (near Park Kultury metro exit)* has a highly commended heated outdoor swimming-pool, free-weight machines, a sauna and hydro-massage. Costs used to be about $100 a month. There is not much in the way of cardiovascular equipment.

◊ **Marriott on Tverskaya** has a nice gym and swimming-pool

• *Judo*
Contact the **Judo Federation** in Moscow *(tel/fax: 322-0833).*

• *Multi-purpose*
Tsentr *(tel: 952-7828; 3 Kholodny Pereulok, opposite Tulskaya metro, open 11:00 - 05:00).* Entrance charge is about $1 if you buy tickets between 11:00 - 18:00 and $3 afterwards. All facilities except rollerblading incur extra charges. Tsentr opened in October 1998 as Moscow's biggest multi-purpose club offering in-line skating disco, a bowling alley, a children's playroom featuring ball pond and climbing frames (great for adults who want to leave them there while they enjoy themselves on other amusements), Qazar, a restaurant and at least four bars. There are also several video game machines. The children's playroom (ages 3 - 12) is able to host children's parties. Expect crowds on weekends.

145

Expat guide: Moscow **9/Keeping busy**

You can consider **Luzhniki Olympic Sports Complex** a multi-purpose sports centre. To enter by car you will need to drive to the eastern entrance next to the river, just near Novodevichy Convent. If you don't have a permit, you will need to pay about $2 entrance. If you do have a permit, you still need to pay an entry fee, but this is only about 50c.

To obtain a permit, you need to register for the sport that interests you e.g. swimming, tennis, ice-skating etc and pay a sum in advance which will cover your use of the facilities and entrance to the complex at a certain time and on a specific day according to what you have reserved. There are various administrative offices dotted around Luzhniki, so it's best to take a Russian friend with you initially so that the process of finding the right admin person for the right sport is made that much easier.

• Pool

There are many pool bars around the city, you just have to find them. One reasonably large pool bar is at Planet Hollywood. Note that Russian Billiards is often played which involves using a larger ball than other types of billiards games. If you want to buy a pool table, visit the sports shop on Leninsky Prospekt at Gagarina Ploschad. You will find it on the left if you head towards the centre from the Gagarin statue just after the buildings commence.

• Quizzes

On the last Thursday of the month, a pub quiz is usually held at the Fox and Pheasant Pub at 21:00 *(16 Tverskaya/Yamskaya Ulitsa)*. All are welcome for a fun night of trivia and general knowledge questions. The fee is about $4 per person and teams are restricted to five. All proceeds are used in projects for Russian orphanages.

• Rock-climbing

Being flat, Moscow doesn't offer much outdoor opportunity for climbing. You could try the ruins at Tsaritsino for bouldering. Further afield, the best places are to be found in the Caucasus, the Crimea and near Krasnoyarsk and Kemerovo.

The Palace of Children's Sports *(tel: 270 - 2160; 63; Ultisa Rabochaya)* is where you go if you want to practise indoor rock-climbing. The sport has attracted followers since the 1950s. The palace boasts one of Europe's biggest *skalodroms* or rock climbing walls which at 17m in height, is decorated to lull the climber into imagining that he's at a real rock face. It has been the venue for a number of international and national competitions.

Climbing practice is charged by the hour and the centre is open from noon to 15.00 and 19.00 - 21.00. Climbers can also rent special climbing shoes *(kalki)*, a safety harness and tether and magnesium powder to counteract sweaty palms.

Muscovite rock climbers, who were ready to try anything, apparently used to practise on the faces of old buildings, such as abandoned churches and the monuments at the Tsaritsino estate. However, as more city buildings undergo renovation, there is less opportunity for the climbers. 'Industrial alpinism' which involves the washing of skyscraper windows, and the pasting of advertisements on billboards, as well as the clearing of icicles off balconies in winter now serves

146

Expat guide: Moscow   9/Keeping busy

to satisfy the most passionate rock climbers. Try **Alpindustriya** *(tel: 165-0429; 1 Pervomaiskaya; metro: Izmailovskaya)* for equipment.

• *Squash*

Many of the fitness clubs listed above have squash facilities. In addition, you could enquire about use of the court in the compound of the Indian Embassy. *(tel: 917-0820).*

• *Swimming*

Most indoor swimming-pools in Moscow require the production of a medical certificate *(spravki)* before you can swim. You could obtain one from your doctor, or from the doctor on site at the swimming-pool. There seems to be a two-tiered system for charging of certificates with foreigners paying more. To obtain a certificate the doctor or nurse on duty will simply check your blood pressure and heart-beat and ask whether you suffer from any infectious diseases.

You can either try the State-owned pools (which are reasonably priced) such as the one across the road from the smaller Park Kultury metro station - **Chaika Sports Complex** *(tel: 246-13441/3 Turchaninov Pereulok;)* or the one at **Moscow Olympic Centre of Water Sports** *(tel: 369-1086; 25 Ulitsa Tkatskaya).* Alternatively, you could join a fitness centre. Some of the larger hotels have swimming-pools and their own fitness centres, but these can prove to be expensive.

If you have longish hair, it's best to wear a cap. Check that the swimming-pool is not a haven for serious swimmers if you intend a simple splash-around with kids.

Instead of going swimming on an *ad hoc* basis, it's wiser to get a monthly season ticket (these go on sale around the 27/28th of each month), otherwise you have to queue for a free slot which may be of 30 or 45 minutes duration.

Expect a process where you first get a token for your coat; then pay for the swimming; then leave some form of identity as a 'deposit' (often a *'spravka'* or permit with a photo which you have already paid for); find the right changing room; remove your outdoor shoes (take a plastic bag to put shoes in) and replace with rubber ones or flip-flops. Before entry; hand over the correct tag in return for a locker key; get undressed, have a shower; change into swimsuit and put on your swimming cap if required; head for the swimming-pool, the entrance to which may be simply a wet hole in the ground and then dive in, exhausted. After swimming reverse the process.

Other public pools are at:

◊ **Olympic Sports Complex** *(tel: 903-5303; 16 Olimpiskiy Prospekt; metro: Prospekt Mira)*

◊ **Dinamo swimming-pool** *(tel: 212-1483; Dinamo Sports Complex. 36 Leningradsky Pereulok)*

◊ **Luzhniki**, *24 Luzhnetskaya Naberazhnaya, #19 Malaya Sport Arena.*

◊ **Greenway Club** *(tel: 967-6815; 39 Leningradsky Prospekt)* has a recommended 50m swimming-pool. Half the width is segregated into lanes and the rest is open. There is also a range of diving boards that can be used. Membership is not cheap.

147

Expat guide: Moscow   **9/Keeping busy**

Swimming - outdoors
You are free to follow the Muscovites' example and swim where they swim, but bear in mind the cleanliness of the water. The beaches of **Serebryany Bor** where there is a nude beach and a gay beach, are popular as swimming venues in the summer, but water quality again is questionable.

The **Pirogovskoe Reservoir**, 35km outside Moscow is said to be the cleanest option.

Don't be tempted to swim in any natural ponds or pools either in Moscow or on its outskirts. In winter you might see *morzhi* (walruses) taking a quick dip in gaps in the ice. They are the Russian equivalent to the American Polar Bear Club members.

If you can gain access to it, try the American embassy swimming-pool (membership only).

• *Tennis*

Tennis is a comparatively expensive sport in Moscow, ranging in price from $20 to $70 per hour and more. The best bet is the university where there are several courts, but you may have to go there with a Russian friend. There are outdoor courts at Luzhniki and these are popular on weekends and after business hours.

Indoor courts

◊   **Chaika** *(tel: 202-4966; 1 /2 Korobeynikov Pereulok open: 09:00 - 21:00)*
◊   **Druzba** Universal Stadium *(tel: 201-1655; 10 Luzhnetskaya Naberezhnaya)*
◊   **Luzhniki** *(tel: 201-1164; 24 Luzhnetskaya Naberezhnaya; Malaya Sport Arena #19)*
◊   **Gold's Gym** *(tel: 931-9616; 31 Leningradsky Pereulok; metro: Dinamo).*
◊   **Le Meridien**, Moscow Country Club *(tel: 926-5924)*
◊   **Petrovsky Park** tennis club *(tel: 212-7392; 36 Leningradsky Prospekt)*
◊   **Fili** *(27 Ulitsa Novozavodskaya; open 07:00 - 23:00; metro: Bagrationovskaya)*
◊   **Iskra** *(tel: 187-8161; 26 Ulitsa Selskokhozyaystvennaya; open: 09:00 - 22:00; metro: Botanicheskiy Sad)*
◊   **Kirovskiy Sports-Fitness** *(tel: 406-4665; 20 Ulitsa Prishvina; open: 08:00 - 22:00; metro: Bibirevo)*
◊   **Otradnoe** *(tel: 907-1094; 10 Ulitsa Khachaturyana; open 07:00 - 23:00; metro: Otradnoe)*

Outdoor courts

◊   **Nekuschny Sad** *(adjacent to Gorky Park and reached from 14 Leninsky Prospekt)* has two outdoor courts
◊   **Chaika Tennis courts** *(tel: 202-4966 1 /2 Korobeynikov Pereulok; open 07:00- 23:00; metro: Park Kultury)*
◊   **Fili** *(27 Ulitsa Novozavodskaya; open: 07:00 - 23:00; metro: Bagrationovskaya)*
◊   **Iskra** *(tel: 187-8161; 26 Ulitsa Selskokhozyaystvennaya; open: 09:00 - 22:00; metro: Botanicheskiy Sad)*

Expat guide: Moscow　　　　　　　　　　**9/Keeping busy**

◊ **Kirovskiy Sports-Fitness Complex** *(tel: 406-4665; 20 Ulitsa Prishvina; open 08:00 - 22:00; metro: Bibirevo)*
◊ **Petrovskiy park** *(tel: 212-7392; 36 Leningradsky Prospekt; open: 06:00 - 24:00; metro: Dinamo)*

• *Volley-ball*

The **US embassy** courts sometimes hold games on Wednesday and Sunday nights. These sessions last about three hours from 20:00 to 23:00. Cost to non-Embassy employees is about $5. You will need to take your passport for entrance admission. All foreign passport holders (except for Russian) are usually welcome. Call 252-2451 and ask for the recreation department (gym) to find out more.

MGU (Moscow University) has some volley-ball courts next to their soccer pitches indoors. The floor surface is not ideal, but there is no cost and all are welcome.

• *Yoga*

Classes are held at **The Yoga Centre** *(tel: 492-4592; 316-6937; 966-0007)*; the **Indian Embassy Education Centre**, *(tel: 916-0644)* and the **International Yoga Club** near metro Tretyakovskaya *(tel: 313-8389/6683)*. The classes are in Russian ($2.50) and in English on Tuesdays at 12:30 costing $10 per class or $40 for five classes).

The **Iyengar Yoga Centre** *(tel: 313-8389; 43 Ulitsa Pyatnitskaya; metro: Tretyakovskaya)* has six instructors who welcome people of all abilities and all ages, including English speakers. Classes last for up to 90 minutes and are held throughout the week.

Outdoor recreation (summer)

• *Baseball*

Russia's only baseball pitch (donated by the Japanese) is to be found at the University. The pitch may be hired. Contact 939: 2431 for further information. A mini-league for children from the age of six up to 9th grade is run for approximately six weeks from May every year on Saturday mornings. Also contact the Baseball Federation of Moscow *(tel: 924-1067)* for further information.

• *Badminton*

Contact the **Badminton Federation** of Moscow *(tel: 924-1067; 18 Milyutinskiy Pereulok)* for information on courts and games.

• *Boating/sailing*

For sailing opportunities on the Moscow river, contact **Spartak Yacht Club** *(tel: 408-2500; fax: 576-2337)*. If you prefer to be less active on the water and let

149

Expat guide: Moscow   **9/Keeping busy**

someone else do the sailing, you will find cruisers aplenty at **Rechnoi Vokhzal**, *(tel: 457-4050; 51 Leningradskoye Shosse; metro: Rechnoi Vokhzal).* The crumbling, but architecturally interesting 1930s-built North River Terminal is the starting point for a number of journeys on the Moscow river. These include trips on the *Raketa* hydrofoils (the fastest), the much slower ferries, such as the ones you see in Moscow itself on the river, and the large three- and four-deck boats which travel as far away as St Petersburg.

During the summer hydrofoils and ferry boats run from the Northern River Terminal to beaches and stops further north. The hydrofoils are fast (60km/h) and can get you to a number of interesting sites within 40 minutes of the Northern River Terminal if you want to do a spot of picnicking, swimming or simply lazing in verdant birch forests.

Tickets are available on board the boat itself if the cashier *(kacca)* which is on the quay, is not open. Prices are higher on weekends than during the week, but children between the ages of 6 - 10 pay half the adult price whereas those that are younger, go free. The boat has a comfortable inner section where you sit in airline-seat style and are shielded from the teeth-jarring and bone-juddering of the engine's noise that you are exposed to if you choose to sit outside. As the journey begins, a small on-board shop is opened, which sells a small selection of soft drinks and beers (non-refrigerated) as well as sweets and chips.

The second stop (Gorky) after Vodinka (not really worth stopping at) takes a 20-minute trip before you alight into a green, lush, clean and peaceful forest which has toilets (dubious) and volley-ball courts (bring your own net) and plenty of opportunity to find your own picnic-spot. You could swim at the small beach nearby, but the water looks none too clean, although quite a few people do swim there.

If you have a lot of time to pass and you aren't travelling with kids (they get too impatient) you could try the much slower ferry boats *(T/x Moskva)* on which a round trip can take up to six hours (see below).

For longer distance trips, several three- and four- storey boats moored at the terminal sail to destinations as far afield as St Petersburg. You can obtain tickets from the ferry terminal itself. Boats sail from late May to late August on trips lasting from three to 14 days. There is a wide choice of classes ranging from 1, 1b, 2, 2a, 2b, 3, 3a and 3b and prices differ for adults and children.

Destination	Fast boat	Slow boat
Gorky	20min	1h30
Bukhta radosti	30 min	2h15
Solnechnaya Polyana	35 min	2h 30
Gvoinlya bor	40min	3h

Cruising inside Moscow

The river boats run by **Central Lines** *(tel: 277-6678; 277-3902)* begin in May usually and sail until October. It's possible to sail either up or down river. You pay one fee which covers one or multiple stages as long as you sail in one direction. If you reach the terminus, you will need to pay again to sail in the other direction. The boats are ideal for passing the time on a lazy summer's afternoon. They are more crowded and therefore frequent at weekends than during the week.

Expat guide: Moscow   9/Keeping busy

Don't count on obtaining cold drinks on board although warm drinks are sometimes given away as part of the cost of your ticket. Only snacks such as chips and sweets are available. If you take your own (modest) picnic, the staff on board don't seem to mind.

From Kievsky Vokhzal travel downriver, past Novodevichy Convent, Luzhniki Stadium, past the Sparrow Hills, Gorky Park, the Statue of Peter the Great, the Cathedral of St Saviour and the Red October factory, the House on the Embankment, past the Kremlin, the Rossiya hotel, the Novospassky Monastery and finally, the terminus at Novospassky Most.

You can also sail in the other direction past the White House to Fili and Krylatskoye on an hour-long trip.

If you want to organise an unusual venue for a party or outing, the boats on the inner stretch of the Moscow river can be rented from in front of the Hotel Ukraine for about $300 per hour without extras. Food and drink can be organised according to your needs. Or you can choose to supply your own.

A weekend option is the cruise ship 'Georgiy Zhukov' that travels over a weekend to Tver or as far as Nizhni Novgorod from Moscow's Severniy Vokhzal. The boat is approximately $120 a night, including meals and a double room. There are discos, saunas, billiard hall, conference rooms, and children's playroom. Contact Dzhamila Arifulina *(tel: 339-2844 or 331-9444)*.

• *Bungee-jumping*

In Gorky Park you can enjoy two types of bungee-jumping in the summer. The first type is the classic type where you go up to a platform and then jump off over water. This takes place at the pond to the extreme left of the main entrance. The second type (where you are sent up into the air from the ground) is available at the back of the park. Walk in the entrance and continue heading as far towards the back of the park as you can till you get to the swan pond.

• *Cricket*

The Moscow Cricket Club was started a few years ago by those who are even more crazy about the game than the English - the Indians.

The Cricket Club used to play regularly against a number of teams. Games usually last for approximately three hours with 25 overs - one over equals six pitches - for each team. A score of over 150 was considered a good score at the Krasnopresnenskaya pitch.

The Moscow Cricket Club plays every Saturday and Sunday from noon to 15:00 at the Sports Venture, Krasnopresnenskaya Naberezhnaya, behind the Hotel Mezhdunarodnaya from early June until the weather starts to turn cold. A team of 11 can compete for $150. To arrange a game or confirm whether the club is still in existence, call Atul Kant or Samar Shakil at 938-8788/8041/8506.

• *Cycling*

Moscow is neither a second Amsterdam (though it's quite flat) nor like an English county with neat cycle paths, all painted and with arrows indicating which direction you should go in. However, the arrival of spring weather still brings out the bicycles.

151

Expat guide: Moscow   **9/Keeping busy**

If you prefer to get together with other enthusiasts, try the **Moscow Bike Touring Club** *(tel: 267-4468; 20 Staraya Basmannaya Ulitsa, Bldg 2)*. The club meets on Tuesdays 19.00 - 21.00 and organises bike tours varying in length and difficulty for cyclists of varying ability.

Members range in age from 7 - 70; membership is only a few dollars a year and you don't even have to be a member to take part in activities which are publicised by telephone to members.

The club holds family trips where children can ride with parents on baby carriers or on their own bikes.

Weekend tours are usually organised twice a month on Saturdays and outside Moscow with trips lasting in between 35-100 km in distance. Members usually meet at a train station and travel to the starting point by electric train. Suggestions are welcome for route planning but these usually include historical sites and scenic routes.

Annual trips are available to Karelia, Pskov and Novgorod for the more advanced cyclist and these may be over 700km in length. The annual Golden ring trips last about six days. The club also has a White Nights trip to St Petersburg by rail in time for the summer solstice.

Bike rentals are available for children and adults as well as support vehicles. The **Russian Club of Bike Travelling** *(tel: 916-88941; Bloc Tryokhsvyyatitelsky Pereulok. Entrance 3.)* specialises in foreign trips. Meetings are held on Thursdays from 19.00 - 22.00.

The **Caravan Moscow Club of Sports Touring** *(tel: 245-0392; 3/5 Serpov Pereulok)* holds meetings on Mondays from 19.00 - 21.00 and specialises in adventurous trips including weekend mountain bike tours on rough terrain.

Bikes and equipment can be obtained from **Mirida** *(tel: 954-4585 market at Gagarin Square, Leninsky Prospekt.)*; **Sokolniki market***;* **Velotsentr,** *(tel: 123-8119; 24 Nakhimovsky Prospekt);* **Zenit** *(tel: 269-7111; 9 Sokolnicheskaya Ploshchad)*.

Viri *(tel: 134-2546)* at 69 Leninsky Prospekt is rated as being not too expensive but hard to find. As you face the building, walk around the left side and the doorway is near the back corner. Once inside, follow the steps down to the basement.

You can buy super-expensive bikes at **Triatlon** on Ulitsa Maroseika across from the Amacord restaurant. Otherwise try the bike shop on Nikitsky Bulvar. **Global USA** is said to have mountain bikes sold at a better price than many other places. The sporting goods store on Tverskaya-Yamskaya (closest to Beloruskaya station) has a good selection of GT and Giant bikes.

Riding venues within the city
If you prefer to ride individually try the **Krylatskoye Hills** (in the north west) *(metro: Molodyozhnaya)* highly-rated cycling track built for the Olympics or **Bitsevsky Park** in the south *(metro: Chertanovskaya)* which is suitable for tour and mountain biking; **Sokolniki Park** *(just behind the Sokolniki metro station)* has flat terrain and in summer, plenty of *shashlyk* stalls; **Losiny Ostrov** (Elk Island) in northern Moscow is the largest park in Moscow. It does not have much in the way of paved roads, but is very peaceful and quiet; the **Botanical Gardens** (north west) *(metro: Botanischky)* has paved roads, but you can wander off; The

Expat guide: Moscow　　　　　　　　　　　　　**9/Keeping busy**

area near **VDNKh** (All-Russia Exhibition Centre) *(metro: VDNKh)* is interesting for architectural monuments.

Fishing

During the dog-days of July and August, you will often spy fishing fans trying their luck along the central embankments of Moscow's rivers, patiently casting their rods into the dubious looking water. However, if you want to join other afficionados, you could head for the Moscow region's myriad reservoirs. Locations such as Istrinskoye, Mozhaiskoye and Klyazminskoye double as suppliers of the city's drinking water and fishermen's haunts. Here you can find nearly all species of fish existing in Central Russia (some 30 specimens).

The **Moscow City Society of Hunters and Fishermen** *(tel: 230-4439) Building 7, 6 Ulitsa Stroitelei)* advises that the fish most likely to jump in summer are bream, along with roach, perch and some predators, such as pike or pike-perch. You can either fish for free along with anyone else, depending on the location or you can fish in a reservoir that is assigned to a fishing club where you will have to pay a nominal fee.

Club members pay less cover charge for a day's fishing than non-members. You can either pay your fees at the local fishing clubs or at the reservoirs themselves where you can rent boats by the day (two-tiered pricing system for members/non-members).

There are bases at some of the reservoirs where fishing fans can tell their tall stories and relax. The base at **Verkhne-Ruzskoye** reservoir, Fileneno, accommodates 24 people, with up to four sleeping in a room. You can use the base's bed linens and kitchen utensils but you should be responsible for your own meals.

The **Pirogovskoye reservoir** can be reached by commuter train from Savyolovsky train station to Vodniki. It is possible to rent a boat at one of the local yacht clubs.

Klyazminskoye reservoir, closer to Vodniki, along the Dmitrovskoye Shosse is another option.

The **Khimkinskoye reservoir**, near the Vodny Stadion metro stop, and Serebryany Bor, an island in north-west Moscow, can be reached by taking trolley #20 or #65 tram from Pole-zhayevskaya metro.

Lake Senezh can be reached by car along Leningradskoye Shosse or by commuter train from the Leningradsky Station to Podsolnechnaya, where you can catch a bus to the lake. The trip may take up to two hours each way. Lake Senezh is the territory of the Solnechnogorsk Society of Hunters and Fishermen, which means it's the only reservoir mentioned where you have to pay a fee.

Don't expect to rent rods from the fishing stores in Russia. The traditional hunting stores (see one example on the Old Arbat) or the fishing department of a large sporting goods store is likely to be your best bet.

• Flying

There are no expat flying clubs as such, but you may be lucky to find Russian enthusiasts at Vnukovo airport in the south of Moscow. There is an ultra (delta) plane glider club in Tushino, across from the airport.

Expat guide: Moscow   9/Keeping busy

Contact Larry George *(tel: 258-5250)* for further information regarding acrobatic flying.

Also try the Russian Federation of Superlight Aviation (UFSLA) *(tel: 149-4219)* which flies microlights at Tushino airport.

Vadim Kokurin offers air-gliding individually and groups (over the airfield and up around Moscow). Call Anatoly at 941-8347.

Parachuting is offered at the Chekhov airfield in the form of an all-day lesson that culminates in a fixed-line jump.

• *Golf*

Golf is a rich man's sport in Moscow and if you're prepared to pay an annual membership fee running to the tens of thousands of dollars you can take in the relatively short golfing season.

A single Master's membership to the Moscow Country Club confers lifetime memberships and entitles two people to unlimited entrance/golf playing rights. There are no restrictions on resale at a later date. In addition, annual dues must be paid to MCC. This category of membership costs between $45,000 - 50,000.

Trade Express Ltd *(tel: 785-0350; fax: 785-0348, 14 Shosse Entusiastov)* offers golf lessons at an indoor golf centre. Other facilities include a *s*ports and health centre. Sauna, fitness, massage, trainer.

Moscow City Golf Club *(tel: 147-8330; fax 147-6252 1 Davzhenko Ulitsa, vicinity of Mosfilmovskaya Ulitsa)* features golf and tennis in summer and skating and broomball in winter. There is also junior school and all-year-round golf tuition. Highly expensive membership available.

• *Hockey*

Players gather every Saturday afternoon indoors at 16.00 hrs in the sportshall on Krasnopresnenskaya Naberezhnaya.

Also contact Amelia *(tel: 925-1078)* or Julian *(tel: 246-0776)* for games at all levels, with sticks provided.

• *Horse-racing*

Hippodrome *(22 Begovaya Ulitsa; metro: Begovaya)* Races take place throughout the year, specialising in the trotting races which feature the highly-bred Russian and Orlov trotters, as well as horse and cart races. Open since 1834, the racetrack currently holds race meetings on Saturdays from 13:00 with some 20 races taking place. Entrance fee is nominal.

• *Mountain-biking* (see cycling)

• *Roller-blading*

This has become a popular sport in Moscow. Being flat it has a good number of places where you can roller-blade. The best options are the embankment of the Moscow River (in certain places only) and Victory Park. Another recommended option is Izmailovsky Park, with good trails on the north side of the park at metro Piervomaiskaya (left at 11th Parkovaya).

Expat guide: Moscow   **9/Keeping busy**

Most sports shops stock roller-blades starting from basic models ($15 - 20 at kiosks) to much more expensive models.

• *Rowing*

You can rent a boat at Grebnoi Kanal (Rowing Canal) in Krylatskoye every day apart from Sunday from May to September.

• *Skydiving*

One skydiving option available in Moscow involves doing an assisted-tandem jump with an instructor on wing-type canopy. This is offered at the Tushino airfield, and it costs around $70. A wide choice of airfields and airclubs is located outside Moscow. The best known is 3rd MGAK (3rd Moscow City Aeroclub),which has its base in Volosovo, near Chekhov (approximately 100km from Moscow). This club provides initial training for beginners together with the first jump on weekends. It also offers 1500m jumps with or without automatic release advanced training, video and photo capture of the jump. For further details visit the club's website at *www.skydive.ru/index.en.html.*

• *Table-tennis*

Quite a number of parks (Kuskovo and the top end of Gorky Park, just off Leninsky Prospekt to name only two) have all-weather concrete tables. These are not in fantastic condition, but playable, nevertheless. Bring along your net, bats and balls.

Neskuchky Sad in the forest behind Gorky Park (just off the early part of Leninsky Prospekt) has about 20 table-tennis tables for rent. They are open from 10:00 - 22:00. There are also two tennis courts adjacent and if you're into chess and draughts, quite a few people playing games next to the courts.

• *Volley-ball*

Tsaritsino park is recommended as being the best place to find a pick-up game in the summer. The park must have at least 50 volley-ball courts for all different levels of experience, and several badminton courts too. If you want a game, simply find the court with your experience level and you'll be invited to join if they need players. There are also a couple of courts at Kuskovo. See listing on 'Fitness' as well.

• *Windsurfing*

There are a number of reservoirs on the outskirts of Moscow where it is possible to windsurf in the summer. The best place is said to be Strogino, just north of Serebryany Bor. You can join the club there during the ice-free period and it is possible to hire equipment there. Strogino has a club (home of the RFA: Russian Funboarding Association) which you can join for the ice-free period, but it's probably better to hire the stuff on an 'as and when' basis. Wind conditions are not outstanding neither is the windsurfing scene very popular.

The sporting goods store upstairs at Aerovokhzal (metro: Dinamo) has a decent windsurfing equipment department.

155

Expat guide: Moscow   **9/Keeping busy**

Outdoor recreation (all year round)

Horse-riding

Horse-riding is alive and well in Moscow and can be enjoyed at several locations. The three main riding schools are at **Bitsa, Hippodrome and Sokolniki.** In addition to the schools, you can find horses for hire at Tsaritsino.

It is not uncommon to come across riders in the more rural parts of Moscow and on occasion, riders are willing to let you have a ride if you pay a negotiated fee starting at about $5. You may also see horses available for a short walk on Tverskaya and the Old Arbat. For a slightly longer ride, try Filyovsky Park (across from the CD market) during the summer.

Take your own riding hat if this is important to you, as Muscovites don't tend to wear them. It's not easy to come across English-speaking trainers and if you do, you most likely have to fit into their schedule rather than the other way round, unless you arrange a group of block lessons.

◊　**Troika** has an English-language site *(www.horses.ru)* which displays horses for sale as well as histories of the Russian breeds. Troika organises purchase of horses and stabling as well as riding instruction with English-speaking trainers.

◊　**Bitsa** *(tel: 318-5744/318-6028; 33 Balaklavsky Prospekt South; metro: Chertanovskaya)* can be reached from the centre by travelling southwards along Varshavskoye Shosse. Built for the 1980 Moscow Olympic games, though you would not know it, the 40-hectare complex with forest attached is now a decrepit area, surrounding an old collapsing stadium dominated by an imposing sculpture of horses. It's difficult to find your way in initially if you park outside, as there are few signs. It's possible to park outside the Hippodrome area, or you can park inside for a small fee per hour. Visit the bathroom at home before you go to Bitsa.

Bitsa has only two English-speaking trainers and a few ponies used for children aged 7 - 9. Bitsa's stalls are home to about 200 horses, some of which are used for rental to adult riders, while a few ponies are set aside for children. It's possible to stable your horse at the centre for about $300 per month. Lessons in the enclosed school are cheaper during the week than over the weekend, starting with children at about $13 per hour during the week and $16 per hour over the weekend. Adults pay about $16 per hour during the week and more over the weekend, depending on your level of expertise, as costs mount the more complicated the lesson. Apart from individual lessons, you can take advantage of increasingly advanced sets of 10 group lessons each, taking place once a week, with the fourth set preparing the rider for assessment. Experienced riders may take advantage of outdoor group trail rides after first taking an individual lesson in order to demonstrate competence.

◊　**Hippodrome** *(tel: Lena (Russian only) 945-1137 from 07:00 - 09.00; 22 Begovaya Ulitsa; metro: Begovaya)* is Moscow's only racecourse with 35 stables and over 300 horses, some available for rent. There is only one Shetland pony for children, though remember, it's probably better for a child to learn on a small pony than on a Shetland as they can be cheeky. If you

156

Expat guide: Moscow   9/Keeping busy

have any experience you can ride in the 40-hectare grounds of the Hippodrome for an hour or so. Those who wish to pretend they are jockeys can gallop around the empty racetrack on Tuesdays and Fridays. Otherwise you can ride in what is said to be the largest arena in Europe. Lessons are given to children starting at age 10 for 45 minutes per lesson. To reach the riding stables on the far side of the track, drive round the side of the Hippodrome to the back entrance.

◊ **Sokoros at Sokolniki** *(tel: 268-5922/42, fax: 268-3063; 11 Poperechny, Park Sokolniki)* offers both indoor and outdoor riding as well as forest-trail riding. The school is about a 20-minute drive from the centre and features two indoor rings, an outdoor arena, and a forest trail. Several instructors speak some English. Private lessons cost about $25 for 60 minutes of instruction, less for children. The school also has a shop with mostly expensive imported horsy items.

◊ **Tourism and Sport** *(tel: 434-2682)* organises horseback riding trips, winter rides along historical routes at Volokolamsk and Mozhalsk 'Borodinskoye Pole' and riding lessons in Moscow and suburbs.

Equipment:

Yevrovet *(tel: 212-4773; 12 Ulitsa Mishina)* sells riding equipment. You can also try **Equestrian Sport Centre 'Rus'**, *(tel: 494-0111, 495-2060 fax: 495-5405, 103 Svobody Ulitsa)*; **Hippodrome (race-course)** *(tel: 945-0437/4516; 22 Begovaya Ulitsa)*; and **Moscowskii Zavod KonnoSportivnogo Inventarya** which has produced a broad range of horse-related tack.

• *Running - long distance*

Problems encountered by runners include pollution, being chased by large dogs while their owners stood by laughing, being whistled at because you are running in shorts and thus exposing bare legs which apparently makes the men jealous and the women frisky, as well as stares. However, the joys of running are slowly catching on in Russia and it's not as unusual as it was to see runners out in all kinds of weather.

In summer, community road races take place along the Frunzenskaya Naberezhnaya on Sunday mornings. Keep a look out for the International marathon and 10km race in the second half of August (inquire at the Rossiya hotel) and the Moscow running race in April.

The run along the river below Moscow State University, known as Vorobyovskaya Naberezhnaya is touted as the best running route in Moscow. Try the far stretch, beginning almost across from the Novodyevichy Monastery, where the embankment road begins. The area is very quiet and especially beautiful during the autumn. When it's dry, there are also some good (but quite hilly) forest trails that go past the ski-jump and the old abandoned metro station. The trails wind all the way into the Neskuchny Sad area at the western end of Gorky Park, abridging Leninsky Prospekt.

On days when the Gorky Park gate is open, it's possible to continue on down the road, under the highway bridge, past the outdoor art market, all the way to the Peter the Great statue.

Expat guide: Moscow   **9/Keeping busy**

In the summer you can take a run out and come back on one of the numerous tourist boats that ply the river in the area. The boats are slow, and priced for tourists, but there are a few stops along the route.

In winter, runners say that running at -10°C can be more pleasurable than running in a muggy +20°C.

• *Running (Hash House Harriers)*

Moscow Hash House Harriers calls itself 'A drinking club with a running problem' and offers you a run for 30 - 45 minutes (or walk, stagger - your choice) once a week, (meet in front of the Ukraina Hotel) followed by a social at a selected venue. Every Sunday at 14:00 in the winter or at 17:00 in the summer, come rain, snow or shine, you pay a nominal fee of $5 to join in the fun. Like in many other places all over the globe, this is one of the major expat haunts. The club also has occasional weekends away and it's own website *(www.orc.ru/~force10/ or e-mail: force10@orc.ru).*

The group was started in 1938 by three Englishmen stationed in Kuala Lumpur, Malaysia. Since then chapters have been formed all over the world with the Moscow HHH starting in 1983. Now, between 10 and 100 people run in the streets and parks of the city. It's an excellent way for new arrivals to make friends.

• *Rugby*

The Moscow Dragons RUFC welcome participants and spectators to their rugby union games. Practice is usually on Tuesdays at 20:00 at Novoslobodskaya and Saturdays at 15:00. Games take place when whenever they can be scheduled. See the *Moscow Times* Bulletin Board published every Thursday for further details.

• *Scuba-diving*

Over the past year or so, travel before the crisis prompted those who had tasted the joys of scuba diving to open their own clubs. The best established clubs are **Akvanavt**, and **Crocodile** at the Olympic Village sports complex,

Akvanavt *(tel: 288-5645),* was founded in 1994 and is purportedly the largest club in Moscow. It provides PADI training (Professional Association of Diving Instructors) and offers open-water diving certificates for a price of about $400.

The intensive beginner's course includes a theory lecture and five practical lessons in the swimming-pool, here the novice learns the diver's code of behaviour and about 20 vital skills. The second part is more complicated and consists of four open-water dives.

Practice dives take place at the low-visibility Pirogovo reservoir where Akvanavt has built a special diving platform to protect divers from the silt. Students practice on underwater wrecks such as a car, rocket, plane and boat, and these are accessed from a diving boat.

Expat guide: Moscow   **9/Keeping busy**

Dives take place in dry suits until first ice appears. Students who begin the course when the open water is considered too cold can finish the training at a PADI registered dive-club when they go on vacation.

The certificate permits the holder to dive without an instructor and obtain discounts on equipment.

Crocodile (*tel/fax: 437-4765; 2 Michurinsky Prospekt*) is a club owned by one of the 30 or so PADI diving instructors in Russia.

- ## Soccer *(Football)*

MGU (Moscow University) has six-a-side soccer games on Wednesday afternoons. There is some team-playing but individuals seem able to form teams on an *ad hoc* basis.

Some of the embassies, particularly the British Embassy, might have informal soccer leagues. Contact your embassy for further details.

AYSO - Youth Soccer League takes place for nine weeks at Olympic Village from beginning September till end October and is open to a number of schools. Approximately 400 children take part, and fathers volunteer as coaches. Teams vary in size according to age group, and cater to children from the age of five to grade 10, depending on demand. It's a great opportunity for parents to network, and girls are welcome to play.

The Olympic village complex has a coffee shop, pub and supermarket for those wishing to escape from the cold while little Johnny or Jenny are waiting to play. It costs about $45 for the league duration, and this includes team kits and a team photograph. Children are ranked according to ability.

The U.S. Embassy Soccer Team occasionally looks for new players. They play every Monday night from 20:30 - 22:30 at the embassy gym against other teams from around Moscow. They also play in local tournaments, usually held on weekends. If you are interested in playing, contact Glenn Corn (*tel: 956-4139 or e-mail to cornga@moscowpoa.us-state.gov or the US Embassy Recreation department*).

It's possible to rent one of the grass pitches at Luzhniki stadium (*tel: 201-1869; 24 Luzhnetskaya Naberezhnaya; metro: Sportivnaya*). Luzhniki charges $50 - 75 per hour).

- ## Walking, hiking and nature trails

Watch the Community Bulletin Board in the *Moscow Times* from early April for 15km hikes and others, otherwise, contact Sergei (*tel: 937-6232*).

The club organises weekly trips into the countryside outside Moscow every Sunday, all year round, whatever the weather, to an average-length 15km hike across country. On a good day, the hikes can attract up to 40 people, while only the stalwarts go out in the dead of winter, which, apparently, are just as enjoyable as summer hikes.

To purchase hiking supplies try the hiking store **Bivuak** of the Moscow City Tourist Club at 17, Ulitsa. Bolshaya Kommunisticheskaya.

If you want to head out on your own and wish to discover the city and fulfil the need for exercise, stay away from major roads, stick to quiet roads, or head

159

Expat guide: Moscow   **9/Keeping busy**

for Sparrow Hills, Kolomenskoe, Kuskovo, Bitsa or Izmailovsky Park, the Botanical Gardens, or Victory Park.

Moscow is bursting with parks full of noble, ancient trees, shaded walkways and calm and privacy. There seems to be a shared conspiracy by all who do visit the parks to keep them a secret. People wander around peacefully and seem to know that others want to do the same.

Kolomenskoye *(39 Andropova Prospekt; metro: Kolomenskaya)* was originally a royal estate dating back to the 14th Century and today housing a gatehouse and a couple of beautiful churches, Kolomenskoye overlooks the Moscow River. The park is ideal for a picnic and a change of pace from the fume-filled centre. There is also a possibility of taking in a river ride on the two ferries that ply their trade during the summer months. One trip is shorter than the other, but both are over one hour in duration. They afford the opportunity to view the church on the promontory built from different perspectives, although the loud pop music played on board somewhat detracts from the experience. During the summer, children can play on 'bouncy' castles or enjoy reasonably priced go-kart rides. In winter, children can enjoy pony and sledge rides, and possibly skidoos. There is also a selection of small kiosks inside mock-wooden huts which resemble the village that had stood on the site for centuries before. These offer a variety of foods to keep you going if you forget your picnic.

There are entrance charges to the various historical sites on the estates. If you are a woman and wish to enter one of the churches that is still in use, you must have your head and knees covered.

Kuskovo, *(2 Ulitsa Yonosti; metro: Ryansky Prospekt then catch the #133 or #208 trolleybus for six stops).* If you don't wish to enter the actual estate you can take a thoroughly enjoyable walk around the outer perimeter of the pond, periodically strolling off into the thicker forest where you will find a small football pitch and posts for volley-ball courts (you need to provide your own net). There are also some tables for table-tennis, but you need to supply your own net and bats and balls.

VDNKh *(metro: VDNKh)* The former Exhibition of Economic Achievements built on a grand scale to impress the Soviet citizens is now like a giant market. Despite the sad transformation, it's well worth a visit, simply to imagine just what it must have been like in its glory days. Once you've finished exploring the exhibition area (could take a few hours) head for the Botanical gardens (see below) which adjoin the centre at the far end.

Victory Park *Kutozovsky Prospekt* was built in 1995 to commemorate the 50th anniversary of end of World War II. This impressive monument which can be seen from afar is surrounded by rows of fountains that are lit up with coloured lights on summer nights. There are food kiosks aplenty for the hungry, *shashlyk* bars on the weekend, beers and soft drinks are sold. For the activity conscious there is plenty of place to walk, cycle and roller-blade. There are a few amusements for children and short rides can be taken on horses in small automated cars and on a 'train' on wheels that takes you a fair way round the park. Children will enjoy climbing over the old military tanks and artillery equipment. In winter, there are ice-slides and sculpture competitions.

Tsaritsino *(metro: Oryekhova/Tsaritsyno).* Here you can see palace ruins (inspired by Catherine the Great) amidst woods and lakes and hire boats, play in the playground, visit the restaurant (open noon to 23:00 and swim and sunbathe

160

Expat guide: Moscow   9/Keeping busy

around the lake, picnic, ride horses (behind the restaurant) for an hour at a time, or take a ride in a horse-drawn cart.

Serebryany Bor *(in eastern Moscow, set in the Moscow River, about 40 minutes from the centre by car; metro: Polezharskaya; trolley buses #20, 21 or 65)*. Like the secluded paradise that it is, Serebryany Bor jealously guards access during the summer. It's best to visit during the week as weekends are crowded. If you visit by car, you will need to have the address of a house you are visiting to obtain entry.

There are lots of places to explore, you will find Moscow's most popular beach here as well as a naturist beach and a gay naturist beach. There are also several ponds with picturesque bridges and many secluded paths. You may come across play areas for children and can fish as well as hire rowing boats and pedalos. A ferry used to take day-trippers for rides round the island. Many of Moscow's power elite have dachas here, as do high-ranking executives of foreign companies who live in compounds of attractive Swedish-built houses complete with guards. Although you will see people swimming in the river, it's not advisable. In winter, Serebryany Bor is ideal for cross-country skiing.

Gorky Park *(tel: 236-6589; Krymsky Val Ulitsa; metro: Oktyabrskaya/Park Kultury)*. The park features all kinds of amusements for children and adults, some expensive. Watch nervous young men try their luck at bungee-jumping (two sites, one near the beginning and one at the far end of the park). Children can try their hand at a shooting range, ride horses (not much of a ride though, more being led around in a circle) drive automated cars and try the hair-raising rides adjacent to the river. Adults can while away the afternoon at one of a number of food kiosks and *shashlyk* bars. The ponds at the far end of the park house pedalos, ducks and swans which children will enjoy feeding bread. Try to empty your bladder and bowel before going to the Park.

In winter, parts of the park are turned into what's been billed as the biggest ice-rink in Russia.

Botanical Gardens *(metro: Botanichsky Sad)* This is a large, well-maintained green space in the north-east of Moscow, with fountain, pond, paths and many trees. It is said to have an arboretum with 1686 species of plant as well as a Japanese garden. The park is ideal for a picnic, bike-riding or roller-blading, it is also accessible from the rear of VDNKh.

Losiny Ostrov National Park The huge (12,000ha) but little known Losiny Ostrov National Park (Moose Island), several kilometres north-east of the centre is accessible by metro and suburban rail. Rangers organise guided tours with an ecological slant.

Home to 48 kinds of wild mammals from mouse to moose, and at least 170 kinds of birds, the park has been in existence since the 14th century when the tsars used it as a hunting ground.

Suburban trains run from Yaroslavsky Station to Yauza or you can catch #176 trolley bus from metro station VDNKh to the New Drama Theatre stop, near a different park entrance. Three-hour guided park tour cost around $10 per group and these can be arranged by calling 268-2965.

161

Expat guide: Moscow   **9/Keeping busy**

Outdoor recreation (winter)

You might think winter is the time when everyone heads indoors, concentrates on eating and hibernating, but much activity nevertheless takes place outdoors and to overcome those winter blues and SAD attacks you'll need to be brave and take advantage of the winter sports on offer.

With rental equipment available at reasonable prices in many city parks, skiing and skating are two activities you'll have to at least try. If you have your own gear bring it with you as gear is available, but if you're after quality items, these can be expensive. Equipment can be obtained from shops such as : **Alpindustriya** for its mountaineering equipment; **Sports World** *(tel: 925-1128; basement of Detsky Mir, 5 Teatralny Pereulok; metro: Lubyanka)* for down-hill and cross-country ski equipment.

Try the **ski-market** near Avtozavodskya metro ulitsa Saikina) where you can buy practically anything in terms of local and foreign-made equipment.

Sports World also repairs damaged skis or snowboards for $40 to $60. The store charges $20 to install bindings.

Olimp, *(tel: 255-0592; 23 Ulitsa Krasnaya Presnya; metro: Ulitsa 1905 Goda)* has a wide range of equipment. Try the smaller Russian kiosk round the corner, near the pizza restaurant.

You may also find individuals sometimes standing outside sports shops selling second-hand sporting goods at reasonable prices.

• Ice-climbing

This is available at Kant Sports Club near Nagornoye metro in southern Moscow on an ice-encrusted circular brick building that is 40m high and 3m in diameter.

• Ice-hockey

Watch out for games at **TsKA** *(tel: 213-6590; 29 Leningradsky Prospekt; metro: Aeroport/Dinamo)* starting from September. If you want to play, contact the American and Canadian embassies and ask for further details of private games.

• Ice-skating

Black hockey and white figure skates are available at many shops including **Olimp**, *(tel: 255-0592; 23 Ulitsa Krasnaya Presnya; metro: Ulitsa 1905 Goda)* or more cheaply at the Russian kiosk round the corner, next to McDonalds; **Kettler Sport** *(tel: 952-0140; 21 Leninsky Prospekt; metro: Oktyabrskaya);* **Union Sport** *(tel: 242-1614; 48/24 Komsomolsky Prospekt; metro: Sportivnaya)*

Skating at Patriarchy Pond and Chisty Prudy is especially picturesque at night when the rinks are lit up.

It's best to go outdoor skating when the temperature is consistently between -2 - -8°C. At this temperature, the ice will be 'fast' enough for those who are skilled and good for beginners.

Outdoor rinks

• **Chisty Pond** Situated at the end of Chistoprudny Bulvar has long been a popular spot with ice-skaters. There is no admission fee, and the ice is not

Expat guide: Moscow   **9/Keeping busy**

maintained. However, the absence of large crowds makes it a good spot for beginners.

- **Torpedo Stadium Rink,** *(tel: 275-4586; 4 Vostochnaya Ulitsa; metro: Avtozavodskaya; open: 10:00- 21:00).* Situated in the park around Torpedo Soccer Stadium, the rink is well kept and entry is cheap at around $2.00.

- **Luzhniki Yuzhny Rink** *(tel: 201-1164; Luzhnetskaya Naberezhnaya; metro: Sportivnaya)* to the left of the big arena is open: Saturday and Sunday: 17:00 - 21:00; Tuesday to Friday: 10:00 - 14:00 and 17:00 - 21:00. The rink offers skate rental, though the quality is not of the best. You pay an entrance fee and extra for skate hire.

- **Gorky Park** *(metro: Oktyabrskaya and Park Kultury)* Open: 11:00 - 22:00. To reach the three Gorky Park rinks turn left after the main entrance. Entrance is charged to the rinks, though these are connected by iced-up paths which can be skated on for free. Count on large crowds - probably no place for a beginner. From 18:00 - 22:00 you can skate to disco music. You can also rent skates by the hour and change in the changing room. Hot mulled wine and *shashlyk* are usually available.

- **Sokolniki park** The rink *(tel: 268-8277; metro: Sokolniki)* open:11:00 - 21:00. is in the 10th Sports Pavilion inside the park. It boasts a well-equipped skate rental office which rents skates for a reasonable fee plus a larger deposit which also requires some form of identity. Rink use is charged per two-hour slot.

Indoor rinks

- **Kristall** in Luzhniki *(tel: 201-1815; Luzhnetskaya Naberezhnaya, quite near to the Luzhiki Sports Palace; metro: Sportivnaya)* is used by groups which book slots throughout the day. There may be two one-hour slots free for public use, but you will need to phone to find out what the schedule for that particular day is likely to be. Skates (not a huge supply) can be hired by the hour. There is also a skate sharpener at the rink.

- **Lokomotiv Ice Palace** *(tel: 161-9385 125 Bolshaya Cherkizovskaya Ulitsa; . metro: Cherkizovskaya. Open:11:00 - 17:00 daily and from 11:00 - 15:00 on Wednesdays)* skates are not available for rent.

- **Olympic Sports Complex** *(tel: 288-5663; Olympiisky Prospekt, metro: Prospekt Mira; open : 19:00 - 23:00)* Ice-skating at the Ice Training Hall. Tickets for a 45-minute skating session cost $2.40 for children and $4 for adults.

Skiing

Because Moscow is so flat there is very little opportunity for down-hill skiing. This is rather the place for cross-country skiing, and you'll find Muscovites of all ages out skiing in the winter. Equipment is widely available.

- There is a ski shop at the ski-run in the suburb of Krylatskoye which is Moscow's favourite skiing venue. A shop at the ski-run also rents out skis.

- **Vyshaya liga** on Olimpiiskiy Prospekt not far from Penta hotel

- **Sport City** *6 Kuznetsky Most*

163

Expat guide: Moscow   **9/Keeping busy**

- **Skif** (is said to be good for cross-country skis, imported kids' sleds, windsurf equipment and snazzy winter clothes) in a two-storey concrete building on Krylatskaya Ulitsa, on the banks of the canal built for the 1980 rowing, just near the foot of the Krylatskoye ski-run.
- **Sokolniki market** has a ski section which opens around 11:00, otherwise try the ski sports shop on the ground floor of the mall facing the market.

Cross-country skiing

Beginners should try classic skis first. These are longer than skate skis and have tips that are more pointed and used facing straight ahead on tracks found in most parks. They are not as fast as skate-skiing and requiring less skill and balance. Wooden skis are better than plastic skis for beginners. Ski poles should reach your armpit or shoulder. In addition to the actual skis and ski poles, you'll also need ski boots and bindings, and these are available in the older, cheaper pin-style or in the more modern styles more suitable for skate-skiing. Obtain a wax kit for waxing your skis periodically. Some shops offer a binding service at extra cost.

- Skiing in the **Izmailovsky Park** *(metro: Ismailovskaya)* It is possible to ski directly from the road across from the station. The scenery is attractive and varied, and cross-country routes are marked by red paint on tree trunks.
- **Losiny Ostrov** a real forest just several kilometres north-east of the Kremlin; skiing there, you have a chance to see traces of wild animals -- moose, boar, foxes and hares
- **Moscow University area** with some short runs and ice-slides
- **Neskuchny Sad** (adjacent to Gorky Park)
- **Sokolniki Park**
- **Krylatskoye**

Down-hill skiing

With Moscow being so flat there is not much opportunity to ski down-hill. However, you can try small pistes here and there such as at Krylatskoye and the area adjacent to the ski-jump in front of Moscow University.

Lessons are given at Krylatskoye, also watch out for the extreme sports festival which takes place there in February.

Another skiing option, but not exactly in Moscow, is at the Yakhroma hills some 75 minutes drive from Moscow. A new resort **Volen** *(tel: 587-3502/409-7000)* has nine slopes up to 370m long and some vertical drops of 70m with four ski-lifts. Numerous instructors are on hand for lessons for both adults and children over four years of age. Lessons cost under $10 per hour. However, there are no nursery slopes for absolute beginners. It's possible to rent new and used imported equipment at the centre, and both city and regional competitions are held there. The down-side is that the centre gets seriously overcrowded on weekends with thousands of visitors clogging the ski-lifts. To visit the centre, it is recommended that you go during the week, or even at night when the slopes are lit and the lifts operate till midnight. In addition, prices are cheaper during the week and at different times of the day on the weekend.

It's also possible to stay at the centre in three types of wooden cabins, all costing different prices according to facilities. Those with mini-saunas are more

Expat guide: Moscow   9/Keeping busy

expensive but all are reasonably priced (discounted during the week) and all have
a shower, heating and a television. Depending on style, the cabins hold between
three and six occupants, and extra beds can be ordered for an additional 10% fee.
The manager's name is Dmitry Kopein and he speaks only Russian and German.
There are four different catering venues, all cosy and conducive to *apres-ski*.
The centre can be reached by driving north along Dmitrovskoye Shosse and
turning left when you see the sign for Volen.

Buying equipment

There are many shops in Moscow which sell locally made and imported skigear.
Otherwise you can rent some equipment (mostly for adults) at Krylatskoye. Try
Alpindustria *(tel: 165-9081; 18 Ulitsa Pervomayskaya; metro Izmailovskaya,)*
which is expensive or the more reasonably price Sports Store at Aerovokhzal on
Leningradsky Prospekt.

◊ **Krylatskoye, Alpine Ski Centre** *(tel: 140-4308; 51 Ulitsa Krylatskaya;
   metro: Molodezhnaya and then take trolleybus # 829)*
◊ **Alpine Skiing International Club** *(tel: 276-1565; 5 Ulitsa Dubrovskaya 1,
   metro: Proletarskaya)*
◊ **Sport Master School** *(tel: 939-0037; 28 Ulitsa Kosygina)*

• Sledding

Many children slide down small slopes on a plastic sheet from locally-produced
lyedyanki of all shapes and sizes. This is said to be more fun than sledding as
direction is not pre-determined. Other makes of sled are widely available.
Try:

• **Detsky Mir** *(tel: 927-2007; 5 Teatralny Proezd)*
• **Dom Igrushki** *(tel: 238-0096; 26 Ulitsa Bolshaya Yakimanka)*
• **Sport** *(tel: 925-1642; 30 Leninsky Prospekt)*

Many hills are to be found along the Sparrow Hills, Kolomenskoye; Krylatskoye,
in north-western Moscow, near the Academy of Sciences building and in
Neskuchny Sad. There are slopes near the Nagornaya metro station at the Kant
sports club. You can use facilities as a member, or pay per use as a non-member.
The club also offers lessons (in Russian) in down-hill skiing and has a snow-
boarding school, as well as a ski-lift and cross-country trail.

• Snow-boarding

The sport has been in existence in Russia since 1987. Snow-boarders will find
company at the Kant Sports club near Nagornaya metro station; at Krylatskoye
where they can also take lessons, and on the slope below the Olympic ski-jump
near the university. You could also venture out to Volen in the Yakhroma hills
(see listing under down-hill skiing) which has a half-pipe for snow-boarders,
hires out equipment and offers lessons. The centre also holds city and regional
snow-boarding competitions.

In 1999 Krylatskoye held a festival of extreme sports which included free
snow-boarding lessons and daily freestyle competitions among, a host of other
activities. The festival took place over five weekends from late January to early
March.

165

Expat guide: Moscow   **9/Keeping busy**

• *Snow-mobiling*

This is not so widely found within Moscow (try Kolomenskoe in the north) but more so in outlying areas. Try the Moscow Country Club or venture to the Suzdal Touristic centre which has several snowmobiles rented out for $50 per hour. You are able to snowmobile on a nearby frozen river, gloves and helmets are provided. Be careful that the river is frozen solid, as a French expat apparently fell in the river, snowmobile and all, a couple of seasons ago.

The yacht club on Dmitrovskoye shosse, near the Vodo Khronilishche (water reservoir) changes focus to snowmobiles for the winter, and there are occasional races at **Nikolina Gora** (a dacha town outside Moscow). If you wish to purchase your own snow-mobile, Russia now makes the Taiga which sells for about $2,400.

• *Troika rides*

Although one hears about troika rides, they are not easy to find. Try Kolomenskoe Park, as well as Tsaritsino (near the restaurant), the livestock showing area at VDNKh and further afield, Sergiev Possad, a town about 70km outside Moscow.

One enterprising Russian has laid on activities for a day's outing to Sergiev Possad (worth seeing simply for the monastery). She will organise transport for you at $15 per person; a Russian-style meal and drink at $25 per person; a troika ride on a short circular route and a ride on a single horse drawn sleigh through the forest. The rides are another $15 per person. To top off the day, you can enjoy a Russian *banya* for $15 per person and a roll in the snow. Total cost for a day's outing including transport is $55 per person 50% for kids. For further information contact Sveta Kurlikin who speaks good English *(tel: 8-254 21870 or 8-254-4432).*

166

10/Staying healthy

Before coming to Moscow you will need to reassure yourself about medical facilities. There are a number of Western and Russian medical and dental clinics that are modern and well run and can provide services up to a point. After this point, you will possibly need to be evacuated for further treatment in the West. Note that 'Western' does not mean 100% Western in some cases, as Russian doctors do make up part of the staff complement of most clinics. If you need to be hospitalised, neither will you be hospitalised in a Western hospital, but be referred to a Russian hospital.

It must be pointed out that there are many excellent Russian doctors. However, your main problem in using them is likely to be language-related and also in locating a reputable doctor.

Some Russian hospitals are able to provide a similar level of treatment as in the West, but prepare yourself for very limited English-language facilities, and also for culturally alien norms when it comes to visiting hours and other ward practices and rules. Always ascertain before admission exactly what access you will have to a child should they have to be admitted to a hospital, and on discharge, request a copy of the medical record and a translation thereof, so that your own doctor will be able to interpret which procedures and medications have been administered.

Before your arrival in Russia, investigate medical and dental insurance schemes, so that you can put your mind at rest regarding the outcome of any unexpected serious health problems.

Emergencies

Bear in mind that even though you might become a member of one of the Western clinics, they are not in a position to guarantee effective emergency services, in which case, your fate will be in the laps of the gods.

If you are to be admitted to hospital via one of the medical centres, you can expect to be charged a hefty $5,000 deposit if your insurance scheme does not cover hospitalisation. In certain cases, parents of child patients can also pay to accompany their children in hospital overnight, whereas other hospitals may even restrict what you would call reasonable access.

House calls

Before selecting a medical centre in Moscow, find out if they will make house-calls. Those that do charge high rates (over $100) for house-calls, especially if you are not a member of the centre. Russian doctors from Russian clinics usually charge about $8 per house call.

Expat guide: Moscow   **10/Staying healthy**

Sterile disposable needles

These are widely available from most pharmacies in Moscow without a prescription.

X-ray equipment

Always ask how old equipment is and check that adequate protection is provided.

Medical insurance

Arrange comprehensive medical insurance and emergency evacuation coverage in your country before you arrive. Choose a supplier who is not an expert in finding excuses to deny payment for the majority of ailments. You should select one that reimburses costs in full, minus deductables. Policies should cover emergency care; illnesses thought to be of non-emergency nature, including diagnosis and medicine as required, and emergency evacuation for those situations where adequate treatment is not available locally.

When comparing insurance schemes look at :

- annual overall maximum ceiling of cover
- in-patient and day case benefits (does this include a full refund for hospital accommodation?)
- does it cover surgeons, physicians and anaesthetists as required?
- does it cover consultations by other specialists such as radiologists and radiotherapists?
- parent accommodation costs when accompanying a child under 12
- hazardous sports injuries
- out-patient benefits
- emergency local road ambulance up to a certain amount
- nursing and diagnostics procedures
- emergency evacuation (in Russia evacuation is usually to Helsinki or London
- emergency dental healthcare

Some international companies you may consider comparing are:

- BUPA International in the UK *(tel: (44-1273) 32-3563 see their website also)*
- Cigna International
- Coutts
- Care Card International
- ExpaCare International
- Guardian Health
- Good Health Worldwide
- International Private Healthcare
- Medicare International
- OHRA
- PPP Healthcare
- Western Provident

168

Expat guide: Moscow   **10/Staying healthy**

Medical and dental centres
Membership
Many Western-run clinics require that you sign up and pay a membership fee, which offers you various advantages over *ad hoc* consultations. Quite a number of Western firms will sign up on behalf of their expatriate staff. Among other perks, membership means that you don't have to fork out cash every time you visit a doctor. A visit with medicine starts at about $120.

It also helps if you need on-line information. If you are not a member and phone up for advice, you will not be able to obtain information without making an appointment. You will also benefit in terms of gaining priority access over non-members; housecalls may be cheaper, you may be able to use their ambulance for free, and you may obtain certain discounts.

The American Medical Centre, the European Medical Centre and Mediclub do not insist that you take out membership when you use their services.

Medical services
- **American Medical Centre** *(tel: 956-3366; fax: 956-2306; 10, 2nd Tverskoy-Yamskoy Pereulok; metro: Mayakovskaya; open: Monday - Friday 08:00 - 20:00; Saturday 09:00 - 17:00; www/americanmedicalcenters.com)* The AMC is centrally located and situated in the same building as the EMC (European Medical Centre). According to their advert, the centre is fully staffed by Western family practitioners and specialists, and it claims to be the only clinic to have an American paediatrician in Moscow. It offers X-ray, ultrasound, laboratory facilities and medication on its premises. There is a 24-hour emergency service for AMC members who also have priority over non-members in making appointments as well as a discount on housecalls and medicines. Pre-natal care and paediatrics are offered, as is co-ordination with Russian hospitals. They provide a medical evacuation service and also have a pharmacy and dentist.
- **Assist 24 Delta Consulting group** *(tel: 229-6536; 229-2138; 935-8524)* The group organises medical evacuation from any point in the CIS to any point in the world as well as a 24-hour assistance service.
- **British Embassy Clinic** *(tel: 956-7270; fax: 956-7269; 14 Morisa Teresa Naberezhnaya; metro: Borovitskaya; open Monday - Friday 09:00 - 13:00 and 14:00 - 17:30; closed Wednesday afternoon).* Located across the river from the Kremlin, the clinic handles all medical services, including prenatal care and baby clinic. Although British passport holders only may use the clinic and by appointment only, you first have to be registered on their books, and if they have filled up their quota of registrations, you can put your name on a waiting list.
- **Canadian Family Mediclub Clinic** *(tel: 931-5018; fax: 932-8653; 56 Michurinsky Prospekt; metro: Prospekt Vernadskova; open from Monday to Thursday 09:00 - 20:00; Friday 09:00- 18:00; Saturday 10:00 - 14:00).* Membership is said to be more expensive than the other clinics. The clinic's Canadian doctors offer consultations in a wide variety of medical

169

Expat guide: Moscow   **10/Staying healthy**

specialities, as well as full prenatal cae and a pharmacy. A doctor is available by telephone 24 hours a day.

- **European Medical Centre** *(tel: 250-5523; fax: 251-6099; emergency: 956-7999; 10, 2nd Tverskoy-Yamskoy Pereulok; metro: Mayakovskaya; open Monday - Friday 09:00 - 20:00 and contactable round the clock)* The EMC promises access to Moscow's best hospitals. Staff speak English, French and Russian. Provides a wide variety of Western health care by mostly European physicians including diagnostic and laboratory testing, optical, dental and full prenatal care, emergency hospitalisation and evacuation, pharmacy and 24-hour emergency care with after-hour calls re-routed to an off-site doctor. Membership confers a reduction of 25% on costs, which are typically $80 for a general consultation; $100 for a paediatric consultation; $120 for a gynaecological consultation. House-calls cost from $140.

- **AEA SOS International Clinic** *(tel: 937-5760; fax: 280-8677; 31, Grokholsky Pereulok, 10th floor; metro: Prospekt Mira)* Formerly the International Medical Clinic, the clinic offers family practice, paediatrics, emergency medical care and hospitalisation, pre-natal care, laboratory and pharmacy on-site, medical evacuation; 24 hour physician house call service; counselling and 24-hour observation.

- **Medical Centre Urgentum** *(tel: 432-0240/1600; 20, Ulitsa Lobachevskogo Open; 08:00 - 20:00)* The clinic specialises in gynaecology and urology as well as diagnosis and treatment of sexually-transmitted diseases. It also attends to the treatment of skin and tropical diseases.

- **The Medical Centre for Foreign Affairs** *(tel: 237-5843 Russian)* which was originally established for the diplomatic community but is now open to all, is recommended for fast, efficient and reasonably priced treatment.

Dental services

There are some 400 dental clinics in Moscow and these are accessible to foreigners as long as you can speak the language or take along someone to interpret for you. Russian dentists are certainly cheaper than the Western dental practices, though quality varies widely.

It is recommended that you ensure that Western standards of treatment and hygiene prevail at the clinic of your choice and not rely simply on a dentist who has a reputation for not causing too much pain to his patients. Long-term health care should take priority over short-term pain relief.

You should consider a dentist's attitude to infection control, above all. New gloves should always be used by the dentist treating you, not only for his protection but for yours as well. If the dentist does not change gloves between patients, then you are exposing yourself to great risk. You should then be confident that the dentist will seek to conserve a troublesome tooth rather than to simply extract it. You should also be fully aware of what the dentist is doing to you and why, therefore communication between dentist and patient is important.

Oral hygiene

You should consider having your teeth cleaned periodically, as Moscow water causes a higher level of tartar deposits than found elsewhere.

170

Expat guide: Moscow   **10/Staying healthy**

Cosmetic dentistry

Bleaching procedures are offered at several clinics, both Western and Russian, however, the procedure should not be so strong as to remove the surface layer of the tooth. Veneering is also performed involving either same-day application of composite materials which have the drawback of changing colour in five or six years and requiring replacement. The more expensive procedure involves the use of porcelain which does not change colour. One expat recommends **Dmitry Glasov,** (English-speaking and charming) a dentist who does only new teeth (no bridges, therapeutics or preventative cleaning) is at Centralny Nil Stomatologii *(Central Research Institute for Dentistry which is a five-minute walk from the Park Kultury metro station and can be contacted at tel: 246-0392).*

- **Adventist Health Center** *(tel: 126-8767/7554/7906; 21A, 60 Letiya Oktyabrya Prospekt; metro: Academechiskaya. Open from Monday to Friday, and Sunday from 09:00 - 17:30. The centre closes at 13:00 on Fridays)* This dental clinic offers a full range of dental services and has an on-site Western dental lab. Emergency ambulance services
- **American Medical Centre** *(tel: 956-3366; fax: 956-2306; 10, 2nd Tverskoy-Yamskoy Ulitsa; www.americanmedicalcenters.com)* offers routine, preventive and cosmetic dentistry.
- **Dental clinic 'Prestige'** *(tel: 150-1864; 156-7659; 19 Leningradsky Prospekt).* The clinic offers services including bleaching, implantation, anaesthesia, orthodontics as well as 24-hour a day house calls.
- **Dental Centre European Medical Centre** *(tel: 250-0730; fax: 251-6099; 10, 2nd Tverskoy-Yamskoy Pereulok; metro: Mayakovskaya)* is highly recommended by several expats for skill, chair-side manner, wide variety of services at reasonable prices as well as sanitary environment.
- **Neodent** *(tel: 134-3556/196-6520)* Offers cosmetic surgery for teeth using a painless, same-day-service for whitening. Ultrasound tooth caps. X-ray, metal-ceramics method.
- **Russian-American Dental Centre** *(tel: 269-1392; fax: 269-3523; 28 Rusakovskaya; metro: Sokolniki)* offers complete diagnostic services, general and cosmetic dentistry; emergency care, dental implants; teeth bleaching; adult and child orthodontics. Advertised as being owned and managed by American dentists and offering lower fees than other Western dental clinics
- **US Dental Care** *(tel: 931-9909; fax: 931-9910; 8 Ulitsa Shabolovka building 3; metro: Shablovskaya; www.usdentalcare.com; open Monday - Saturday 07:00 - 21:00)* Offers comprehensive dental care involving all dental, cosmetic, and orthodontic specialities. The clinic has an on-site laboratory. Expats say this centre has a good reputation and modern equipment.

Ophthalmology, Optics

- **European Medical Centre** *(tel: 956-7999; 251-6099; 10, 2nd Tverskoy - Yamskoy Pereulok)* Treatment of visual defects, eye infections and injuries, (24-hour service) all ocular examinations using latest Western technologies, Western glasses and lenses.

Expat guide: Moscow   **10/Staying healthy**

- **LensMaster,** part of an international optical retailing chain, recently opened in Moscow *(tel: 928-4009; 19 Nikolskaya Ulitsa (in the centre near Manezh))* and is advertised as offering a one-hour turnaround service
- **Paris Optik** *(tel: 290-5496; 4 Ulitsa Malaya Bronnaya)* is said to offer a quick and reliable service and is highly recommended by several expats.

There are many *'optik'* shops around, some of which supply glasses with a same-day service, so ask Russian colleagues for recommendations. Soft contact lenses are available in Moscow, but bring your own lens solution as it is difficult to find.

Pharmacies

In Russia, people usually only go to the drugstore or pharmacy to buy medicine, however, a chain of supermarket-style pharmacies has recently opened in Moscow. Presented like an American style drugstore or British Boots chemist, the shops boast shelves loaded with goods other than medicine such as toiletries and cosmetics. You can walk down aisles with a trolley and pick what you need rather than attempt your Russian on the harassed attendant. Called '**36.6**', the store *(25/9 Tverskaya Ulitsa)* owned by the Vremya company, also runs a 24-hour hot-line dispensing medical advice. Another company, ICN is developing its own chain of retail drugstores (one outlet is at *(tel: 232-6600; 24 Usacheva; metro; Sportivnaya).*

In the meantime, you will be able to spot many Russian pharmacies all over the city from the sign *'apteka'.* These are generally inexpensive and most medications are available without a prescription.

Some of the better pharmacies in terms of supplies are reportedly:

- **Aero-Komek** *(tel: 578-56-86)* features a broad selection of prescription and non-prescription medicines at the Arrivals level of Sheremetevo-2; Open every day round the clock. Their optical department can do eyeglasses, frames.
- **Akademicheskaya** *(tel: 125-2104; 24 Dmitriya Ulyanova. Open Monday - Friday 08:00 - 20:00, Saturdays 10:00 - 20:00; metro: Akademicheskaya)*
- **American Medical Centre** *(tel: 956-3366; 10, 2nd Tverskoy-Yamskoy Pereulok; metro: Mayakovskaya)* has a well-stocked Western pharmacy. It is open every day round the clock.
- **European Medical Centre** *(tel: 956-7999; 19 Nikolskaya Ulitsa; metro: Lubyanka, Teatralnaya)* offers a well-stocked pharmacy. The prepared medications department *(tel: 928-4777)* is open from Monday to Saturday from 08:00 - 20:00 and on Sunday from 10:00 - 18:00.
- **Multipharma** *(tel: 721-3050/1/4/5 19 Marshala Zhukova Prospekt; metro: Polezhaevskaya; open Monday - Friday 09:30 - 18:00)* Prepared medications, medical treatment and prophylactic cosmetics, medical supplies.
- **Novy Arbat** *(tel: 291-2063; 16 Novy Arbat Ulitsa; metro: Arbatskaya; Open Monday - Friday 08:00 - 20:00; Saturday 09:00 - 20:00)*
- **Old Arbat** *(tel: 291-7105; 25 Arbat Ulitsa; metro: Arbatskaya; open from Monday to Friday from 08:00 - 20:00 and Saturdays from 10:00 - 18:00)* said to have a delivery service of American and European medicines.

Expat guide: Moscow   **10/Staying healthy**

- **The Medicine Man** *(tel: 915-7218; tel/fax: 915-6817; 3, Goncharnaya Naberezhnaya; metro: Taganskaya; open Monday - Friday 09:00 - 20:00; Saturdays 10:00 - 18:00)*
- **Eczasibasi Drugstore** *(tel: 928-9289; fax: 921-9709; Ulitsa Maroseika; metro: Kitai Gorod)* is the Turkish licencee for Western preparations at reasonable prices.

If you can read Russian, you can find out which pharmacy stocks which drug at what prices by visiting *www.mosmed.ru.*

Gynaecological/obstetrics

- **The Family Planning Center** *(tel: 301-1502 (Russian) and 918-4331 (English, staff member - Elvira);17 Federativni Prospekt, building 10, Centre of Family Planning and Pathology of Reproduction)* at the Women's Wellness Centre at Saviour's Hospital for Peace and Charity (in partnership with Magee Womancare International) is recommended by expats. Professional staff are trained annually in the US, and are said to be business-like and thorough. Equipment is Western. The centre offers birthing classes and practises partner-assisted births. It's also possible to obtain a wide variety of contraceptives including diaphragms which are said to be difficult to find in Moscow, and diagnostic tests for sexually-transmitted diseases. Prices are said to be reasonable.

HIV testing

The AEA SOS International Clinic formerly IMC (International Medical Clinic) offers a test with results in a couple of hours.

Chiropractice

- **Lena Vorontsova** *(tel: 466-0869, 10:00 - 22:00; Russian only)* is not a chiropractor but is a trained nurse and masseuse with more than 15 years experience and is highly recommended. She is said to have extensive work experience with foreigners. Her massage style is said to be intensive, she does house-calls and charges $20 per hour.
- **Dr Charles Register** *(tel: 234-9656; fax: 433-2245; e-mail: spinedoc@aha.ru; 16/20 Ulitsa Malaya Tulskaya; metro: Tulskaya)* is a chiropractor who has a degree from Life College in the US (one of two main chiropractic colleges in the US).

Acupuncturists

- **Anya Lepilina** *(tel: 440-7112)*
- European Medical Centre has a resident acupuncturist

Influenza

Flu epidemics are expected annually in January/February and early March. The Ministry of Health's department of sanitary epidemiological monitoring reports on the spread of the epidemic with forecasts issued down to the day. Russian doctors define an epidemic of registered flu cases as exceeding 1,317 per 100,000

Expat guide: Moscow　　　　　　　　　**10/Staying healthy**

per week. In 1998, the flu left Russia for the West in April. Anti-flu shots are available at most of the medical clinics listed above, and should be taken from the last week of October/early November, though their efficacy depends on the strain of virus in existence every year.

Keeping warm in winter

The district heating system keeps most apartments warm, though impediments such as ill-closing windows and other draught-traps might cause you to seek to purchase other forms of heating. Space heaters are available at **Gorbushka** market at metro Bagrationovskaya (weekends only) with radiator-type heaters starting from $70. Russian heaters are usually available at **Sveti** stores. Also try **Domino** and **Partiya** stores.

Most draughts through ill-fitting window frames or under doors can be reduced by placing a rolled-up towel, cloth or small rug in front of the draught.

You could also make a sausage shaped container out of a piece of cloth and fill it with sand or small dried beans or uncooked *kasha*. Some expats swear by foam strips (available in most hardware shops) and masking tape (though watch you don't leave a hard-to-remove residue - ask your landlord first) to keep out draughts.

You will not need to bring electric blankets with you, as Moscow apartments are kept warm enough for you not to have to use these.

Long underwear

Cheap and cheerful models can be bought at any clothing marke or from babushkas standing outside metros. More expensive models can be found at Next, British Home Stores and Ramstore.

Barometric pressure

Russians attribute changing air pressure to heart-related illnesses, blood pressure, headaches etc. Occasional rapid changes from a day of relatively warm weather to cold, rainy or icy weather tends to have adverse effects on the ability of some people to adapt. It affects sleep patterns and in general make it difficult for some people to physically adapt.

Banyas (bani)

This typically Russian cultural activity is very popular in Moscow *(see Chapter 9 -Keeping Busy)*. Remember that banyas involve extremes of temperature which can cause stress to the body, especially to those who suffer from heart disease, diabetes, stress or high-alcohol consumption.

Water

To be on the safe side, most expats drink bottled water or buy recyclable 20 litre containers of water, expensive but worth it. Infectious diseases such as hepatitis A, dysentery, typhoid fever and cholera can be transmitted from unsanitary water. If you have to drink from the tap, boil water for 12 - 15 minutes, though some

174

Expat guide: Moscow   **10/Staying healthy**

embassies advise their nationals to boil for only five minutes. *(see Chapter 6 - Eating and Drinking* for suppliers of bottled water).

Food

Check expiry dates on all tins and keep away from blown or dented tins. Always make sure food is thoroughly cooked. When washing vegetables such as lettuce or those that won't be peeled, soak in salted water for 5 - 10 minutes to kill any bugs.

Alcohol

Always make sure you buy recognised brand-name vodka as you can get hundreds of varieties, many of which are only fit for cleaning windscreens. Its integral part in Russian history has meant that people have devised a variety of uses for it. Apart from cleaning windscreens, it can be used for de-icing windows, and is used for a variety of medical ailments.

Never accept drinks from strangers, no matter how attractive, unless you see the bottle opened and you pour it yourself.

Vomiting and diarrhoea

At any time, as in any country, this can strike those of a more sensitive disposition with highly debilitating results. Make sure you know the rules of diarrhoea control, otherwise you may end up in hospital.

Some expats say that you should be careful of eating *shashlyk* from roadside stalls, while others have never experience any problems from these. When buying tinned food, check to see if a 'sell-by' date appears on the tin and don't buy any that are discounted and beyond their 'sell-by' date.

When such a bout does strike, it's best not to eat anything, and take sips of rehydrate solution until the frequency of stools or vomiting subsides. If you must eat, then only take dry bread or non-fatty biscuit, or even better some rice water.

Vomiting is more dehydrating and therefore more dangerous than diarrhoea, and in combination, an adult, and a child (even more so) can become very quickly dehydrated. Always consult a physician before attempting to take treatment into your own hands.

TB (tuberculosis)

There are constant stories about a TB epidemic in Russia, and with the potential release in 1999 of 10,000 prisoners (TB is rife in prisons) it's wise to make certain that you are inoculated against the disease.

Radioactivity in food produce

Some years ago it used to be the case that expats used Geiger counters to check fresh produce for radio-activity, though many now say there is no need to. However, others warn that you should not purchase fresh fruit or vegetables from Kievsky *rynok* as these may come from the Chernobyl area. Nor should you buy food from other markets that are known to come from that area. Although you

175

Expat guide: Moscow   **10/Staying healthy**

can purchase Geiger counters at some of the electronic markets, their efficacy in correctly detecting levels of radio-activity is said to be questionable.

Pest control

It's not much help using Combat, or trap-a-roach roach 'hotels' as long as your neighbours have a cockroach problem which they neglect. Even if you use a cockroach treatment (see below) you will need to have this done at least twice a year to be effective. The cockroach problem is exacerbated by the summer heat, nor do they disappear over winter, due to the warmth of most apartments. If your neighbour is doing a renovation, this can also cause them to migrate to your apartment. Some expats recommend Israeli products SANO k-900 and Antikan as being particularly effective, as well as the British-made 'Gett' and Cobra

With spray-type preparations it is recommended that you spray around ventilation grilles in the bathroom and kitchen as well as floors, skirting, doors and windows, around and under fridges, cookers and cupboards. The process should be repeated after two weeks and then once every three months.

- Cockroach service **Svelena Company**, *(tel: 179-6238; 590-2775 10:00 - 19:00 except weekends)* guarantees American-made treatments for six months. The compound they use is said to be harmless for people and pets.
- **Insect Racisid Group** *(tel: 135-7012)*

Allergies

These usually begin in May with the start of the *pukh* season *(see Chapter 15 - Weather)* when the poplar trees start flowering and discharging clouds of fluffy seeds. Those most susceptible to *pukh* are lucky, in that their discomfort lasts only four to five weeks, but others continue to react to dandelion pollen other plant and grass pollens, as well as pollution.

Heat makes the spread and distribution of pollens that much more efficient, while dust, smog and pollution all exacerbate the allergic condition.

The greatest incidence of conjunctivitis, head colds, and asthma occurs in June and decongestants and antihistamines are the best treatment.

De-sensitisation may be used if symptoms become intolerable. Winter allergies usually occur in response to fur or dust.

Winter blues/SAD

Seasonal Affective Disorder is the name for the relationship between daylight exposure and moods. SAD is a form of depression that develops from of a lack of sunlight. It is said to affect up to 10 percent of the population in Finland, Iceland, Alaska and the former Soviet Union.

Light therapy has been shown to be the best treatment for SAD. Simple exposure (15 - 30 minutes a day) to luminous fluorescent light can have beneficial effects in three days. If treatment is stopped, symptoms invariably return. Typical symptoms of SAD are lethargy, appetite changes, a general depressed feeling and a change in sleep patterns.

176

Expat guide: Moscow   **10/Staying healthy**

Frostnip and frostbite

Frostnip is not as serious as frostbite and appears most commonly on exposed skin on the face, ears, fingers, toes and wrists. After turning very red or white, skin may tingle, sting or partly feel numb.

Frostbite causes skin to appear waxy, hard, blue, or blistered and may feel painful or totally numb. Symptoms probably call for treatment. Immediate steps to be taken include the following: change sufferer into warm dry clothing and immerse the affected area in lukewarm water, ensuring that skin is not rubbed or that any blisters are not broken.

To prevent frostnip and frostbite, dress properly for the cold, making sure gloves are worn, and wear boots with at least two pairs of socks and a hat. Avoid prolonged exposure by going indoors frequently to warm up.

Water-based moisturisers should not be used during winter, to avoid freezing on the skin with resultant frostnip or frostbite.

Sensitive skin

Quite a number of expatriates experience sensitive, cracking and peeling fingertips, usually worse during the winter. Cornhusker's Lotion is recommended for treatment, and if you're prone to this condition, bring a supply of that or Neutrogena with you. Some expats recommend Dead Sea hand cream from Israel, sold under the trade name of Biotherm or Ahava in the Hotel Moskva, or Lacticare which is a lactic-acid based skin cream.

Mental health

This is just as crucial, if not more crucial than physical health, and it pays to be on your guard against any depression.

A pep talk for those who need it

Moscow seems to conspire to work against you, and this perception helps to engender feelings of negativism or at least to counter any optimism you might have left, after your first week or two, when your initial enthusiasm and shock merge and you realise this is what life is going to be like for the next x years.

For some people, coming to live in Moscow is like comparing your life to a thousand piece jig-saw being flung into the air and scattered all around. You feel intense pressure to gather the pieces together in a hurry, just so you can carry on. It takes a while to find and establish comfort zones, so don't feel as if you're the only one it's happening to. Many men seem to hit the ground running and effortlessly get into the swing of Moscow life, but this can also prove to be a good case of cover up. Don't be afraid to let your misgivings show, for after all, it's only then that other people will realise you need help and are likely to offer it.

If you pretend you are okay, people will think you don't need help.

Remember, you are very likely to encounter culture shock - when you assume everything is possible, and then you discover it's not. It takes a while to rediscover that in fact it is possible, but not in the ways you are used to.

177

Expat guide: Moscow   **10/Staying healthy**

It's important to define your parameters of what's possible for you and what's not, as well as to establish a routine. Routines help to package Moscow into bite-sized chunks rather than one bewildering morass.

It's worth also not expecting too much of yourself and remembering that Moscow is a demanding posting. After a while you'll be grateful that you are posted in Moscow and not in Beijing, though even long-term expats have their moments of being down. Also remember that those that make it to Moscow and survive, can claim to have a certain pioneering spirit which not all people have.

If things get really bad do the following:

1. List the good things about being in Moscow on one page.
2. Then list the bad things about being in Moscow on another. Then screw up the bad page and throw it away.
3. Concentrate on the good page.

When you've overcome the first hurdle, which for most is finding their accommodation, then you begin to discover small things that no-one thought of telling you: the phone that should have been connected is not, it's a long weekend and you have to wait five days till it can be connected. The Kosmos TV that was included as part of your rent isn't, the electricity that goes off in the middle of cooking dinner and you can't find the fuse box, let alone know what to do with it when you have found it. You don't know where to buy a particular favourite item, and you don't know how to cope with the currency and unfamiliar brands you see in the shops.

One expat said that when they arrived he and his family found the going tough but told themselves that things would get better. "Don't kid yourself, things don't get better", were his encouraging words. Others give estimates for settling in ranging from eight weeks to six months.

Rely as much as you can on fellow expatriates. They've all 'been there' before and they know what it s like, and most of them are prepared to help even if it's in recounting their first faltering steps in their new environment. Which at least gives you the feeling that it's not because you're you that frustrations keep occurring.

Once you find your feet, however, don't concentrate only on your own national enclave, which in itself can cause feelings of isolation from the culture around you. Although it may seem difficult to form links with Russians, particularly where language problems exist, it will be these links that will eventually enrich your stay and lead to you feeling more at home.

Telephone crisis lines

These have been developing in Russia since Perestroika. Russians by nature are not inclined to discuss their private lives with strangers, being mistrustful of them, but a growing number have come to realise that the call is under their control, as they can always put the phone down without identifying themselves.

In Moscow, distressed expats suffering from isolation in the midst of the frenzied activity around them, can call a free confidential 24-hour crisis line *(tel: paging operator at 244-3449 or 931-9682; give the code name: 'crisis'; then leave your phone number and a counsellor will call back in English).* There is also Moscow's AIDS Open Line run by expatriate volunteers along the same principles the Samaritans employ in Britain. The professional volunteers don't

178

Expat guide: Moscow   **10/Staying healthy**

give advice, but instead just help people find their own solutions. The service occasionally seeks new volunteers, so if your skills lie in counselling, then give them a call.

Psychologists/psychiatrists

- Dr Robert Sharpe *(tel: (44 7074 742-773; e-mail: rs@psychology.gg or view www.psychology.gg/rs.htm)* a chartered psychologist from the UK periodically visits Moscow to consult with expats. He has had more than 30 years of experience in his speciality of stress and exhaustion management, marital and family therapy, and post-trauma therapy. He has also worked extensively with expats at other locations.
- The American and European Medical Centres have professional staff that can help if you don't feel a help-line will do the trick.
- American (Russian-born) psycho-therapist who speaks both English and Russian *(tel: 723-6406; e-mail: goldan@cityline.ru).*
- A German-speaking psychologist offering individual, group and family therapy, Boris Novoderschkin, can be contacted at *(tel: 489-6917/790-4280 or e-mail: ciborisn@cityline.ru or at www.user.cityline.ru/~ciborisn/gestalt.htm)*
- A psychotherapist, specialising in cross-cultural and family therapy, formerly a fellow at Harvard Medical School, can be contacted at *tel: 301-1036* (between 20:00 - 22:00)
- Dr Jean Hoareau at the European Medical Centre *(tel: 956-7999; 34 Ulitsa Konushkovskaya)* speaks English, French, Russian and Spanish, and offers anti-stress treatment as well as treatment for psychosomatic illnesses, detoxification (alcohol, tobacco and drug addiction) and treatment for mental disorders.

Work and the need for balance

Another form of stress that should be considered is the heavy toll exacted from working expats. Reasonably speaking, expats who come to Russia are well paid, and they are expected to provide value for the relatively high salaries many command.

Typically, expats put in 12-or-15 hour days, while the spouse sits at home with a child or children, isolated. Having no contacts with Russians and not speaking the language result in maladjustment within an unfamiliar culture. Without keeping a properly balanced lifestyle, too much attention can easily be paid to work, leaving little time for relationships. It's not unusual for wives to lament: What on earth are we doing here?

To reassert some balance in your life, you need to pay attention to the four major aspects of life: physical activity; work and achievement; friends and family; and hopes, dreams and wishes which encompass the spiritual side of life.

Instead of limiting your social contacts to working colleagues only, efforts should be made to broaden social horizons and make friends outside the work environment. Don't shy away from making friends with Russians as you will gain valuable insight into their culture and also find that they are as eager to find

179

Expat guide: Moscow   **10/Staying healthy**

out more about you. Many of those who can speak some English are only too glad to get an opportunity to practise what English they have.

Cross-cultural romantic relationships *(see Lyn Visson's book: Wedded Strangers)* may encompass clashes over the woman's role in the marriage, misunderstandings due to the language barrier and different cultural expectations.

The importance of families

Many expatriate women, when asked, cite the distance from their families, and their mothers in particular, as being a significant cause of stress. Extended family support and advice is lacking, as is the very valued option of being able to leave children for a few hours with their grandparents. One way of reducing the effects of this separation-anxiety is to focus on maintaining ties between grandchildren and grandparents, urging the children to send home drawings and letters to keep bonds intact.

When, for one reason or another, you don't have family to turn to, you will find yourself adopting 'family'. It's not unusual to warm to older women or men and then on analysing the situation, find that you do so because they provide some guidance and role-modelling that you miss from your own parents.

English-language Alcoholics Anonymous

The **AA** *(tel: 243-1420; 202-7219; 290-4814; 37 Dmitriya Ulyanova Ulitsa, building 3)* meets six times a week at 19:00 Sundays and 19:30 Tuesdays and Fridays; 19:30 Wednesdays and Thursdays and 17:00. Saturdays at the Anglican Church at 8 Voznesensky Pereulok.

Spiritual health
Religious services and groups

Since Soviet times, religion has come out of the closet and is now freely practised (with limits). Certain religious groups such as the Jehovah's Witnesses are frowned upon, while anti-Semitism keeps on rearing its ugly head.

Whether you are a regular churchgoer or merely seek some spiritual inspiration, the following churches are recommended for foreigners. In all instances phone beforehand to confirm times of services:

- **Calvary Chapel** (Protestant) *(tel: 499-2447; 29 Ulitsa Presnensky Val; Krosna Cinema; metro Belorusskaya)* English services with Russian translation are held on Wednesdays at 19:00 and Sundays at 11:00.
- **Christian Science group** *(tel: 417-9028/158-6096 evenings; 14 Ulitsa Sushovskaya; metro Novoslobodskaya)* Services in Russian/English are on Sundays at 22:00 and at 19:00 on the first Wednesday of every month.
- **Church of Jesus Christ of Latter-day saints (Mormon)** *(tel: 247-1136/198-1018/198-2040) Dom Kultury Krasny Oktyabr, 7 Vyshnyovaya Ultisa; metro: Tushinskaya)* Holds English services on Sundays from 11:00 at 16 Stolyarny Pereulok; metro: 1905 Goda.
- **German-language Catholic Mass** This is held every Sunday at the German Embassy at 56 Mosfilmovskaya. For information call 245-0297.

Expat guide: Moscow   **10/Staying healthy**

- **International Baptist Fellowship** *(tel: 971-3558 15 Ulitsa Druzhinnikovskaya, 5th floor, room 5; metro: Krasnopresnenskaya).* Bible study is on Sundays at 10.00 with a service at 11:00 at the *Kinotsentr.*

- **International Christian Assembly** *(tel: 338-1150; 10 Krymsky Val: metro Oktyabrskaya)* The assembly holds Christian Growth class at 10:00, Sunday services in English at 11:00 in the Concert Hall of the Central House of Artists, opposite Gorky Park.

- **Mission Living Faith** *(tel: 959-6110; 21 Shmitovsky Proezd; metro: Ulitsa 1905 Goda)* This is a non-denominational Protestant church which holds services at 11:00 Sundays and 19:00 Wednesdays at the Detsky Tsentr Kultury,

- **Moscow Catholic Chaplaincy** *(tel: 243-962; 78 Leninsky Prospekt; metro: Universitet)* English mass is on Sundays at 10:00 and in French at 12 noon Additional masses are 18:00 Saturdays in English and French; 19:15: Italian, and 18:00 Sundays in English at 7/4 Kutuzovsky Prospekt, Building 5, Entrance 3, Apartment 42.

- **Moscow Charismatic Church** *(tel 461-9874; 97 Ulitsa Pervomayskaya; metro Pervomayskaya)* Russian Services with English translation are on Thursdays at 19:00 and Sundays at 22:00.

- **Moscow Christian Centre** *(tel 344-1344; 24 Ulitsa Novy Arbat; metro Arbatskaya)* Services are on Fridays at 19:00 and Sundays at 10:00 in the Oktyabr Cinema.

- **Moscow Protestant Chaplaincy** *(tel: 243-9621/143-3562; 36 Prospekt Mira)* English services are on Sundays at 11:00 and French language services at 12.30 Sundays.

- **Mosque** *(tel: 281-3866; 7 Vypolzov Pereulok; metro: Prospekt Mira)* services are on Fridays at 13:00.

- **Russian Orthodox Church, Church of St Catherine** *(tel: 231-8226; 60/2 Ulitsa Bolshaya Ordynka; metro: Dobryninskaya)* English services are on Sundays at 10:00.

- **St Andrew's Anglican Church** *(tel: 229-0990/275-6221; 8 Voznesensky Pereulok; metro: Tverskaya)* Services are on Sundays at 10:00 and 11.30 and Wednesdays, Fridays and Saturdays at 19:30 (phone to confirm). During Easter and Christmas, other services may be put on specially during the week and are usually announced in the press. Sunday school is available for children from 3 - 14 split into different age groups.

- **St Louis Church Roman Catholic** *(tel: 925-4665/925-2034; 12 a Ulitsa Malaya Lubyanka; metro: Lubyanka)* Masses in English, French and Latin, Russian and Polish. Although it continues to strengthen, especially since 1991, the Catholic church's presence is difficult, especially as a consequence of a recent law passed that creates obstacles to the activity of the Catholic and other churches in Russia. It has an uneasy relationship with the Russian Orthodox church, which is said to be fearful of its power. There are about one million Catholics in Russia. Easter Mass is nevertheless broadcast from the Vatican on Ren TV which may require a special antenna.

- **The Community of the Holy Spirit** *(tel 133-8166 from 10:00 - 18:00)* A Christian Interdenominational group, the community provides spiritual counselling and support.

181

Expat guide: Moscow   **10/Staying healthy**

- **The International Congregation Hineini** (Reform Judaism) *(tel: 161-1673/270-9343/918-2696; 26 Ulitsa Novoryazanskaya; metro: Komsomolskaya)* Services are on Fridays at 17:00 at the autoworkers Palace of Culture.
- **Universal Church** *(tel: 133-8166)* Acting as a spiritual SOS and part of the Community of the Holy Spirit, it provides spiritual counselling for those who are in despair.

Jewish Community

There are seven Jewish secondary schools in Moscow, at least two yeshivas, three restaurants of varying degrees of kosherness and, finally, separate singles clubs for the Orthodox and not-so Orthodox. Some sources say that the Russian Jewish population in Moscow is 500,000, making it the fifth biggest Jewish community in the world.

- **Moscow Synagogue** *(tel: 923-9697; 14 Bolshaya Spasoglinishchevsky Pereulok; metro: Kitai Gorod)* Services are on Fridays at sunset and Saturdays at 09:00 at 14 Ulitsa Arkhipova.
- **Polyakova Synagogue** Chabad Lubavitch *(tel: 202-7393/7696) 6 Bolshaya Bronnaya Ulitsa; metro: Pushkinskaya)* The synagogue holds services at sunset Fridays; 10:00 Saturdays and 8:00 and 10:00 Sundays.

Jewish restaurants

- Call Agudas Chassidei *(tel: 202-7696)* for kosher meat, bread or matzoh or visit the store run by Alla Nazarova at the Choral Synagogue *(tel: 924-3025)* but not for kosher dairy products.
- **King David Club** *(tel: 925-460; 16 Spasoglinishchevsky Pereulok, Entrance 1, intercom code 77; metro: Kitai Gorod; open 08:00 - 10:00)* Reservations are advised. This is not an official restaurant, more like a club. It serves gefilte fish, kosher wine and offers free delivery.
- **Eshel Lubavitch** *(tel: 229-8796; open Sunday - Thursday 12:00-22:00)* is said to have the most kosher menu in town, but also attracts gentiles for its Caucasian menu. Live music nightly. Free delivery.
- **Karmel** *(tel: 200-5763; 7, 1st Tverskaya-yamskaya Ulitsa; metro: Belorusskaya. open 12:00 - 00:00)* This is not strictly kosher, more kosher-style. It offers free delivery.

Exercise

To ward off illness, it's best to keep your activity levels up. Judging by the list of activities in *Chapter 9: Keeping busy*, you have no excuse to laze around, either in winter or summer.

Snow-shoeing, skiing, snowboarding, snow-mobiling and cross-country skiing are just some of the outdoor sports you can take part in winter. If you want to go 'native' you could even try ice-hole swimming and ice-hole fishing and the sauna-and-snow treatment.

Health clubs have burgeoned in the past few years, as Muscovites grow in understanding of the importance of fitness. They also serve a valuable social purpose.

11/Staying safe

Stop press: The following was written before the awful bombings occurred in Moscow in September 1999. Instead of deleting this and starting all over again, I believe it's worth leaving as it is, simply to show what life was like before the bombings and to show what life may return to once the terrorist activities cease. Moscow will never be the same again after these bombings, security will be much tighter, people will be more suspicious of foreigners. At the time of writing, the Duma and Presidential elections still have to take place, and it's anybody's guess as to how bloody the fight for the control of Russia will be. Nor can anyone predict how or if the Chechen problem will be resolved.

If you have lived through this wave of terrorism in Moscow, you will know what procedures to follow to safeguard your security. New arrivals should contact their embassy for advice regarding which procedures to follow.

The major risks to your safety in Moscow were likely to be, in order of likelihood traffic accidents; being robbed, and becoming ill.

Before you arrive you may have been so prejudiced by Western news reports that you might think it is unsafe to go out on the street, in case you walk into a stray bullet. However, once you arrive and get out and about you will soon see that this is not an everyday occurrence. Many expats cite New York City and other US cities, as well as London, as being far more dangerous, and say that they feel much safer in Moscow. The Mafia is a constant presence, but they are not likely to seek you out unless you are making a lot of money which they may believe they might like to share.

Emergency telephone numbers

Fire	01
Police	02
Ambulance	03
Gas	04

These calls are free from a public phone booth (taksofon). You will need to be able to speak in Russian to these services. Either call a neighbour who can call on your behalf, call your office and get a Russian speaker to contact the service for you, or as a last resort, know your apartment address in Russian and simply give the address with the word 'Pamagite meniya' (Help me!) used liberally. If you lived at 24 Frunzenskaya Naberezhnaya, flat 20, you would say:

Expat guide: Moscow   11/Staying safe

Adres Frunzenskaya Naberezhnaya, dom 24, kvartira 20.

International SOS Assistance (24 Hours)   *280-7133*
Lost children   *401-9982*
Lost American Express cards   *755-9001/9900*
Lost Visa, Master cards, Diners club, JCB 956-4806

Safety procedures

It's a good idea to know the location and telephone number of the nearest police-station to your home and office. You could also try contacting 02 giving them your location. Ask a Russian friend to help you draft a 'help' message.

Some useful words to memorise are:

pamagite meniya	**help me**
adres	**address**
kvartira (give number in Russian)	**apartment**
zdanie	**building**
podezhd	**entrance**
etazh (supply number in Russian)	**floor**
srochno	**emergency**
ograblenie	**robbery**
telefon (supply number in Russian)	**telephone**

If you can't speak Russian, ask someone who can to prepare a script or scripts which you can tape next to your telephone in case of emergency.

Personal security

One of the first things you should do on arrival is to register with your embassy. In the, hopefully, unlikely event of mass evacuation, at least your embassy will know where you are, and if they are organised enough, they will see that you get the latest security briefings, if not an invitation to a flight out of trouble.

If there is unrest, keep up to date on the situation by visiting the US government website *(http://travel.state.gov/travel_warnings.html)* and the UK government website*: www.fco.gov.uk/travel*

The majority of crimes are said to be non-violent, involving pick-pocketing and the subsequent loss of passports. As you are required to carry your passport and visa details around with you at all times, it is advisable to keep these in a safe place which is not easily accessible. Some say that you are not allowed to carry around photocopies of these documents. The GAI/DPS will tend to stop those who look like foreigners, especially if you are darker-skinned and ask you to show them your passport and registration details. Some expats say you should not rely on carrying a copy only of passport and visa as this may not be regarded as sufficient in terms of identification, nor will a notarised copy of these documents be regarded as sufficient, although, others say they carry copies only and never get harassed.

Expat guide: Moscow   **11/Staying safe**

The US Embassy advises that US citizens carry original passports as these are easy to replace, however, you should carry a copy of your registered visa because it is difficult to get a new one, if lost.

If you have to submit your visa and passport to an agency for application for a new visa, don't forget to ask the agency to provide you with a letter explaining that they are handling your documentation for the interim period until you receive your updated documents. This should be accompanied by a copy of your documents. All three documents should be stamped with the agency's registration number with the Ministry of Foreign Affairs.

Photocopy all your identity documents and credit cards just to facilitate things if you do lose them. Also brace yourself for a possible visit to your embassy to replace a lost or stolen passport. If you lose your visa, it's worth being *au fait* with the procedure used if you do need to replace it. Contact some of the travel agencies who might be able to organise one for you in a hurry. You may need to leave the country in order to obtain a new visa which could cause all sorts of costs and complications.

Make a copy of credit card company hotlines so that the moment your credit card disappears, you can contact them and alert them to this fact.

Dealing with the GAI/militsia

Car drivers and pedestrians are often stopped by militsia or GAI or DPS depending on their latest name (GAI - *Gosudarstvenniye Avtomobilniye Inspektsia* has recently changed its name to DPS - *Dorozhnaya Postovaya Sluzhba*) and asked to produce their documents.

Some expats have been let off with a $10 fine, depending on what documents are missing or faulted. Others choose not to pay out of principle, in which case they may have to spend a few hours in a police cell. If you run the risk of not having all the correct documents when stopped while driving a car, then you are likely to get into trouble. This is one instance where photocopied documents will not do.

Try calling the following numbers:

- You could try calling 02 to report undue harassment on the part of the police services. The calls are recorded and the duty officers must display that action has been taken for each call. However, the misdemeanour probably will need to be quite serious in order for it to be taken seriously. When it comes to document checking, which is normally not in front of witnesses, the officer could defend himself by saying you were acting suspiciously or behaving aggressively, or seemed to be intoxicated, in which case, you won't be able to defend yourself. However, it might still be worth complaining, because if only one or a handful of the same policeman consistently elicit complaints about their behaviour, something is then likely to be done. Calling the 02 number may not work if the poor-English-speaking female receptionists do not consider the call important, in which case they may hang up or ignore it.

- If calling 02 doesn't work, try calling the GUVD Moscow City police duty officers at 200-9561 who are said to be high ranking officers with better understanding of English.

185

Expat guide: Moscow   **11/Staying safe**

- If you feel a militsia officer has overstepped the boundaries of the law you can report him to the Self-security service of MVD/Interior ministry *(tel: 924- 6572)*.

- If you speak Russian, you could check whether the hotline supplied by Novaya Gazeta *(tel: 291-7011)* is still open. The hotline offered legal advice to victims of unlawful behaviour by the Moscow Militsia.

If the militsia are simply being a nuisance and want to intimidate you, they may ask you to enter their vehicle so that you can accompany them to the station. However, if you call their bluff, they may find some way out of the game, perhaps settling for a 'fine'. Don't accept a favour such as a ride home or the offer of their vehicle as a taxi home as they may, having found out where you live, from then on come and pester you for small amounts on a regular basis.

Some suggest that you do not pay a 'fine' of more than $20 if you are caught without your documents. Instead, insist on going to the militsia station. In most cases, the officer is likely to be of low rank and would be intimidated if you threatened to speak to officers higher up. You are entitled to ask the officer to show you his service ID, and to write down his name, position and the telephone number of his regional police station.

If you are stopped the best way to get out of trouble is to only speak English or your mother-tongue. If you try some of your basic Russian, they will believe that you can, in fact, speak Russian and will not let you off the hook, whereas if you speak English, they will soon give up trying.

Expat conventional wisdom has it that the police tend to pick on those who seem more scared than those who smile, are friendly, and behave in a calm manner. However, don't smile too much as this might convey that you are trying to be too friendly.

It would seem that the police have right of access, but not the right to search your property without a search warrant.

You have the right to ask the militsia (who may not necessarily be in a uniform) to produce his identification. This comes in the form of a card with a red cover and states the name of the department he works in. Inside you should see the militsia's photo with an identification number, expiration date, name, rank, position, date of issue and authorising signature.

Street mugging

The most frequently encountered type of street mugging involves crowding by gypsy children or women and this usually occurs only in summer time. They tend to swarm all over you and attempt to prick you with needles which will have the effect of disorienting you. In the ensuing confusion they pick-pocket your valuables. Therefore, always attempt to keep them in inside pockets preferably with zips and buttons.

It might help if you carry a small can of mace spray or pepper spray or if you really feel vulnerable, a small gas cylinder especially made for self-defence, though it must be stressed that carrying such items is not the norm among expats unless they expect to be in dangerous situations. If you do feel threatened, take the defensive item out so that your potential assailant can see it. Use it if necessary. You could also carry a can of hairspray which burns the eyes if sprayed into them.

Expat guide: Moscow   **11/Staying safe**

Other mugging techniques involve an accomplice pretending to be intoxicated, bumping into the intended victim and another fleecing them in the confusion.

A popular scam which is said to be copied from the movie 'The Sting' involves one person dropping directly in front of you, and making a big show of finding a wad of notes. They enlist your help offering you half the pickings if you promise to keep quiet. Another person will then come up to you, visibly angry that his money has been stolen and demand that you empty your pockets to show that you have not stolen it. As you do so, and in the confusion, they will make off with some or most of your money. If anyone drops money near you, it is best to ignore them completely and refuse to become involved.

In the past, there seem to have been a number of scams at the airport after an arriving passenger exits the building. It would seem that anyone approaching you after your exit may have been tipped off by Customs staff inside the building who know whether you are carrying a large amount of money on you, or not. Simply refuse to co-operate as their assessment of whether you may enter Russia ends once they let you through the gate. Nor should rely on nearby militsia who may also be in on the scam. Your best bet may be to return into the airport and report the matter to officials there.

Sometimes a person will pretend to be deaf and communicate with you with excessive body-language, but all they are doing, in reality, is casing your body for telltale wads of notes in pockets.

To get yourself out of a tight corner you could use a decoy wad of small denomination notes and throw them aside to distract the attention of the potential muggers and then run off while they examine it.

To be on the safe side, stay away from dimly lit areas and parks at night. If you think someone is following you, do not go home, but enter a shop or restaurant, instead.

If you are entering an apartment lift and there is another person travelling in the lift, find some reason not to get in the lift, as muggings do occur in lifts.

Be extra vigilant when entering or leaving metro stations, as many pickpockets find rich pickings in the crowds and confusion of these areas. Other hotspots include watching out for gypsy kids harassing you at cashpoints, and the possibility of forewarned accomplices waiting for you if you come out of an exchange booth with large sums of money.

The queues at fast-food restaurants are also favourite places as are crowded evenings at the Bolshoi and Conservatory. Be wary in markets or at souvenir stalls where in the crush it is easy for someone to slash your bag with a knife and run off with the contents. Do not wear the small fashionable backpacks, or haversacks, especially on crowded buses or metros where it is easy for someone behind you to somehow remove the bag.

Some expats say that you should not speak and therefore reveal you are not Russian in a full lift. It would also help to know your floor number in Russian e.g. 1st, 2nd etc.

Beggars

Before the crisis, beggars were similar to those you find elsewhere in the world. There was the usual assortment of homeless and drunks, and also a gypsy

Expat guide: Moscow   **11/Staying safe**

presence, more so during the summer than the winter. Now there seem to be many more pensioners rooting around for the odd ruble, and even digging in dustbins for something of value to salvage, such as food, or empty bottles which can be returned to the bottler for recycling.

The latter do not seem intent on being aggressive, whereas with the professional beggars, avoid eye contact, hide behind sunglasses or simply yell something in your own language and give a nasty look. One expat said that hurling a well-aimed gob of saliva worked a treat with a persistent hassler.

Watch out for favourite places of congregation such as metro entrances, railway stations and markets. Keep aware of crowds and steer far away from suspicious looking people. If you are approached by a child or woman, do not hesitate to defend yourself as well as you can. You could also shout loudly : 'Militsia!'

Some say that Russians equate broad smiling with stupidity, perhaps that explains why they all look so grim on the street and on public transport.

By shaking your head sideways in a negative way and holding up your palms upward and to the sides, transmits that you're not interested in a transaction.

You should avoid shaking of your fist which can be thought of as aggressive in any society.

If you're a woman, don't go onto the metro wearing lots of jewellery, and leave your diamonds at home, as you could only be tempting fate.

You're more likely to be at risk if you're a visiting businessperson and are staying in a non-five-star hotel. People have copies of keys made and can enter in the middle of the night.

If involved with prostitutes, be careful of being thought to be double-crossing on a deal, as the pimps will no doubt come to collect their 'debt' at one time or another.

Changing money

When changing currency, use only reputable money changers otherwise you risk landing up with counterfeit bills. Don't accept to change money with touts outside money-changers as with sleight of hand, they can ensure that you land up with less money than what you started with. Don't wave money around if doing a transaction in the street. What seems like a little money to you could look like a fortune to someone who is out of work and hungry.

Hole-in-the-wall scams

A recent scam involved the placing of false ATMs around Moscow. People desperately looking for dollars during the crisis would go round to every ATM they could find to see if it was dispensing dollars. They would insert their card and pin number and find that the machine registered empty (like so many others at the time) and go off in search of a new one to try. However, in the process the machine had recorded their card details and pin number and was able to access their account in their home country. They would only discover the scam once they received their monthly statement. The solution to avoiding this scam is to only use ATMs that are known to dispense cash.

188

Expat guide: Moscow   **11/Staying safe**

Racism

Never let yourself into the situation where you are alone on the street late at night as this can be an open invitation for a more serious type of mugging. This is of particular concern to black or dark-skinned people.

You should also be particularly careful when you visit places like Fili CD market where there can be crowds of skin-heads. Also be wary of metro-exits, especially those at Oktyabrskaya after 20:00 and Dinamo especially before and after football matches and where crowds of football fans are involved.

Anti-Semitism

Despite the authorities avowed aversion to anti-Semitism it certainly does exist. Synagogues and gravestones have been attacked and desecrated in the past. Don't unnecessarily flaunt the fact that you may be Jewish.

Home security

You will have noticed from your first few weeks in Moscow, that most homes are protected by what we, in the West, would call tough security measures. Metal doors, up to seven locks on a door, intercom systems, concierges, video phones and personal security guards all add up to the impression that life is not safe in Moscow.

Quite a few of these are hangovers from the past and the early days of democracy, when other people's possessions seemed to provide a free-for-all situation. Nevertheless, there is no knowing whether the economic situation will get worse and put ordinary citizen's security at risk again. Of course, home security also depends on just where you live. Some areas might be high security risks, while others are not.

Even if a door has two parts to it and the outer part is fitted to a metal frame, don't underestimate the avid burglar's determination, as these will not prevent him from removing the door from its frame. Likewise, it's not unknown for locks to be drilled out even in operations that take three or four hours of drilling. You might ask why neighbours do not intervene - well, would you?

You could examine how securely the door frame is mounted to the surrounding wall, the type of metal that has been used in the construction of the door and the frame, the type of lock fitted (the more the merrier, especially those with lots of bolts), and whether there are any gaps between the door and frame.

One way of determining security is to look at access at the front door of your building. Lobbies staffed by babushkas are not to be sniffed at, as these ladies take their jobs seriously and make it their business to know just who goes in and out of the apartment block. Domophones or intercoms use a code system, but even those are known to be vulnerable to penetration, especially where an intruder slips in after someone who has legitimate access.

Always use your spy-hole (you should have one in your door) to check who is knocking. If you don't see anyone or you see someone unfamiliar, don't bother to open the door. Only open the door to someone you know, and always ascertain if they are alone, or being forced under duress to gain your confidence.

It would be wise for you to obtain, from your landlord, the telephone number of your apartment block's maintenance office (ZHEK) so that you can

189

Expat guide: Moscow   11/Staying safe

verify if workmen need to gain access to your apartment. Do not offer your home address to a stranger, but give them your business address instead.

It might be an idea to ask the landlord if you can have the locks changed immediately on moving in. You never know who may have a copy of the keys (e.g. landlord's relatives, previous tenants or locksmiths who previously installed locks). You don't need to change all the locks, only one will do.

Car theft

Cars are always at risk of being stolen. Park your car in a secure area that is well-lit. Always use anti-theft devices or an electronic cut-off switch. Although burglar alarms are much in evidence (sometimes too much in evidence), their use is questionable (*see Chapter 5 - Getting Around* for further information).

Driving hazards

It's wise to be cautious while in traffic if someone approaches you to ask for information. Keep your door locked and window only slightly open when talking to them. Several expats have had items taken from the back- or passenger-seat of a car during traffic, someone even had his trunk opened while in traffic, while he was distracted in the front of the car *(see also Chapter 5 -: Getting around)*.

Road rage

Keep away from road-rage situations. You never know who you might be dealing with. Road rage incidents are not as evident as they are in the UK, and given the fact that there is plenty of potential for road-rage, judging by the way drivers change lanes without a second thought or signal, or by impatient hooting if you are too slow off the mark at the traffic light, there is remarkably little evidence of it.

Hailing taxis

Although hailing ordinary cars for use as taxis is widely practised and is an effective way of getting from A to B, you should never enter such a car if it contains more than one occupant. If you really want to make sure you are safe if catching a taxi, first order it by phone through the organised taxi services, however, many expats jump into gypsy cabs with a total stranger without any mishap. Try to avoid travelling alone late at night in a taxi, unless you have pre-arranged your lift.

Moscow City Government Emergency Rescue Scheme

The American Chamber of Commerce has presented on its website, *(www.amcham.ru)* information prepared by the Moscow City Emergency Rescue Department intended to help Americans and other foreigners in Moscow to understand how to use the 911 rescue service.

190

Expat guide: Moscow   **11/Staying safe**

RESCUE SERVICE
(tel/fax: 276-4072; 276-7712; 276-1877; 276-4402; e-mail: rescue@co.ru;
4a Ulitsa Abelmanovskaya)
The Rescue Service comprises an information centre, prompt reaction groups,
and a reservists institute. The information centre gathers, analyses and reroutes
information about accidents to the city emergency services. Specially-trained
prompt reaction groups which include a professional doctor are required to render
aid (free of charge) to accident victims before special services staff arrive.

12/Staying solvent

Before the financial crisis, Moscow was known for its soaring costs and stratospheric rentals. Alongside Tokyo and Hong Kong, Moscow was ranked as one of the three most expensive cities in the world, and in 1997 it also kept its position as Europe's most expensive city for the second year running.

Now that the crisis has introduced a measure of restraint in many spheres in Moscow living, things are improving, for in this time of collapsing demand, those who are setting prices no longer can count on the next customer being able to pay, and the next customer might be a long time coming.

There are a number of ways you can aim to stay solvent in Moscow, and apart from avoiding scams and pickpockets, probably the most important is knowing how and where to shop.

Obtaining (your own) money in crisis-times

Before you can shop you need to have access to money. It's hoped you won't have to resort to holding up a bank to obtain your money, as was attempted by a disgruntled depositor in early 1999. As the banking situation remains unstable, it's worth finding the best possible, but rare, refuge for your money: an account with a foreign bank but with a branch in Moscow. The other option is to use a bank from home with a tele-banking/online facility. If you place your money in a Russian bank, you run the risk of further devaluation, as occurred during the crisis of August 1998.

Withdrawing from your bank account via ATM

Before moving to Moscow, ask your card provider about the following:

- whether security issues regarding hacking into ATMs for retrieval of pin numbers have been resolved and what advice can be offered regarding this issue
- which services are provided
- which additional services you need to subscribe to and how much they cost to use, if they are not automatically provided with the card
- how to obtain express cash with your card
- how much interest is accrued daily on cash advance
- which daily/weekly/monthly withdrawal limits apply and what fees are charged according to the size of the transaction
- how to pay your bill by phone from your cheque account and what fees are charged for this procedure, if any

Expat guide: Moscow   **12/Staying solvent**

- be certain to confirm all fees and finance charges, as well as procedures for paying finance charges you have incurred (which, with some providers, is charged for even before you've been billed)
- how to monitor your card account on-line or by telephone
- procedure in case of loss/theft

Using a card to withdraw rubles or dollars from an ATM should not be a problem as long as the ruble is reasonably stable and security of access to one's bank account through an ATM is assured. During the crisis, finding an ATM which would deliver rubles or dollars was a time-consuming occupation. Sberbank, Most Bank and Alfa banks had reasonably reliable ATMs in the first quarter of 1999. However, the banking situation is so volatile and because anything can happen in Russia, by the time you read this the situation may have changed.

Always scrutinise your statements to ensure that withdrawals have not been made without your knowledge.

Using Alfa/Sobin/Sberbank you should be charged a commission in line with international withdrawal charges (0.75%) When using ATM machines to collect dollars on a UK or US bank account you should confirm the rate being charged as although there is no charge or 1% the rate is sometimes very low.

Some ATMs (most of which are open 24 hours a day) that have been suggested are:

- The former SBS-Agro ATMs accept PLUS network cards and offer rubles only
- Alfa Bank in the Artists' Gallery Shopping Mall at Pushkinskaya accepts Plus, as does Avtobank (on Pervaya Tverskaya Yamskaya Ulitsa) and the cash machine in the Marriott Grand Hotel
- 41 Prospekt Mira, (Visa, Master, Amex); metro: Prospekt Mira
- 16/2 Ulitsa 1st Tverskaya Yamskaya; (Visa, Master, Amex); metro: Mayakovskaya
- GUM, Red Square, 3rd aisle open from 08:00 - 20:00; (Visa, Master, Amex); metro: Ploschad Revolutsii
- Hotel Metropol, Teatralnyy Proezd; (Visa, Master, Amex); metro: Teatralnaya
- 2 Novy Arbat; (Visa, Master, Amex); metro: Arbatskaya
- 33 Kutozovsky Prospekt; (Visa, Master, Amex); metro: Kutozovskaya
- 10a Ulitsa 1905 Goda, ; (Visa, Master, Amex); metro: Ulitsa 1905 Goda

Some expats use Cirrus and say that the majority of ATMs withdraw funds from a cheque rather than a savings account by default while others offer an option.

Find out if Bank Austria Creditanstalt and Raiffeisenbank Austria have set up their proposed ATM system (still under discussion at the time of writing).

Obtaining dollars from a bank/ATM through debit/credit card

In Moscow, you will always need to present your passport, visa/work permit for any kind of banking transaction inside a bank.

Visit the sites for major Western banking institutions to locate ATMs nearest to you: *www.mastercard.com; www.visa.com*

Expat guide: Moscow   **12/Staying solvent**

The best Alfa bank ATMs seem to be those at Pushkinskaya, Tverskaya, 4 Old Arbat and metro Krasnopresnenskaya and these are said to dispense rubles and dollars up to a limit, though they do not work 100% of the time. At present, Alfa bank reliably supplies dollars at a commission of 1% over the counter but not at the ATM.

Alternatively, if you wish to clear a transaction over $1,000, it's recommended that you contact the customer service department of your home bank in advance (number on back of credit card) and warn them of your intention. This will help speed up the transaction from a potential few hours (while the anti-fraud system holds up the process) to ten to fifteen minutes or so.

Credit-card security

Because passports are used for identification when cards are used in banks, it might be the case that your date of birth is spotted and used as a potential pin number to obtain funds fraudulently from your card (assuming you use your birthday as your pin number).

If you use any of the mail suppliers in Moscow, be careful of your new credit card arriving in the same batch of mail as the separately posted PIN number. Rather ask your bank to courier the card directly to you.

ATM clearing agents have been known to make errors in recording of transactions. Always check your statement that amounts have been correctly withdrawn and only withdrawn once.

Keep a lookout for fake ATMs which are dotted around Moscow and which can be identified by their lack of familiar Visa/Cirrus etc logos. If you put your card in them, it reads the details before spitting it out again without any cash. Only use a machine that you know has given out money either to yourself on a previous occasion or to someone else in front of you.

As in any other country, be wary of the people around you when withdrawing cash from a machine.

Credit card fraud in Moscow is on the increase and recently seems to now include even those ATMs previously thought to be 'safe'.

Opening a bank account

Most Russian banks are to be considered as risky, given the debacle that occurred after the start of the financial crisis when small depositors lost cumulatively large sums of money when these banks either would not repay the money or repaid at vastly different sums compared with the sums initially invested.

Some foreign banks that have guaranteed offshore funding include: Bank Austria, ABN Amro, ING, Garantibank and Finansbank, as they have Russian Banking licences. The banks allow you to open personal accounts, meaning you can transfer money into Moscow and withdraw US dollars. Likewise you can transfer money offshore as long as it matches or is less than the amount transferred into Moscow.

There seems to be great confusion regarding just which bank will or will not open individual accounts, and some say that if they do, they will only do so under the aegis of a corporate account, meaning that your employer should be a healthy depositor at the bank before you would be allowed to use its facilities. Bank

195

Expat guide: Moscow **12/Staying solvent**

Austria was planning to expand in local retail banking with services aimed at corporate clients, and employees of companies with corporate accounts at the bank. Private depositors are welcome as long as they deposit a minimum of $5,000. Private depositors must submit a letter of recommendation from his employer stating his job title and which services are required. Upto 2% commission will be charged for cash withdrawals.

Another Austrian bank, Raiffeisenbank Austria was also planning to expand its retail services.

Others say that you can bank at ABN Amro (if you deposit a minimum of $10,000) but you can only deposit cash if you have a *spravka* or Customs declaration.

Personal cheques

Cheque accounts are not popular in Russia so don't expect to be able to use cheques. Rather access your money from your home bank with a debit card linked with a Visa or Mastercard account. Alternatively, if you have an Amex card, you can cash personal cheques at their office on Tverskaya Ulitsa. Five percent commission is charged.

Traveller's cheques

As traveller's cheques seem to be exempt from the rules governing the exportation of funds, they are becoming more and more popular. American Express, Visa and Mastercard traveller's cheques are said to be cashable at the representative offices of these companies.

Playing the money game in crisis times

During the crisis, the major impact on foreigners was caused by the rapid exchange-rate fluctuations, the great difficulty in obtaining rubles from ATMs and the dearth of establishments that were willing to accept credit cards. Those that did accept credit cards charged a premium to cushion themselves against any losses as a result of the unexpected fluctuation.

When the ruble is stable for long periods there is no problem using credit cards. However, when the ruble was on a roller-coaster ride from one day to the next, many shops and restaurants banned the use of many credit cards and insisted on cash.

Credit card companies will always charge the transaction at the highest rate on the day of calculation which will be a few days to a few weeks after you actually used it. So if you bought when the rate was Rs15/$ and the rate went down a week or so later to Rs10/$ you will be charged at that. They are also hedging their bets against the ruble going the other way.

Some say that credit card merchants have up to a year to submit their claims which could lead to fluctuating statements.

To get around the problem when buying an air-ticket in a crisis, it's suggested that you call the airline you intend to fly with in your home country, order the ticket and obtain that country's price, then go to that airline's office in Moscow and pay for the ticket by credit card, signing the bill with the USD, RUR and GBP price on it and you should be billed the correct price when you receive

Expat guide: Moscow   **12/Staying solvent**

your statement. You could also pay over the phone by phoning your home country, and ask them to issue the ticket in Moscow.

During the crisis, there was much confusion regarding how payments could be made, whether credit cards were still in use (they were temporarily suspended).

Often, totals were designated as *y.e.'s* which are equivalent to dollar units, although it has been reported that it is against the law to price items or services in dollars. However, that allowed you to make a quick calculation to find out which interest rate applied at the time. The rate was so fluid that at first many shops simply closed as they could not keep up with the speed at which they needed to change prices. Sometimes, service providers such as restaurants or hotels quoted their own exchange-rate which was more advantageous to them, charged the customer in rubles, and then reconverted a process which 'hid' another percentage increase. Always make sure you know what the stated exchange-rate of the day is, if the ruble is in a state of fluctuation, as this should be displayed in a prominent place in the store, although it won't necessarily be in English, and therefore easily discernible.

At times of crisis, don't rely on being able to use a credit card to pay for your shopping, otherwise you may be caught short. Always make sure credit cards are accepted before doing your shopping to avoid embarrassment.

If there is a sudden devaluation, as there was in August 1998, you need to make sure that you buy all you need for the next few weeks at least, as retailers sometimes get caught unprepared and don't have an opportunity to raise prices as quickly. The worst time to buy is when a shortage occurs after the initial frenzied buying, for at this time, stock is marked very high to offset any losses. It's best to skip this period unless you absolutely have to buy, and wait until prices have settled down again.

To offset any unexpected devaluation, it is always wise to change as much as you need only for a given transaction or day in order to avoid loss.

Paying deposits

Unfairly, some organisations ask you to pay a deposit for a service in rubles to a dollar-equivalent amount, however when it comes to the time to refund you your deposit, you will receive the same amount you paid originally in rubles. So, for instance, if you paid say Rs100 when the exchange-rate was Rs6/$1, that would have been worth approximately $16, however if you had to reclaim your deposit at a time when the exchange-rate is say, Rs25/$1, you will only be receiving $4 instead of roughly $16. See if you can wangle things so that you get a better refund deal before you sign the contract.

Converting rubles vs dollars online

For up-to-date exchange-rate information consult:

- *www.infoart.ru/money/currency/currency.htm*
- *www.oanda.com*
- *www.xe.net/ucc/*

197

Expat guide: Moscow
12/Staying solvent

Exchange booths

These are known as *obmyen valuiti* and are wide-spread. Shop around for the best rates. Most will not ask you to produce identification but will provide a receipt if requested. Be careful if changing a large amount of money. It has occurred that accomplices were tipped off outside the exchange booth so that they were aware of what money the customer had when he came out.

Deutschmarks/French francs

Many '*obmyen valuiti*' or exchange booths will exchange rubles against the DM. It is less frequent to find one that exchanges French francs. One which might still do so is the exchange inside Hotel Tverskaya. There is also an exchange on the Old Arbat that is said to do a range of currencies. It is rarer to find an exchange booth for pounds, but you might be lucky close to the centre.

Internet banking

This involves obtaining software from your bank in your home country, which you load onto your computer and which enables you to access your account whenever you wish. Many such programs also allow you to pay bills from your computer. One major benefit is that you will know far more quickly if your credit cards have been used fraudulently in any way, rather than having to wait for the time it takes for your bank statement to reach you by snail mail.

Sending/receiving a money order

Before you can send money out of Russia, you will need to present a permit *(spravka)* which proves that the money you wish to send out has been exchanged legally. If you are sending money through the bank from which you have withdrawn the money, you automatically have proof that this transaction was legal.

Cost of living

Life has become cheaper for foreigners since the August crisis. Instead of being rated as the most expensive city in Europe and third most expensive in the world for expatriates, it is now rated 88th most expensive out of 123 rated cities, according to the Worldwide Cost of Living Survey.

Expats paid in dollars say that utility bills, transport and rent have all become significantly cheaper. Despite such optimistic news, many expats had their previous salaries reduced which meant they did not have the opportunity to reap as much of a bonanza as they might have done.

American expats say that most things are available at a cost which is either equal to, or up to 50% more expensive than at home. UK expats who do their weekly shopping in places such as Ramstore, find their weekly grocery bill to be consistently less than what it would be buying at a typical UK supermarket, for example.

Accommodation is still expensive, while petrol is reasonable, restaurants can be either expensive or very good value for money, but you need to seek out the latter. Clothing in general is more expensive. One benchmark is: if you buy

Expat guide: Moscow   **12/Staying solvent**

Russian, you are likely to get the item at a much better price, but it might not last as long as an imported item.

If you wish to research the cost of living before arriving in Moscow, visit a good reference library and ask if it stocks the country report published by Craigshead International. Alternatively, visit *www.homefair.com/calc/ salcalc.html* which will show you what salary you should aim for in Moscow if you wish to match a salary from your current place of residence.

Benchmark food basket (March 1999 = Rs24/$1)
Apples 55c/kg
- Bananas 62c/kg
- Grapes $1.06/kg
- Kiwi fruit 20c/unit
- Mandarin 25c/unit
- Potatoes 13c/kg
- Onions 33c/kg
- Garlic 35c/kg
- Tomatoes $2.34/kg
- Cucumber 66c/kg
- Cabbage 17c/kg
- Butterhead lettuce $1/each
- Flour 44c/kg
- Butter $2.26/kg
- Cheese $1.25/kg
- Meat/fish (wide variety from cheap to expensive e.g. fatty mince at $2.20/kg, pork roast $3/kg; bacon $2.30/500g)
- Fruit juice 86c/litre
- Milk 60c/litre
- Baltika beer 30c/500ml

Alternatively, visit www.cyber-grocery.ru where you will be able to browse the different and current costs of a wide variety of items.

Shopping

It's all very well being told you can get everything in Moscow, but when you have to travel long distances to find what you want (that is, if you are only intent on getting something specific), it becomes a tedious chore and makes it difficult to plan ahead. Making lists becomes a daily routine as does a visit to the supermarket which because of the language problem and the unfamiliarity of the brand names (apart from Russian brand names, you'll also find French, Italian and especially Finnish brand names) is stressful in itself. Unless you visit Ramstore (two branches and more coming) or Stockmann in Smolensky Passage, what you hoped would be a one-stop shopping experience turns into getting what you can, when you can.

Of course the experience is made so much simpler if you have a driver who can stop outside a supermarket for you so that you don't have to battle finding

199

Expat guide: Moscow   12/Staying solvent

parking as well as getting the goods to the car, neither will you be limited to one or two bags that you can carry on your walk home or on the metro.

If you don't have a driver, you can always hire a taxi to take you from shop to shop.

Availability of goods

Forget about the dark old days of the Soviet Union, you can get whatever you want in Moscow, however, it might take some time to find it. Be prepared to have to shop around. Some notable items that are missing from the Moscow shopping scene are:

- Marmite/Vegemite
- Velveeta cheese
- pull-up nappies/diapers

You may not be able to find all brands of cosmetics (though many are available), especially if you favour supermarket brand names such as Boots/ASDA, in which case, bring your own supply or a substitute. Some of the malls have upmarket cosmetic stores which stock most of the well-known European brands such as Lancome and Dior.

Pricing policy/double price standards

You are also likely to encounter this price variance in the tourism industry when you purchase airplane, hotel and museum tickets. This may be because these are supported by state subsidies, and unless you are a permanent resident and therefore a taxpayer, you will not be eligible for the discounted rate.

One expatriate took exception to having to pay more than a local on an internal flight, and took a case of two-tier pricing to court on the basis of a decree by Boris Yeltsin which stated that it was illegal to have two prices, and won his case (though he was paid only a nominal fee of about $1.50, at least he made his point). Despite this precedent, you will no doubt encounter two-tier pricing again. You could try to draw attention to this decree (Article 426 of the Russian Constitution), but there's no telling how far it will get you. In May 1999, and despite the Constitution, the Railways Ministry moved to close loopholes that allowed 'accredited' expats to buy train tickets at the Russian rate though enforcement was irregular and ticketing agencies were not unified in charging the foreign travellers' rate. In July 1999, the way was cleared for all train journeys to be charged at a single rate.

The double standard also works in some hotels, where two identical rooms can be charged different prices according to the passport of their occupants. Some expats say that if, as a foreigner living in Moscow and paying taxes, you are able to prove your status by a document in Russian, then you could pay the price charged to the Russians in museums. Whether it works in hotels or on airlines is debatable.

There is also an informal two-tiered system in Moscow. This is: expensive for foreigners and cheap for locals, but this depends on whether you shop where Russians shop, or stick to the more expensive Western supermarkets.

If you are able to shop at the market with the help of a bilingual driver or nanny or even a friend, you can get superb cuts of meat, fish, fruit and vegetables

Expat guide: Moscow   **12/Staying solvent**

at prices well below that of the foreign supermarkets. However, if you choose to go it alone you will make yourself conspicuous by your lack of Russian and prices are likely to go up as a result. You will also need to know which markets are the better ones.

One tip worth knowing is to take along a small notepad on which you can write quoted prices as you understand them and obtain confirmation that these are the prices you have agreed upon, otherwise you might end up paying a lot more than you bargained for.

Security in shops

Most shops have security doormen who usually take their jobs very seriously and won't admit you unless you check your bags or other shopping into a stall or security cubicles. Don't try to argue with them. It won't help.

Shopping hours

Remember that shop hours differ from those in the West. Many open at 10:00 only, closing for lunch from 14:00 - 15:00 and re-opening for an afternoon stint until about 18:00 or later depending on the type of business.

How to pay

(See also under *Supermarkets* below.) In general, not all shops accept credit cards, so you should be prepared for those which don't - always ascertain that they do before filling your basket, or trolley. At the height of the economic crisis, many shops stopped accepting credit cards until some sort of stability returned to the ruble/dollar exchange-rate, while others accepted them but at their own rates (always beneficial to them) whereas others displayed prices in *y.e.'s* which denoted a price in dollars while not actually being dollars, and which you would simply convert back into rubles at the rate of the day. Although there was a time when dollars were acceptable, nowadays only rubles are regarded as legal tender.

Some shops have a select-and-pay system, while the more traditional ones have a kiosk or counter (*kacca* pronounced 'kassa') where you pay after you have decided what you want. The saleslady (at the counter where you have indicated your interest in an item) will mark down the price of the item, you then take the note to the *kacca*, pay and then return to collect your goods with your receipt to prove that you've paid. Many expats find this system hard to deal with as it takes the spontaneity and freedom out of shopping, though it helps if you can speak Russian. However, over time, these more 'soviet' practices are dying out in Moscow.

Some Russian shops are subdivided, meaning that you buy your sweets, alcohol and cleaning fluids on one side, paying for them at that till. Then cross a few metres to the other side of the shop and buy bread milk and eggs, and then again to the far end where you buy fruit amd vegetables. If you don't know what to ask for, take a sample of what you want and hold it up quoting the number in Russian (if you've got that far, or using your fingers or writing it down).

201

Expat guide: Moscow   **12/Staying solvent**

Russian service

It used to be the case that shop assistants would bark at you, ignore you and treat you with disdain, managing to thoroughly put off the Western shopper used to smiles, greetings, courtesy and assistance. You will still come across this Soviet attitude these days, but even Russians admit things are improving markedly.

You can make your own contribution to this evolution by always complaining when you feel you have been hard done by. Don't be afraid to give constructive advice either, as you will find that it is gladly accepted on occasion. Every shop is required to have an official governmental comments book which you are entitled to ask for and use to vent your spleen or pay compliments.

Where to buy:
Clothes

You can choose to frequent expensive shops such as those at **Manezh** where a fur coat can cost more than a car, to **Gum** on Red Square, and then **TsUM**, behind the Bolshoi, Stockmann at Smolensky Passage, or to numerous designer shops for instance, on Tverskaya Ulitsa, Kutozovsky and Kuznetsky Most. On the other hand, you could go local and buy perfectly adequate clothes in the subways or at the markets, where quality is not marvellous, but will do for a season or more.

If you are buying from a small kiosk in a subway, instead of trying to explain to the attendant that you want the striped blue dress at the back of the display, just note down the number and show it to her and she will retrieve the item from the stocks in the inner sanctum of her shop.

In general, European sizing is used, so if you are used to UK or US sizes, try to have them converted to European sizes to make your shopping task easier.

There are a number of other shopping centres, and it's up to you whether you want to spend the time finding out just who does what and at what price.

- Clothing boutiques at the two **Ramstore complexes** (which being under one roof and because they are not charged exorbitant rentals, are more likely to be more affordable).

- **Smolensky Passage** *(Smolenskaya Ploschad, Smolensky Bulvar, opposite metro: Smolenskaya)* opened at the end of 1998, contains the 20,000sqm Stockmann, billed as Moscow's first department store, plus space for 40 boutiques. The anchor tenant, Stockmann's, has a department store above its food hall.

- **Petrovsky Passage** *(10 Ulitsa Petrovka; metro: Kuznetsky Most; open: Monday - Saturday 09:00 - 19:00)* is a shopping mall containing designer-type shops.

- **Valdai Centre** *(2 Novy Arbat. Open: 10:00 - 19:00)*. Boutiques within a department store set-up where you pay for each item at its place of purchase.

- **Mothercare** *(tel: 202-5250; 83/1 Leninsky Prospekt)* sells children's wear.

- **Detsky Mir** *(tel: 927-2007 5 Teatralny Passazh)* is a children's department store.

- **Manezh** (subterranean mall just near the entrance of Red Square and exit for metro: Okhotny Ryad). A wide variety of expensive boutiques. Might be worth a bit of window-shopping if you like that sort of thing. Watch out for sales by shops closing down. Fast-food hall.

Expat guide: Moscow   **12/Staying solvent**

- **Actor's Gallery** *(16/2 Ulitsa Tverskaya; metro: Pushkinskaya)* another mall with a variety of small and expensive boutiques.
- **TsUM** (just to the side and back of the Bolshoi theatre) is a vast department store made up of open plan independent shops.
- **GUM** (right next to Red Square) is a collection of designer boutiques.

Clothes markets

There are numerous clothes markets around. Quality and price vary depending on the market. Try Izmailovsky and Savyolovskaya markets (don't forget the Vietnamese market adjacent to the latter for cheaper clothes).

Catalogue shopping overseas

Some recommended US catalogue companies are:

- **Land's End** order on-line
- **California Style** *(tel: 1-760-918-3700 or 1-800-477-7722)*
- **The Territory Ahead** - Travel Clothes *(tel: 1-800-882-4323)*
- **Signals** - (public TV- mall stuff) *(tel: 1-800-669-9696; 01-651-659-4310)*
- **Cold Water Creek** *(tel: 1-800-968-0980)*

Fur coats

These can be bought at the most expensive shops such as Manezh and at GUM and also at markets. A vast number of women wear them mostly out of necessity, and there does not seem to be any antipathy as in the West to the idea of wearing fur. Some Russians go abroad to buy their furs, believing local-quality pelts to be inferior.

Try the following places:

- the market next to Tushinskaya metro
- Ismailovo market (remember to bargain and check quality)
- A large market just near Konkova metro
- The *dublonki* shop at 6 Leninsky Prospekt.

Fur coats should be cleaned and stored in the summer by hanging in plastic in a dark closet. Two recommended fur coat repairers are:

- **Armen** *(tel: 430-3268)* who collects and delivers from home/office and whose quality of work is good. Charges are said to be reasonable.
- **Atelie Zima** *(corner Pervomaiskaya Ulitsa and 15ᵗʰ Parkovaya Ulitsa)*

Hats

There is a reasonably wide variety of hats that can be purchased both inside shops and from street vendors or at markets, ranging from the typical Russian fur hat to much slinkier models in different kinds of fur and at much higher prices. Hats are mandatory for winter.

203

Expat guide: Moscow   **12/Staying solvent**

Shoes

Numerous shoe shops abound, but you won't guess from the displays outside, unless you recognise the word that looks like *'obyb'* or Bata.

Shoes tend to be of reasonably good quality and you can choose from a vast selection of full boots or ankle boots (mostly high-heeled) which women favour. Most designs are conservative and don't tend to follow the way out trends of UK and the US.

Prices are also generally reasonable, except of course in the obviously expensive shops.

Shoe repair

There are many shoe repair shops around *'obyb remont'*. It's best to ask for recommendations from work colleagues and friends. One expat recommends the shop at 48 Leningradsky Prospekt while another recommends the shoe *remont* near the Belgrade Hotel. You will regularly find shops that combine photographic, key cutting and shoe repair services situated near metro entrances.

Fabrics and haberdashery supplies

Generic *'tkani'* stores are found all over Moscow.

Tailors

Tailors are generally to be found in generic *'atelye'* or studios, look out for the unobtrusive signs. Some that are recommended are:

- **'Regyer'** *(tel: 253-6281 Russian only); 5 Presnensky Val; metro: 1905 Goda.* The *atelye* is recommended as being speedy on service, reliable, very reasonably priced.
- A tailor on *(tel: 290-5253 Russian only) 24 Bolshaya Nikitskaya* through a small archway, to the left, and down steps. Staff at the shop can do repairs and adjustments as well as create a garment from a drawing (without a pattern). Prices are reasonable.
- **Oleg** *(tel: 113-0356 Russian only)* does suit and shirt alterations and can make an item from scratch if you give him the fabric. He is said to charge reasonable prices and comes to your home or office to take measurements and drop the finished product off.
- An *atelye* at 20/1 Pokrovka (door round the back of the grey building)
- **Fatima** *(tel: 493-1359)* Russian only, custom design, extremely reasonable pricing
- **Adal** *(tel: 151-1538; 6 Baltiiskaya)* work is recommended as being of top quality with low prices in quick turnaround time.
- **Lika** *(tel: 562-040; Russian only)* does designer clothes, repairs and alterations for a reasonable price.
- **Lena** *(tel: 137-1706 evenings)* makes housecalls.
- **Tanya** *(tel: 467-5624)* makes housecalls, work is good quality and prices are reasonable.

Expat guide: Moscow   **12/Staying solvent**

- **Armen** *(tel: 430-3268)* will collect and deliver work to your home or office, reasonable prices.
- **Lika** *(tel: 561-0401)* designs and does alterations.
- **Wintex** and **Executive Fashions** are companies which are both run by expats. They will generally measure you for suits and shirts which are made in Hong Kong. Depending on the fabric you chose, suits cost around $450 and take three to five weeks from order to delivery. Executive Fashions: Johnny Manglani/ Sandy Kumar *(tel: 785-2136; www.efashions.aha.ru)*. For Wintexm, contact Sammy Kotwani *(tel: 926-5015; www.wintex-international.com)*

Laundry/dry-cleaning

Quality and reliability are not comparable to Western standards in general as shrinkage and slight colour changes may take place. Don't entrust anything precious until you are satisfied that you have found a decent dry-cleaner. Ask about compensation for lost/damaged items, and rather don't risk having expensive items cleaned. Don't allow a verbal brush-off for poor quality work. If you feel really upset about it and need some form of compensation write your complaint down and post it to them by recorded delivery, threatening to sue if they don't co-operate. This way they are much more likely to be co-operative.

- The **Aerostar Hotel** *(tel: 21- 9000)* offers dry-cleaning services to non-guests. Quality is said to be good.
- **Diana** will pick up and deliver twice weekly, prices are said to be reasonable. Diana has a number of different locations around the city, and each is independently owned and run. Look in the MBTG for one near you.
- **California Cleaners** at Park Place *(113a Leninsky Prospekt)* said to be expensive
- Laundry service **Quick and Clean** *(tel: 977-6691; 11 Ulitsa Vavilova; metro: Leninsky Prospekt)* will collect and deliver. Friendly and helpful staff.
- **Express Dry Cleaners** near the Moskovsky Univermag, metro: Komsomolskaya, is said to have decent prices, and speedy service.

Self-service laundry/dry-cleaning

The laundry service *(tel: 977-6691: 11 Ulitsa Vavilova; metro: Leninsky Prospekt)* costs about $1.50 for 6kg and the dry-cleaning about $4 for 10kg. The process takes about one hour.

Cosmetics

Usually in shops marked *Kosmetica* (in Cyrillic) where 95% of what is sold is cosmetics, often only Russian brands. There are a few upmarket shops dedicated to selling Western designer-name cosmetics such as Lancome and Estee Lauder.

Expat guide: Moscow   **12/Staying solvent**

Toiletries

These, including well-known Western brands, are widely available in supermarkets. The only problem is that you will need to be able to understand the Russian labels otherwise you will not know whether you are buying shampoo for greasy or dry hair, for instance.

Haircuts

It's difficult to find a decent haircut in Moscow without paying inflated prices. You can choose to go native, but then you run the risk of a language problem which could have very unwanted consequences. The difference in the prices you are likely to pay could range depending on location between some $10 - $100 or more. Some say there's no reason to pay more than $30 for a decent haircut in Moscow, while if you speak Russian, you can find hairdressers who will do your hair for between $4 - 10. It might be an idea to take along a picture of what you want and hope that the hairdresser can reproduce the style, alternatively, you could translate a list of basic words such as short/shorter, long/longer, curly/straight, shaved, layers, etc.

Some suggestions that have been tried and tested include:

- The **Metropol hotel** *(tel: 927-6000)* just by the Bolshoi theatre, has separate salons for men and women with haircuts in the $30 range.
- **Tressals** *(tel: 959-3147; 2/20 Ulitsa Serafimovich)* which was originally Irish and now Russian-owned is said to be friendly and offer reasonable prices with a few English-speaking staff and a British hairdresser who does women's hair (if he's still there). The basic plan gets you a wash, cut, blow dry and gel.
- **Adolpho** at the National Hotel *(tel: 258-7179; 15/1 Mokhovaya Ulitsa)* is said to do a good job, but for a high price. If you don't mind giving Adolpho free licence you might be pleasantly surprised.
- **Charodeika** *(tel: 290-5339)* on Novy Arbat. The salon's senior hairdresser is said to be skilled, friendly and considerate of your wishes, although things are rendered somewhat difficult by a lack of English-speaking staff.
- **Jacques Dessange** *(tel: 215-9780)* sometimes has French hairdressers who charge over $100 per cut.
- **Fit and Fun Sports Club** *(tel: 924-4315)* has a competent salon and prices are on the reasonable side.
- **Mod's Hair** on Mayakovskaya Square, directly across the square from the Mayakovskaya metro exit. Charges about $30 for a head massage and haircut.
- **Wella** *(tel: 290-5137)* next door to the Canadian embassy, 2nd floor.

The following are freelancers who have been recommended by expats:
- **Yvetta:** *(tel: 917-8126)* Experienced Russian male/female hairdresser in Kurskaya region, charges competitive prices:
- **Larissa** *(tel: 153-7003 after 21:00; speaks a little English)* charges $20 per adult cut and $10 for children and will come to your apartment on evenings and weekends. Good with children

206

Expat guide: Moscow **12/Staying solvent**

- **Nadia** (speaks Russian only) *(tel: 229-3396)* can create new hairstyles and do colouring. She only works on alternate days so you will need to make a reservation. She is highly recommended and also reasonably priced.
- **Nastya** at Figaro *(tel: 928-2695)* is highly commended.
- **Irina Olympieva** *(tel: 393-1701)* does house-calls and cuts, colours, gives permanents, styles; speaks some English and is reasonably priced.

Medical/health/optics

See *Chapter 10 - Staying healthy.*

Sporting goods

There is a wide variety of sports wear and equipment around (no baseball gloves though). Locally-made equipment is much cheaper than imported equipment and sometimes does not tend to last as long. *(See Chapter 9 - Keeping busy)*

Cigars

If you are a cigar lover in Moscow, you won't have any problem finding shops that sell them:

- **Havana (Gavana)** on Komsomolsky Prospekt, between metro Frunzenskaya and Park Kultury metro. Although it also sells food products, look for the cigar section along a side wall. Ask for Feruz, their specialist tobacconist. The shop has a decent selection of accessories, as well as chewing tobacco and hookah pipes. You need to check for quality before you buy although the staff will probably help you do this.
- **The Embassy Club** *(tel: 229-7185; 8/10 Byusov Pereulok)* in the House of Composers features a cigar bar and cocktail lounge. The cigar bar part of the club is open from 12:00 - 20:00, Monday to Saturdays. It sells Cuban, as well as Dominican and Jamaican cigars. The Embassy opened in the midst of the crisis in late 1998. An on-site tobacconist said to sell the best quality and selection of Cuban and other cigars which are more expensive than many other cigar shops, because of strict quality control.
- **Davidoff** *(22 Tverskaya north of Pushkin Square across from Hotel Minsk)* is said to have a very high pricing policy but with a good selection and storage facilities.
- **La Casa de Cuba** at Manezh shopping center on the intermediate level. It has a good selection of Dominican cigars but also high prices.
- **Troubki** on Pokrovka, just inside the Bulvar Ring. The shop is clean and it has a good selection with reasonable prices.
- **VDNKh** exhibition centre. There is a small store opposite Moskva pavilion - with a small selection at good prices.
- Restaurants, clubs and kiosks also sell cigars. You might also be able to get them from Cuban students who smuggle them into Moscow in order to earn some pocket money.

Expat guide: Moscow   **12/Staying solvent**

Cigarettes

If you are a smoker and enjoy smoking, Moscow will seem like seventh heaven to you. The locally manufactured cigarettes are cheap (Camel light - 80c a pack of 20 (June 1999)) whereas it's almost impossible to obtain brands such as Silk Cut unless you buy them in duty-free at the airport.

Cigarettes are widely available and prices may vary from kiosk to kiosk. It is also socially acceptable to smoke virtually everywhere, although not inside shops, on public transport and in offices, where smokers are expected to smoke outside.

Despite this, there is no 'politically correct' movement afoot as there is in other countries, to make smokers feel like social outcasts. If anything, if you don't smoke, you will probably suffer more as you try and dodge the cigarette smoke.

Passport photos

There are a number of small studios in Moscow that can do passport photos. Always make sure you ask for non-glossy (matte) otherwise the ink from the visa stamp runs the risk of being rubbed off and invalidating your visa.

A place on Komsomolsky Prospekt on the opposite side of the street from metro Frunzenskaya in the block on the corner of Timura Frunze Ulitsa can do a same-day delivery if you have the picture taken early in the day. As the photos are cut manually, show them an example of the size you need.

Also look out for passport photo machines which are becoming more and more prevalent in metro lobbies. Kodak studios are also able to supply photographs within a few minutes.

Advantix film

*   **Sivma** in the Promradtekhbank building on Kutuzovsky Prospekt and its other branch on Gogolevsky Bulvar stock and develop Advantix film.
*   The photographic shop on the ground floor of **TsUM** as well as the Kodak shop in **Gum**, both process Advantix film. TsUM offers a one-hour and one-day service.
*   Two photographic laboratories: **TASS** laboratory near Kievsky Vokhzal *(tel: 243 4344)* and **RIA-Novosti** laboratory: *(tel: 201-3943)*

Film-developing

There are many small 'express' photo shops all over town. You just have to find them. Ask your friends and colleagues to recommend those that have worked well for them. Automated photo booths are not as thick on the ground as in the UK or US, but are in existence.

*   **Soyuz** in Ramstore *60A Ulitsa Sheremet'yevskaya; metro: Prospekt Mira*
*   **Kodak professional lab** and mini-lab offer a free pick-up and delivery service (minimum order over $18). Call 733-9612 from 09:00 - 18:00 Monday - Friday to arrange for a courier. Slightly more expensive than many express booths, but more reliable in terms of quality.

Expat guide: Moscow   **12/Staying solvent**

New and second-hand camera equipment

A wide variety of new camera equipment is available locally but if you want to buy reasonably priced second-hand camera equipment walk halfway down the Novy Arbat to the store that sells camera equipment and you are likely to see freelance sellers standing in front of the shop selling their wares.

A shop in Yasenevo is rumoured to be a good place for swapping and selling of photographic equipment between hobbyists

Camera repairs

Canon *(tel: 258-5600)* has an authorised service centre at its office in Moscow. Try the small 'foto-*remont*' shop at 5 Komsomolsky Prospekt which is said to offer good service at reasonable prices, though service can be slow. Also try 52/3, floor 5, Kosmodamiansky Naberezhnaya, and Agfa at *(tel: 234-210)* Trekghorny Pereulok and **Technosoyuz** *(tel: 274-7093)* in Manezh mall. On the web, if you have a faulty Minolta, consult *www.minolta.ru*.

Flowers

To order flowers for delivery in the US, Proflowers at *www.proflowers.com*, is highly recommended for reliability, choice, good delivery times and price.

Locally, flowers are available at many kiosks on the side of the road (look out for a sign which looks like: *цветы* Prices vary according to demand so if you need to buy flowers for all the important ladies in your life for Women's Day on 8 March, you can expect to pay a premium.

Florists who deliver include

- **White Lily** (Belaya Lilia) *(tel: 152-2014; 62 Leningradsky Prospekt)*
- **Interflora** *(tel: 926-5412; 23/2 Komsomolsky Prospekt)*
- **Elite-Flora** *(tel: 254-3992; 4th floor, 32 Gruzinskaya Bolshaya Ulitsa)*

Plants

There are no big plant centres, rather small selections are sold in flower shops. Prices are quite steep compared with the West, but it is possible to buy bags of compost and plant pots and tubs.

Food
Farmer's markets

Ask others for recommendations of what they regard as being the best markets. These are open throughout the year, all week long. Farmer's harvests are sold here as are imported fruit and vegetables.

Even if you intend to shop in supermarkets, just visiting a market is a worthwhile experience. It is said that if you live by Russian prices and shop in the markets, you can live very cheaply.

If you can't speak Russian, take a local who can speak English and order on your behalf otherwise the chances are that you'll get ripped off. Also take wads of small change in notes and bring your own supply of plastic bags.

Expat guide: Moscow   **12/Staying solvent**

Tips and pitfalls

When shopping for produce/meat at the *rynok* or on the street, beware of being undersold in terms of weight. Sometimes a kilogram on the street can weigh as little as half that amount. Watch when your produce is being weighed, and don't accept any pre-bagged goods without having them weighed again. Always check that the produce at the bottom of the bag is as fresh as that on top, if it was packed out of sight.

If you are worried about BSE or Mad Cow Disease, don't risk buying beef at the market as there are no checks against the disease. However, regular shoppers praise the fact that the meat is fresh (not frozen and refrozen) and hormone-free. If the meat is still soft, pinky/red in colour and with evidence of blood, then it should be fresh. But if it's dark red and dry and crusty to the touch, it's not as fresh.

It's also possible to sample the dairy products, honey and pickles as well as vegetables and fruit before buying. Haggling will often result in small discounts Toiletries and pantyhose prices are also said to be very good. It may help if you find one supplier for one type of food and stick with them every time you visit that market as you will build up a relationship, they will get to know what you like and they are less likely to rip you off.

Watch out for products that are date-stamped and check them for expiry dates. Do not buy produce with a crossed-out date stamp or any label that has been crossed out.

You will need to find out if pieces are sold by item or by kilogram. You will also need to be vigilant in seeing that you are given the correct change.

Some recommend markets are:

* **Dorogomilovsky** Market *10 Mozhaisky Val; metro: Kievskaya.*
* **Rizhsky** Market *Prospekt Mira*
* **Tishinsky** Market *50 Bolshaya Gruzinskaya;*
* **Leningradsky** Market *11 Ulitsa Chasovaya: metro: Aeroport/Sokol*;
* **Cheryomushkinsky** Market, *3 Lomonosovsky Prospekt;*
* **Novocheryomushky**, probably the best and widest selection - also most expensive
* **Tsentralny** Market, *15 Tsvetnoy Bulvar. Near the Circus. metro: Tsvetnoy Bulvar*
* **Kievskaya** and **Tulskaya** are said to be very good for fresh meat and vegetables though some say that as some of the fresh produce is likely to come from Ukraine, there is an increased risk of radio-activity.

Supermarkets

* **Irish house** $$$$$
  Novy Arbat *(tel: 291-7641; Open: 10:00 - 21:00)* sells food, alcohol, electronic equipment, some clothing and pub. Selection of meat, fish and frozen meals, cheese.
* **Eldorado** $$$$$
  (tel: 230-3662; 1/3 Ulitsa, Bolshaya Polyanka; metro: Polyanka)
* **Gastronom**$$$
  (tel: 291-7625; 11 Novy Arbat)

210

Expat guide: Moscow   12/Staying solvent

- **Global USA $$$**
    * *(tel: 151-3354) 78 Leningradsky Prospekt*
    * *(tel: 189-1967) 27 Ulitsa Menzhinskogo*
    * *(tel: 274-5539) 12 Ulitsa Simonovsky Val*
    * *(tel: 245-5657) 35 Ulitsa Usacheva*
    * *(tel: 229-8786) 6 Tverskaya Ulitsa*
    * *(tel: 290-4168) 17 Ulitsa Bolshaya. Nikitskaya*
- **ItalMarket $$$**
  (tel: 437-3298; fax: 437-4935; Michurinsky Prospekt Olimpiiskaya Der.2;metro: Yugo Zapadnaya; open Monday - Saturday 10:00 - 19:00; Sunday10:00 - 15:00). An Italian cash and carry outside the rear of the Olympic village complex. They advertise fresh mozzarella, a wide selection of freshly-cut prosciutto and sausages and other ingredients imported from Italy.
- **Kalinka-Stockmann $$$$$**
  (tel: 953-2602; 951-1924 opposite metro/train station Paveletskaya). This is a smallish but very well stocked food supermarket, with some home hardware goods
- **Kalinka-Stockmann $$$$$**
  Smolensky Passage Opened in November 1998. Similar to a department store, also with a food hall downstairs. If you can't find something you are looking for, you are likely to find it, but at a price.
- **Mega Centre Italia $$$$$**
  (tel: 132-3233; 10 Ulitsa Akademya Pilugina) Some Italian brands, fruit and vegetables excessively expensive.
- **Progress $$$$$**
  (tel: 246-9078; 17 Zubovsky Bulvar) Open 24 hours. Many French products. Has paid guarded parking. Currency exchange outlet. Also look at shop on ground floor which sells books, toys, gifts.
- **Sadko $$$$$** Sadko's has two stores.
    * **Sadko Arcade** Expocentre *(12 1st Krasnogvardeisky Proezd. Open: 09:00 - 21:00)*
    * **Sadko Foodland** *(tel: 243-6659; 16 Ulitsa Bolshaya Dorogmilovskaya; metro; Kievskaya. Open: 09:00 - 21:00)*
- **Seven Continents $$$$**
    * *(tel: 241-0761; 241-3401; 54/2 Old Arbat)*
    * *(tel: 137-0093; 61/1 Leninsky Prospekt)*
    * *(tel: 928-9527;12/1 Bolshaya Lubyanka Ulitsa)*
    * *(tel: 292-2248; 2 Ulitsa Okhotny Ryad)*
    * *(tel: 959-101; 2 Ulitsa Serafimovicha)*
- **Ramstore $$** *Head Office: 19 Yartsevskaya Street; tel: 937-0440; fax: 937-0441; e-mail: ramenka@co.ru;19 Ulitsa Yartsevskaya; metro Molodezhnaya; also 60 Ulitsa Sheremetyevskaya; metro: VDNKh from where you can catch a free shuttle bus to the mall every 20 minutes or so)* Ramstore is the first, the biggest and the most Western-like of the supermarket genre in Russia and is likely to make you feel most at home. For this reason alone it deserves its own detailed and unapologetically

211

Expat guide: Moscow   12/Staying solvent

enthusiastic entry. The chain (now with two stores open) offers plenty of variety, plenty of stock, fresh fruit and vegetables and fish and meat. The shops are in outlying districts which can take some 30 or 40 minutes to get to from the centre, but they are definitely worth visiting as they have introduced the idea of one-stop convenience shopping and value-for-money to Moscow. Two other stores in different areas are in the pipeline. Ramstore offers electrical goods, gardening, cooking, clothing, cosmetics, cameras, hi-fi equipment, televisions, fans, barbecue equipment. They also follow a seasonal format in terms of display, for instance filling shelves with Christmas-type items just prior to the start of the season, and summer barbecue and swimming gear in time for summer.

Local Russian supermarkets
(Cynepmapket/produkti/gastronom)

There's absolutely no reason not to venture into your local shop, be it a kiosk or proper shop. Take your time to wander around and figure out which shops have which products. Bacon is often much cheaper and better quality in these shops, as are ham and cheese, for instance. Quality seems fine in most instances. Remember to take your own plastic bags. If plastic bags are available you might be able to buy them for a ruble or two.

Vegetables and fruit

It does no harm buying your fruit and vegetables from stalls on the street which are usually much cheaper than the supermarkets. However, some say that depending on the length of time the fruit has been on the street, it might have absorbed toxins from passing traffic. This applies in particular to the watermelons during September and October which are shipped in from the south and piled into outdoor cages or containers and left there until sold, which could be a few days, a week, or even longer, depending on turnaround.

Special/unusual foods

Despite its price, Stockmann has a wide variety of more exotic/ethnic products. Otherwise consult *Chapter 6: Eating and drinking.*

New Age and health-food

- **Put' K Sebe** (The Inner Path), which is just past the watch factory on the right as you go up Leningradsky Prospekt from Belorussky Vokhzal is similar to a New Age store with a small but interesting food section featuring vegetarian products as well as other health foods and vitamins.
- **Lavka Zhizni** on Prechistenka, to the right within the first block from the Ring Road (heading to metro Kropotkinskaya). has a homeopathic section featuring Nature's Way herbals.

Expat guide: Moscow   **12/Staying solvent**

Alcohol

Can be brought from many places. Be careful of buying Russian vodka unless it is the best - Stolichnaya. See also *Chapter 6: Eating and drinking.*
Wine is more expensive than the very palatable Russian champagne of which the sweet stuff abounds. If you like very dry champagne, ask for Brut champagne, but remember you won't find it everywhere. *Soekhoi* is off-dry while *pol-soekhoi* is half-dry.
It's worth trying Georgian and Moldovan wines while you are in Russia as they are very reasonably priced.

Markets for non-food items

You might be tempted to visit the other general markets (such as Luzhniki), but be guided by Russian friends before going as these are said to be plagued by thieves and ethnic trouble erupts now and again. You'll also be a very visible target as a foreigner if you don't speak Russian. Make sure you carry your valuables close to your body, and leave any jewellery or expensive watches at home.
It's not unknown for vendors to be willing to return your money if you return your purchase instead of insisting on exchange. Of course, keep whatever documentation you can, or get him to sign the box or instruction leaflet to prove that you purchased the item from that particular stall.

- **Mitino** Radio/electronics market; *(Pyatnitskoye Shosse; metro: Tushinskaya; open daily from 07:30 -18:00).* See under 'Purchasing electrical appliances' below.
- **Gorbushka** *(Ulitsa Barklaya, next to Bagrationovskaya metro station. Open Saturday and Sunday)* Small household appliances and home electronics such as television sets, video recorders, blenders, kettles, toasters and irons. You will find low- and mid-range models here, not expensive or top of the range equipment. Prices vary according to brand rather than between vendors. The majority of vendors are registered as private companies and have city-based shops or offices. Guarantees are usually offered and you might be asked to take the guarantee to the store for an official stamp. You can exchange purchases for up to two weeks after you buy them.
- **Savyolovskaya** electronics and clothes *rynok (metro: Savyolovskaya).* Two large indoor markets together comprising the electronics *rynok*, with prices up to 20 or 30% less than in the centre. There is also a clothing market which forms part of the same building. Look out for the Vietnam market on two or three floors next door with cheap clothing from Vietnam.
- **Fili** *(metro: Filyovsky Park; open weekends)* Very overcrowded, be careful if you take children there as it's difficult to keep tabs on them. Sometimes it's difficult to even get near to the stalls. Wide variety of pirated audio cassettes, video cassettes (English movies too), computer programs for sale. Many vendors will be willing to test play the item before selling and give you a signed receipt stating their stall number in case you wish to return a faulty product.
- **Pet market** *(42 a Bolshaya Kalitnikovskaya Ulitsa)* this is the place to come to if you want to buy a pet or pet supplies.

213

Expat guide: Moscow   **12/Staying solvent**

Buying CDs, audio and video cassettes, English-language films

The main CD market is Fili Park *rynok*, though Izmailovsky has reasonable stocks. Several blocks from metro Bagrationovskaya, the market is separated from Fili Park by a road. It is open only on Saturdays and Sundays. The vast majority of recorded goods sold at the CD market are unlicensed or pirated. If the item is unlicensed some say that it is the vendor who is breaking the law for selling it, and not you for buying it although you could be accused of supporting piracy.

Some vendors, if not pushed for time, will try out a CD for you before you buy it. It depends on your morals and your sense of indebtedness to Bill Gates whether you will choose to buy a pirated item. Local authorities seem to turn a blind eye to the practice, although repeated efforts are being made by local performing artists to introduce some type of copyright restriction. If you prefer not to purchase pirated work, then you can always buy them at UK high-street prices in a shop in the centre (Try Soyuz on Old Arbat).

You can buy compact disks and audio and video cassettes, software programs, also playstations and other paraphernalia. It is possible to buy games cartridges for the playstations. Playstations that have been bought over by expats from the UK do not seem to play games bought at the market (perhaps they have some built-in anti-pirate device?)

You should be forewarned that the risk of buying a dud is rather high but at the prices at which these products are sold, ($3 per CD (computer/audio) ($1 per audio cassette) ($6 per video cassette, English movie), you can afford to take a risk. The chances are that duds will be replaced if you return them. Simply ask the vendor for a receipt stating his stall number, the date and his signature.

Note that there are also many outlets in subways which stock CDs tapes and videos. Some of the best for English-language movies are the underpasses at Smolenskaya and Oktyabrskaya. The bookshop at Progress stocks a limited but up-to-date range of videos.

Remember to check whether a tape is VHS or PAL format and whether it is compatible with your video system if it is not a multi-system machine.

At the time of writing, the mayor had plans to consolidate all street sales into two or three markets only so as to control sales and levy extra taxes on CDs and videos.

Carpet market

It's possible to buy carpets from Central Asia at the Izmailovsky Market. If you are after a good price, go nearer to closing time or on a bad weather day when customers will be fewer than usual. Prepare for some hard bargaining otherwise. One expat recommends a Turkmeni carpet dealer *(Melegoch tel: 463-6688)* who has a wide range of rugs from Dagestan to Afghanistan. His prices are also said to be reasonable.

Expat guide: Moscow   **12/Staying solvent**

Furniture

There are many *'mebel'* stores in Moscow, all varying in price and none so eagerly awaited as Ikea which is billed to open its largest outlet in the world in Khimki on the north-west outskirts of Moscow, very close to Sheremetyevo airport. The 30,000sqm Ikea store will be linked to a mall with some 25 boutiques, a food court, entertainment centre, multiplex cinema and bowling alley. Ikea plans to complete a further three shopping centres in Moscow in the next few years.

Beds

Until Ikea opens its first Russian store in Khimki in March 2000 (if it does, given its dispute with the government over projected import duties), try the following:
- **Home Sweet Home** *(tel: 248-4054; 12 Savvinsky Pereulok)* sells Sealy Posturepedic beds.
- **Domino** *(tel: 231-9388; 39 Ulitsa Pyatnitskaya)* furniture sells simple beds of Scandinavian/Italian design.

Electronics repairs wizards

These can usually be found by word-of-mouth. Two names that have been recommended are:
- **Yura Zhdanov** *(tel: 459-0434 (w); tel: 732-2664 (home after 19:00)* is also able to fix telephones, fax machines and most electronic items.
- **Vartan** *(tel: 232-0000 pager # 14941)* repairs all electronics, computers, CD drives, hard disk and installation problems. He is said to be excellent and reasonably priced.

Purchasing electrical appliances

- **Mitino** Radio/electronics market *(Pyatnitskoye Shosse; metro: Tushinskaya; open daily from 07:30 -18:00)*. Stalls sell short-wave radio parts, electronics, small appliances and computer parts. You can also find old parts and trade in your computer. Some say it has the best and cheapest selection of computer software and hardware and also electronic and electric goods. Very busy on weekends, good prices, though quite far from the centre, and there's quite a crush if you go by car over the weekend. It is not as crowded during the week and you don't need to pay an entrance fee. Thursdays or Fridays are said to be better bets than a Monday
- **Savyolovsky rynok** *(metro: Savyolovsky)* is a more comfortable, enclosed market (open during the week) which features some stall holders from Mitino with slightly higher prices and a smaller selection of appliances. Nevertheless, prices on some items are cheaper than what is available in the centre.
- **Dial Electronics** *(tel: 916-0010)* which has more than one outlet, is said to have reasonable prices.
- **Domino** *(tel: 231-9388)* and/or **Partiya** are part of the same chain although Domino also has furniture and Partiya usually has a larger selection. Prices are reasonable, delivery can be arranged, and you can enjoy the perk of a

discount card after the first purchase. The largest and the newest of the Domino shops is at Oktyabrskaya Ploschad.

- **TsUM** store near metro Okhotny Ryad and the Bolshoi has a good selection
- **Gorbushka** is the weekend market at metro Bagrationovskaya near Fili Park. (The big market right outside of the metro, not the famous CD market
- The market at **metro Rizhskaya** is supposedly better than Gorbushka.
- The electronics kiosks inside the exhibitions center at **VDNKh** also offer good prices.

Air conditioning and a/c appliances

Try the **Planet Klimat** *(tel: 923-7340)* shop on 24 Ulitsa Bolshaya Lubyanka which is said to have a good selection.

Washing-machine repairs

Byt-Lyuks *(tel: 457-3188/452-1134)* is recommended. An engineer will come to your home at the appointed time and provide satisfactory service for a reasonable price.

Christmas trees

Artificial trees are available at a wide variety of stores, prices can be steep.

Real Christmas trees

These *(yolki)* are usually to be found in various markets (try Rizhsky *Rynok*) and even at the side of the road selling for about $3 per metre for locally-produced trees and $10 - 15 per metre at least for imported trees, from about mid-December.

Bookshops

- **The Anglia British bookshop** *(tel: 203-5802; 2/3 Khlebnyy Pereulok; metro: Arbatskaya)* houses Moscow's largest English-language bookshop. Open Monday - Wednesday 10:00 - 19:00; Thursday 10:00 - 20:00; Saturday 10:00 - 18:00 and Sunday 11:00 - 17:00. Order service available.
- **Biblio Globus** *(tel: 928-3567/ 925-8232; 6 Ulitsa Myasnitskaya; metro: Lubyanka; open Monday - Friday 10:00 - 19:30; Saturday 10:00 - 19:00)*. Sells both English and Russian books
- **Dom Knigi** (House of books *(tel: 290-4507/290-3580) Novy Arbat; metro: Arbatskaya* sells children's books, art books icons, maps, books in English, old records, stamps, computer supplies, cards - worth a visit simply to explore.
- **American Bookstore** *(tel: 241-6558; 8/10 Denezhnyy Pereulok; metro: Smolenskaya)* sells US, Canadian and Latin American books with Russian interest. Open Monday - Saturday 10:00 - 15:00; 16:00 - 19:00. It is associated with the British bookshop but is much smaller. Try the Russian bookshop adjacent which stocks stationery and sometimes sells English books at better prices than the American bookshop next door.

Expat guide: Moscow   **12/Staying solvent**

- **Shakespeare & Co.** *(tel: 231-9360; 5/7 1st Novokuznetsky Pereulok;, metro: Paveletskaya; open 11:00 - 19;:00; Sunday: 12:00 - 17:00)*. New and used books most of which are in English.
- **Progress bookshop** *(Zubovsky Bulvar; metro: Park Kultury; open 10:00 - 19:00)* is worth looking at for its small range of English books, used to be well known for its Russian/English translations of literary works. Also good for stationery, gifts, wrapping paper.

Buying tickets for Bolshoi and other venues

- **Anton** *(tel: 438-7217 after 21:00; speaks only Russian)* is able to deliver tickets for orchestra stalls, or amphitheatre and also cheaper seats, from about $35 for the best seats.
- **Intourist** desk *(tel: 924-2585)* Can sometimes offer you good quality and cheap seats and may still deliver tickets.
- **Ludmilla** *(tel: 919-6660)* can get you good seats at good prices. Specify what type of seat you are looking for when booking.
- Touts outside the Bolshoi sell tickets before performances, but go as late as you can to get the best price and always check the date on the ticket before you buy.

Antique markets

Try the market down the small street off Bolshaya Nikitskaya (near the Tass building). Look upstairs as well.

- **Russkaya Starina** Ulitsa Petrovka, selected items, expensive
- Entrance to the **Shon Gallery** at the museum of Arts of Peoples of East, Nikitsky Bulvar.
- **Gelos** sells icons, jewellery, furniture but do not offer help with export permits.
- **54 Frunzenskaya Naberezhnaya** look out for the basement run by Valeri who used to be a museum restorer.

Purchasing serious art and antiques

When looking to buy art from a gallery, the owner or staff should be knowledgeable and helpful, and it helps if they speak English. They should also have a good selection of high quality art at good prices, and the cost of processing the Ministry of Culture paperwork, shipping and valuation for insurance documents should be clearly specified.

Do not pay and then leave it to the gallery owner to ship the paintings otherwise the paintings may not be guaranteed to arrive at their destination.

The Tretyakov Gallery offers official valuations which includes documents citing origin and valuation. The gallery will also list the painting in their database and you will be charged 100% of the valuation price when you eventually take the painting out of Russia.

- **Lida** *(www.aha.ru/delya)* has a booth at Izmailovo
- **NB Gallery** *(tel: 203-4006)* is at 6/2 Sivtsev Vrazhek (suite 2) e-mail: *nbgallery@glasnet.ru* and speak to Natasha or Anya
- **Mir Iskusstva** in Petrovksy Passazh caters for the upper end of the market

217

Expat guide: Moscow　　　　　　　　　　**12/Staying solvent**

Framing artwork

- The small shop in front of the **Central House of Artists** *(Centralniy Dom Khudozhnika)* has a selection of frames for sale at very reasonable prices. You purchase the frame and then take it and the artwork to the framer (Oleg) who has a tiny office just to the right of the front entrance.
- **Rosizabaget** on Pokrovka *(tel: 924-9827)*
- **House of Artists** at 228 Kuznetsky Most, across from an English-language bookstore has a large selection of frames and mounting. Turn-around time is about a week.
- **NeoArt** *(tel: 250-4499)* 22, 1st Tverskaya-Yamskaya offers a good selection of frames and fillets and will take about a week to complete the order. However, orders can be fulfilled overnight if you pay a premium. You could also negotiate a discount if you have a few things done simultaneously.

Exporting souvenirs/antiques

You need to have all VAT receipts and any other receipts otherwise goods will be confiscated.

You should obtain an export certificate which is valid for about one month. You need to take photographs of the furniture, together with your passport to the Ministry of Culture. Phone in advance to ascertain processing hours. The certificate is issued in the name of the exporter. If you are using a moving company (strongly recommended), ask them if they can take care of this for you. You may or may not obtain a certificate depending on the rarity or age of the item. You could also try asking the store from which you bought the item to give you a written guarantee of repurchase.

Jewellery repairs

A recommended jeweller has a shop at 6 Ulitsa Baltiiskaya (turn right off Lengingradsky when the road splits). The shop is round the back. Work is said to be quick and impeccable.

Purchasing sheet music

There are a number of places where you can purchase sheet music:

- **Mir Muzyki** on the Garden Ring, just to the east of metro Mayakovskaya and south of metro Novoslobodskaya
- **Nocturne** on Leninsky Prospekt
- **Accord** on Nizhnaya Maslovka

Paying for travel by credit-card

During volatile movement of the ruble you open yourself to risk if you are billed in rubles at that day's governing rate as the credit-card merchant has up to a year to submit it when they would reconvert it back to dollars at the ruling rate (some months later). If the ruble keeps sliding, you stand to win. The best way to hedge your bets is to call an agent in your home town and ask them to issue a ticket in dollars or whatever currency suits you, in Moscow.

Expat guide: Moscow   **12/Staying solvent**

Always check your credit-card statement and see that details match the transaction. There have been instances where statements have shown amounts in currencies other than rubles and dollars, and amounts have been for more than the quoted ticket price, and for aircraft carriers other than the one you actually flew on.

Insurance (household and medical)

John Wason *(www.johnwason.co.uk)* is recommended as being easy to access for expat insurance via their website. They are also said to be professional and reliable.

Accommodation

See *Chapter 4 - Finding accommodation* for tips on staying solvent in that context.

Customs duty

Judging by the experience of a number of expats, it would seem that if parcels are sent to an office address they are more likely to be charged import duty (around ECU7/kg at the time of writing, but check for current rates). If you wish to use an address other than an office address, you could rent a box at the International Post Office on Varshovskaya Shosse which costs just under $10 per month.

When ordering or arranging for a package to be sent to you, try and arrange confirmation from the sender saying that the contents of the box are items for personal use and not for resale.

There appears to be a limit of $100 stated value, which when exceeded may cause the item to be saddled with import duties.

Never enclose any money in shipments of any kind as it is likely to be stolen. Many expats have also found that part of the contents of a box or package are missing upon receipt if the box is routed through Customs. One way of getting round this (if you can) is to ask for a complete list of contents to be faxed to you and a copy attached to the box so that you can compare copies when you arrive to examine the contents of the box.

The sender should not put a high value on the contents list of a package as duties as high as 30% (after postage) are being levied on the value of the contents. With pressure being put on Customs to raise revenues, incoming expats with more than 50kg personal baggage are now being charged duty on the excess. In March 1999 the charge was ECU4/kg for each kilo over 50kg if the goods constituted your personal belongings and were not for resale. The charge increases to ECU7/kg if it was not declared as part of your baggage whether arriving separately or not. Try to obtain a bill of lading which proves that the goods are for your personal use. Rates are different if the goods are processed under your company's name or under your own name.

Expat guide: Moscow   **12/Staying solvent**

Leaving or entering Russia - how much money to take in or out?

In late summer of 1999, this became a very grey area following the promulgation of a law regarding just who and who could or could not take out money. It proved to be an open day for Customs officers in terms of their flexible interpretation of the law. Check with your embassy for the latest details regarding what is or is not allowed. At the time of writing, it was not worth bringing in more than $500, for despite the law saying that you have the freedom to take in as much as you like, the airport police may choose to see this differently and even charge you a 'premium' for the 'right' to bring in the extra amount.

Don't fall for Customs officers asking for a bribe to let you bring in large amounts of money, nor asking to confiscate the money and offering you a 'receipt' in lieu of the money which you would receive once you flew out of the country again. According to the current law, expats say that as a non-Russian citizen, you can bring in any amount you wish as long as you declare it. On the other hand, some expats say the law is of little concern to the Customs officers and it's worth bringing in only $500 and using your debit and credit cards to get extra money out while you are in Moscow.

Up until the change in law, it was the case that you could not take out more than $500 without supporting documentation proving that you have legally brought the money in with a completed and officially stamped Customs declaration.

Some departing non-residents were given the option of changing their dollars for rubles at an extortionate rate at the exchange window near the Customs section or changing it into traveller's cheques, though on occasion, the exchange clerk sometimes said that traveller's cheques were not available, thus leaving you with the option of changing to rubles or handing your money to friends. However, as the law clearly does not discriminate against taking traveller's cheques out the country, more and more travellers are resorting to converting their money into traveller's cheques. Try American Express, Visa and MasterCard.

Be careful once you step outside the airport after leaving Customs if you have declared a large amount of money - there is speculation that the Customs staff may be advising accomplices outside the airport of the fact that a person with a lot of money is passing through the airport.

Airport baggage overweight fee

Seemingly the Customs staff at the airport have informal quotas to fill and as airport traffic has decreased since the crisis, the focus is on those passengers who visibly have overweight baggage.

It seems that if you go through the red line to declare $500 plus, you are likely to be assessed for overweight baggage as well.

One expat recommended that you pay a porter to ferry you through the Customs maze quickly and cheaply. Another says that it's only Russians and CIS citizens who are likely to be targeted, while yet another suggests going through the green line.

220

13/Working matters

It used to be the case that expats could flock to Moscow and expect high salaries and excellent packages. Then things changed. First, an increasing pool of experienced Russian managers began to compete with the expat sector, although some doubted how quickly it would take to replace the 'expert' expat in the long term. Nevertheless, it was always accepted that many top posts in most Western-owned businesses would still be taken by expats, while second-level expatriate management would be replaced within an estimated three or four years.

The major factor in this equation is the high cost of employing expats contrasted with employing a Russian manager who can often offer similar expertise (depending on the circumstances) at a far lower cost.

Depending on the sector, and particularly in those sectors where Russians still aren't up to Western standards, job requirements have become more stringent in the sense that professional qualifications, work experience and, invariably, Russian language skills, are all now expected.

In addition to this tightening up of expectations, the economic crisis in Russia has certainly thrown a spanner in the works in terms of expat employment opportunities. Apart from anything else, most Western firms downsized dramatically in the wake of the breaking crisis, once the dust had settled, the wait-and-see period had expired, and they accepted that it might take between two and five years for economic conditions to return to the level of activity that was at play before the crisis broke.

All will depend on what happens with the succession to the Presidency which could take place anytime up to June 2000. Not many firms are likely to invest in Russia until they know just which way the economic wind will blow, and this won't be determined until the new president has outlined his policies, a process which could last several months after his appointment. In the meantime, many firms keen to maintain a presence in Russia, and indeed, loathe to put at risk their financial commitment to Russia, will continue to maintain a skeleton staff at worst, and a fully-functioning but slimmed-down operation at best.

What happens once Russia picks itself up off the ground and dusts itself off is anyone's guess. However, the major factors that drive firms to invest in Russia in the first place are not likely to go away. The fact that Russia is an emerging market is attractive in itself. Add to this the potential 146 million consumers and it becomes difficult to ignore. There are those who dismiss the size of the market, saying that the only market worth pursuing is in Moscow, which is 9 - 12 million in size. Others say that competition has reached such a peak in their own countries that they have no choice but to look at Russia for further development.

These positive reasons to invest in Russia are contradicted by the notorious taxation and legal systems as well as the endemic cancer of corruption. Although many firms believe these are surmountable, others are simply not interested in

Expat guide: Moscow   **13/Working matters**

facing this challenge. To muddy the waters further, there was evidence in April 1999 when new visa restrictions were introduced, that expats were not wanted in Moscow.

Business visa

Agencies both inside and outside Moscow offer services whereby they can either obtain and/or organise the renewal of your visa. As mentioned above, increased complications are being added to the visa system and you will need specialised assistance in obtaining your visa.

Two companies with significant experience in assisting expats are:

- **Andrew's Consulting** *(tel: 258-5198; fax: 258-5199; 25/3 Tsvetnoy Bulvar; e-mail: visa@actravel.com)*
- **Infinity** (formerly IRO Travel) *(tel: 234-6555; fax: 234-6556; 13 Komsomolsky Prospekt)*

Consult the book **Russia Survival Guide** by Paul E Richardson, published by RIS Inc, Vermont, for in-depth (though not necessarily up-to-date) detail on the nitty gritty of what is required. Do not take any chances with your visa, either in overstaying your limit or losing the visa.

Accreditation/work permit

A new decree promulgated in March 1999 states that foreigners working for Western representative offices need to obtain work permits. This directive is in contrast with previous requirements which stipulated personal accreditation only. This would force companies with expatriate employees to explain why Russians could not be substituted for foreigners in that particular position.

It is estimated that a large amount of paperwork and bureaucracy is required to process a work permit, which may take up to two months and cost about $300. **Andrew's Consulting** *(tel: 258-5198)* can do the necessary paperwork on your behalf and they also offer discounts for group applications.

Temporary employment

It is possible to obtain temporary employment. You can either approach Kelly Services *(tel: 956-6066/961-1407; e-mail: kelly@kellycis.msk.ru)* or network like crazy. Alternatively, try posting your needs on the Expat-list. You will need to have the correct paperwork, otherwise you and the company you are working for would get into trouble with the tax authorities.

Severance pay

Make sure you have a clause in your contract that concerns severance pay. With Russia being such an unstable business environment, it is worth covering yourself in the event of the next crisis, which is seemingly always round the corner.

Evidence for this was seen after the August 1998 crisis when a number of foreign companies simply closed their doors with no regard for the future welfare of their employees.

Expat guide: Moscow   **13/Working matters**

Employment agencies

If you are in Moscow and want to either swap jobs locally or seek a job elsewhere, try the following recommended agencies:

- **Antal International** *(tel 935-8606; fax: 935-8607; e-mail: antalrus @online.ru)* has offices all over the world
- **Korn/Ferry International** *(tel: 956-4387; fax: 956-4388)* based in Moscow, has a global network which consists of 71 offices in 42 countries
- **Heidrick & Struggles** *(tel: 232-1145)*
- **Commonwealth Resources** *(tel: 755-6868; fax: 956-6849; e-mail: map@cr.dol.ru; www.cr.ru)*

Before signing a contract

Issues which concern companies in Russia, and which should therefore be discussed with your employer before signing a contract, concern his policies on:

- Redundancies
- Terminations
- Voluntary vacation (unpaid)
- Leave (paid how?)
- Salary reductions (what percentage in what circumstances?)
- Bonus system frozen/cancelled (under what circumstances?)
- No reductions or actions taken (guaranteed?)
- Salary payment:
  - ⇒ Ruble-based salary
  - ⇒ In rubles, tied to the US$
  - ⇒ In US$ (rubles converted)
  - ⇒ In US$ (from abroad)
  - ⇒ Other
- How does the company that is interviewing you plan to pay salaries to local employees in the midst of a crisis?
- If you are to be paid in rubles what method will be used;
  - ⇒ Fixed ruble salary
  - ⇒ Fixed ruble salary, indexed monthly
  - ⇒ Fixed ruble salary, indexing possible, but not certain
  - ⇒ Short-term measure until exchange-rate stabilises
- Would company consider changing to a ruble-only based salary?
- Ask if firm would reduce any expatriate benefits such as
  - Housing costs (to what degree)
  - Rest and recreation opportunities
  - Living allowances
  - Home leave
  - Other
  - No reductions
- Ask if your company is considering introducing 'cost-sharing' of benefit costs with employees?
  - ⇒ Health insurance

223

Expat guide: Moscow ___ 13/Working matters

⇒ Meals
⇒ Car
⇒ Salary US$/Ruble conversion cost
⇒ Other

- Potential for continued tenure with the company, should your position be made redundant in the event of a crisis
- Contingency planning scheme in the even of unrest/evacuation

Personal income tax services

Though there are a number of companies which could assist, International Audit *(tel: 230-1135)* has been suggested as a personal tax service for expatriates living and working in Russia. Tax returns are prepared in Russian and English.

Business culture

It is recommended that you read the book **From Nyet to Da** by Yale Richmond. Although the book is slightly out of date, it still has a lot of valuable advice to offer whether you are a business person or not.

Some people say doing business in Russia is a nightmare. However, if you go to Moscow with the understanding that Russians will have a different understanding of business and not expecting them to be clones of your country, the culture shock will not be as profound as it could be.

Some tips include:

- Always confirm appointments and don't be disappointed if you are let down
- Use business cards, the more stylised, the better. Your card will be printed in Russian on one side, and in English on the other side. Always check that your name does not translate into something funny, or rude. This is not unknown.
- Always make contingency plans for heavy traffic in Moscow which can ruin plans, especially during snowy weather.
- Don't rely on verbal agreements.
- Business women are not as regularly encountered as they are in the West.
- Priorities are calculated in a different way. Westerners tend to rely on getting the task done in the quickest, and most practical way, whereas to Russians, relationships come first. It is worth taking time to build up a relationship before relying on trust.
- It is not unusual for vodka to be served during a business meeting. Your worth may be judged by your ability to make toasts, drink vodka, and hold your liquor without collapsing. If you find this difficult or inconvenient, you might be advised to find imaginative ways of disposing of your vodka without offending your hosts.
- Despite the forward-thinking strides made by Russians in business, they are still dogged to a certain extent by the more rigid, hierarchical mentality left over from Soviet days when it was expected that you were told what to do and were not expected to show initiative. Managers in charge of Russians have been heard to lament the lack of initiative and creativity in their

Expat guide: Moscow　　　　　　　　　　　**13/Working matters**

Russian employees who seem to prefer the more autocratic rather than the *laissez-fair* Western style of management.

- Precedence is given to the period from New Year's Eve through Russian Christmas (7 January) for festive celebrations although work continues as normal on 25 December. Men are honoured on Defender's Day in February, and women are given gifts and flowers on Women's Day in March, so be sure to buy flowers or a small gift for any woman working with you or for you. May Day/Victory day celebrations in early May are also very important, with business taking a back seat.
- If invited by Russian business colleagues to visit a *banya*, try to go. It's a Russian way of breaking down barriers and getting to know you on a less formal basis.

Unemployed spouses seeking employment

There are many openings for native English speakers, especially those with teaching English as a foreign language (TEFL/TOEFL) qualifications and experience. Some companies seek teachers (especially with group-teaching experience) to teach their Russian employees English. Some will ask for American-English experience while others will prefer British-English experience. You may also find freelance work, as well as unpaid work where you teach English to a Russian, in return for Russian lessons.

You will need to clear your visa conditions with regard to working, for if you don't have permission and an entry visa does not automatically entitle you to work, you will be infringing Russian law.

If you have any medical experience, or any teaching experience, you may very well be able to obtain a job on site with one of the international schools established in Moscow.

If you want to use your brain and money is not your main motivator, there are many opportunities for employment, especially within the international schools and in several charitable organisations.

Looking for a job outside Russia, from inside Russia

If you happen to have a job in Russia which looks as if it will be terminated, either by yourself or your employer, try the following websites:

- *www.ntl.ids.ac.uk/eldis/ukstruct/uk_govl.htm*. **Eldis** is a UK-compiled jobs database listing aid organisations around the world and others.
- *www.iscworld.com* **International Jobs Report** offers free notification of all overseas jobs. Automated mailing lists allow you to select categories by discipline.
- *www.overseasjobs.com/index.html* **Overseas Jobs Web**
- *www.monster.com* **The Monster Board** allows you to select jobs by category, location or keyword and tenure.
- *www.aesc.org/* **The Association of Executive Search Consultants** shows a member listing of global head-hunter agencies.

225

Expat guide: Moscow   **13/Working matters**

- *www.pinkertons.com/pgis* **Pinkerton Global Intelligence Services (PGIS)** posts the Eye on the World, every Monday, on e-mail, for free.
- *http://browse.help-wanted.net/* **AOL NetFind** allows you to search jobs as posted on Internet News Groups. Post your resume for free, or search extensive resume database.
- *www.escapeartist.com/expatriate4/jobs.htm* **Escape Artist** lists links to expatriate jobs overseas.
- *www.avotek.nl/jobs.htm* **Avotek International** jobs and links page; international headhunters, address guides; world-wide employment contacts, jobs, links, recruiters.
- *www.worldbank.org/html/extdr/employ.htm* employment opportunities at the **World Bank Group.**
- *www.expatexchange.com/career.htm* business and career centre.

Other international career resources

The following is a list of international jobs resources for expatriates. Use your search engine to locate the sites listed:

- **ADIA** - Adecco in 40 countries around the world.
- **Career Magazine Online** - Job openings, articles - resume data-base.
- **Council on International Education Exchange** - Student programs - work abroad for US students.
- **Cornell University** - International Jobs
- **Fred's International Job Pages** - Fred's career bulletins list current job openings in major multinational corporations, most are investment-banking companies.
- **Hunter Associates** world-wide placements
- **Harrison Jones Associates** - International recruitment consultants
- **IREX** jobs and internships: IREX maintains a resume bank to fill long and short-term positions in five field offices in Central Europe and the New Independent States.
- **Internet Job Locator**
- **JobServe**: Overseas positions - the JobServe Database features current permanent positions.
- **MSI International** - a search firm placing highly qualified senior management candidates in executive positions with Fortune500 and other leading businesses across the country.
- **Interskill Services** provides specialist professional services, particularly in the area of information technology, to blue-chip companies internationally.
- **International Computer Professional Associates** assists multinational companies in recruiting technology, marketing and finance professionals for jobs in Japan, Hong Kong, Singapore, China and the US Pacific Coast.
- **Prospective Management Overseas** - Belgium
- **Recruiters On Line (RON)** The network is a virtual community of employment firms world-wide. With over 5,000 participating companies it boasts that they are the world's largest online association of recruiters, search firms, employment agencies and professionals.

Expat guide: Moscow   **13/Working matters**

- **ProNet Global Business Directory** lists over 200,000 online businesses from 76 countries.
- **Top jobs on the Net** -a UK-based international job site includes a jobs search engine.
- **USAID** *(www.usaid.info.gov)*

14/Visitors

Inevitably, you will have much interest from friends and family who might wish to take advantage of the opportunity of your stay in Moscow to visit you.

On the surface this might sound wonderful, but after you've been round Red Square for the umpteenth time and explained the significance of St Basil's, you will start to tire of the novelty.

If you work and still have to organise the entertainment of visitors, your task will be even more taxing as your visitors are likely to be entirely dependent on you for almost all their needs.

Arranging visas for your visitors

This can be a complicated and seemingly trying procedure and is best left to the professionals. Try:

- **1st Travel** (*tel: Tourism - 246-7278; 247-1399; airline tickets - 247-1416/1694; visas, hotels - 247-1936; fax: 247-1399 or www.1st.ru.*
- **Infinity (formerly IRO Travel)** *(tel: 234-6553/55; e-mail: visa@infinity.ru)* Has a range of invitations and offers free registration. They also offer a single entry visa processed in four days or a faster 'express' service.
- **Andrews Consulting** *(tel: 258-5198; e-mail: visa@actravel.com)*

Medical insurance

If the country where your visitors originate expects medical insurance from Russians entering that country, then all visitors from that country will be expected to supply proof of medical insurance. These include Estonia, the Schengen countries: Austria, Belgium, Germany, Holland, Spain, Italy, Luxembourg, Portugal, France) and Israel and Finland.

Accommodation

If you are unable to accommodate visitors at your home, you will need to find adequate and safe accommodation for them. Several of the more up-market hotels are open to negotiation on their rates, especially with regard to high/low season and whether accommodation is taken during the week or over the weekend. Breakfasts are sometimes included in the tariff. See list of accommodation options in *Chapter 3 - Your first weeks.*

Expat guide: Moscow   **14/Visitors**

Entertaining visitors

There are a wide variety of tourist guide-books available both in Moscow and in your visitor's country of origin which will help you and them decide just what they would like to see during their stay in Moscow.

However, if you're stuck for ideas, the following are tried and tested attractions and activities which may help fill time over a ten-day holiday:

- Meal in a Russian/Georgian restaurant
- Visit to Izmailovo Park (souvenirs)
- Visit Fili park (CDs).
- Red Square/ St Basil's/Armoury/Kremlin/Gum/Manezh
- A walk down the old Arbat
- A walk down the New Arbat
- Historical museum
- Pushkin Museum
- Tretyakov Gallery
- Ride on a river boat (spring/summer)
- Cross-country skiing in park (winter)
- A visit to Gorky Park for *shashlyk* lunch and look at the entertainment, try a bungee-jump, in summer, or go and see/join the ice-skaters in winter.
- A visit to the KGB Lubyanka museum to view its workings from the inside
- A walk in any one of Moscow's numerous parks, Krylatskoye, Kolomenskoe, Fili, Sparrow Hills, Sokolniki, Serebryany Bor, Botanical Gardens simply to show your guests that there are oases of calm and beauty right inside the hustle and bustle of Moscow.
- To see Moscow from another angle, take your visitor on a trip right around the Garden ring on the '6' bus (a Cyrillic 'b' and not a '6').
- A day trip to any of outlying towns: Sergiev Possad to see its monastery, Suzdal to see one of Russia's oldest towns; Leninsky Gory to see where Lenin spent his last days
- An overnight trip to St Petersburg by train
- Other options include hiring a private guide to take your visitor on a tailor-made tour while you are at work or contacting Patriarchy Dom Tours and registering your guest on some of their tours. Remember Patriarchy Dom does individual tailor-made tours as well. Nadia *(tel: 433-1692)* a former Intourist guide and now freelance speaks English fluently and is recommended.Also try the travel agents listed under 'Arranging visas for your visitors' above.

15/Weather

The weather is an important factor in anyone's choice when determining whether to live in Moscow or not. If you come from a similar climate you will not be deterred by this city of extremes, where winter temperatures can plummet to -30^{0}C and summer night-time temperatures can soar to +32^{0}C. In Moscow you will definitely find all four seasons, some longer and others shorter than what you might be used to. It's worth being mentally prepared for what you are likely to face throughout the year.

The section below attempts to paint a picture of the seasons and their various delights. Bear in mind that with increased global warming, winters are getting noticeably warmer.

Spring

'Mud, mud glorious mud' and 'A time of dirt, slush and puddles' basically summarises spring. There is hope in the air and friends will want to point out budding trees to new arrivals. There are no early daffodils and bluebells like there are in the UK, but sooner or later you will see displays of bulbs emerging which have lain dormant over the winter.

Don't be fooled that spring, actually means spring. In the first half of April 1998, Moscow had its heaviest snowfall of the entire winter, just when everybody was gearing up for the end of winter. This was followed by temperatures of 25 the following week.

Don't imagine there is a gradual blending of the seasons. Like most things in Russia, weather can change from one extreme to another: one day being winter, the next day but what you or I would call summer, but which is called spring, punctuated by the odd, cloudy and coolish day.

You'll go from wearing coats one day to shorts and short skirts and t-shirts or summer suits the next. So be prepared.

Some say that Moscow is at her naked worst in the month of April. There is no snow to camouflage the dead dogs, the turds, the rubbish which all emerge before they have a chance to be cleared away. After being smothered since October, the grass looks as if it will never grow again. 'Bleak' and 'drab' are probably apt words to describe the landscape.

May Day, (1 May) or Worker's Day is unofficially the start of spring and the dacha season, meaning that the weather is good enough to provoke a mass exodus of those who have 'dachas' or country cottages. They leave the city en masse on Friday nights (so schedule any trips to the airport at other times to avoid heavy traffic), taking with them seedlings and potatoes to plant. They even take piglets who have been purchased several weeks before and hand-reared in city apartments.

Expat guide: Moscow   **15/Weather**

Another sign that spring has officially arrived, is that you will see pleasure boats plying the river once again. (*see Chapter 5 - Getting around*).

Summer

The great unwashed

There comes a time in every Muscovite's life (i.e. unless he or she has a power shower or boiler), when for two or three weeks, hot water will be shut off for the routine, annual cleaning out of the hot water pipes that service individual apartment blocks.

There can't be any routine to this ritual, for no one seems to know exactly when, in advance, hot water will be shut off. When it is your turn, however, you will be notified by a notice stuck to your apartment block's entrance which will give the dates between which you can expect to have no hot water. If you are lucky, you can coincide your annual summer holiday with this period, or if the temperature reaches sweltering thirties, a cold bath could well prove to be a blessing in disguise.

No matter, one is expected to take the burden stoically, as does everyone else apparently, and just make do either with a teeth-clenchingly cold shower or with constant boiling of kettles and giant pots to make one's bath at least tepid.

This can play havoc with women's hairdos, and bad hair days are therefore far more frequent during this time. Some make do with the minimum *abloutissements,* making rides on crammed trams and metros even more of a nasal experience. Well-heeled friends out at Rosinka or Serebryany Bor are not even aware of the problem, but you could always offer to house-sit while they go on their annual vacation.

It's worth bearing this problem in mind before signing the lease on an apartment if it's something that's going to bother you, and either negotiate that the landlord agrees to install a hot water heater if you move in, or choose another flat that does have its own hot water supply. In addition, if you have more than one child, remember that it's hard enough getting them to take a bath when the water's warm. It will be doubly difficult if the water's cold.

Moscow sizzles

For a number of weeks in 1998, temperatures during the short four hours of darkness sometimes did not dip below 30. The temptation is to cool down, but all the water visible around is suspect, though you will find many Muscovites taking a dip from the banks of the Moscow river. It's jokingly said that you lose a few centimetres in height after swimming in the river, owing to its polluted nature.

Despite the pollution, or perhaps because of the pollution, fish still seem to thrive in the river sometimes producing large specimens which can actually inflict a painful bite.

Daylight

At this time of the year, hours of darkness are reduced to a minimum of about four around the summer solstice on 21 June. This is conducive to late evenings at pavement cafes and restaurants, whose gaily coloured awnings seem to bedeck most street corners. The temptation to stop off for a beer and chat after work is ever present and easy to give in to.

232

Expat guide: Moscow   15/Weather

Rain

Rain occurs mostly during the warmer months usually or when temperatures reach close to freezing. During June and July and August 1998, Moscow received an inordinate amount of rain for a place which everyone tells you is dry. Rainfall is not as light and lingering as it is in the UK, but rather short and sharp cloudbursts tending to be followed by sunny spells.

Mosquitoes

For a place that's slap bang in the middle of a temperate continental zone Moscow can be home to a plague of mosquitoes during the summer months. This is apparently because of the large amount of water lying around in ponds and marshes.

The mozzies are big and mean, but don't carry malaria.

Pukh or 'snow in summer'

Pronounced 'pookh' or if you want show the sick side of your sense of humour, 'puke' as some may do unintentionally.

You didn't know Moscow had snow in summer? No one told you? Well, you won't be able to ignore it.

For two to three weeks every year, say from the last week of May till mid-June, you can count on an irritating bout of 'summer snow' caused by the fluffy white pollen released by the female poplar tree. It will get up your nose, in your hair, in your food, and if you dare open a window, into your home. What makes it even more irritating is that it can coincide with a really hot spell when you really do need to open that window.

There's really nothing that can be done. If you are (heaven forbid) allergic to pollen and the like, it can cause much discomfort so be sure you have a good stock of effective anti-histamines and sunglasses.

The blame for this phenomenon can be laid squarely at the door of Moscow's Soviet urban planners who in 1934 instituted a quick-fix programme that set out to make Moscow green as an antidote to Stalin's mushrooming concrete jungle.

The tree was chosen as it is the fastest growing out of Russia's 30 varieties. The planners made a critical mistake by planting more females of the species (one wonders how they would differ between the two) which produces the *pukh*.

Being highly inflammable and easily collecting in corners, it poses a fire hazard especially where discarded cigarette butts are concerned, thereby increasing the fire department's workload at this time. For some reason, lift-shafts are susceptible.

For those who are curious about whether anybody has found a use for this abundant resource, it has been known that paper can be made out of it and it has also been successfully spun, though no export industry has evolved out of its abundance.

Mayor Luzhkov's known dislike of *pukh* has meant that new trees planted currently are more likely to be maples, limes and rowans - slower growing but *pukh*-free. Estimates put the population of poplars in Moscow at 400,000.

Expat guide: Moscow   **15/Weather**

Dacha season

From early June till the end of August, many families ship their kids out to their country houses or dachas, which can take the form of a luxurious country house with all mod cons to a hand-me-down two-room shed with an outside latrine and no electricity. Most dachas have in common one thing, and that is some ground usually rigorously planted to provide a harvest which is then turned into jam or pickled to create much needed reserves over the winter months.

This explains why Moscow is largely child-free during the summer months as children spend this time with their grandparents or cousins while mum and dad, if they have jobs, work in the city and join the mad crush Friday night exodus to the dacha for a weekend of planting, 'shashliking' and general escape from the oppressiveness of the city.

As a foreigner you too can benefit from dacha season. Many companies hire a 'corporate' dacha, where senior level staff are able to use its facilities, usually over weekends, on a roster basis. It's also possible for individuals to club together to cover the rental of a dacha with telephone, running water and indoor toilet within reasonable driving distance from the city over the summer season.

If you're keen on doing so, it's worth starting to scout around from around February onwards. Note that the majority of dachas are used during the summer, as they don't normally have heating.

Rents can range from $100 a month to $20,000 per month depending on location and amenities.

Aktiv Estate agency *(tel: 229-7768/fax: 292-5418)* is said to have a specialist in dacha hunting

Shashlyk!!!!

It's all around you, all year through, but hidden in darkened cafes and kiosks, and it's not the same as in summer, when freshly cooked off the grill, it can give a whole new meaning to why you came to Moscow in the first place.

Once you become hooked you will, no doubt, like many expats, want to do your own *shashlyk* cooking. It's possible to buy a grill called *mangal* or *shashlychnitsa* in many a hardware store or market (try the one outside metro Sokol for dinky fold-away barbecues costing about $18).

You can use beef, pork, chicken and even fish cut into cubes of three to five centimetres square and marinated overnight. Keep your skewers away from direct heat, letting the smoke and subdued heat gently cook it. (Consult *Chapter 6: Eating and drinking*, for a recipe)

Although *shashlyk* was originally a Caucasian dish, it is now a firmly entrenched Russian institution.

Autumn

The leaves start falling in late autumn, though don't expect a Vermont-like panorama, as some leaves turn red and yellow but not all do. Leaf fall is relatively quick and simply serves to inform that summer has ended and winter is on its way. Long forest walks on balmy autumn days can be a pleasure to savour, and you will notice many fellow walkers collecting sheaves of fallen leaves to take home.

Expat guide: Moscow   **15/Weather**

Winter

Snow - there's plenty of it, enough to keep the ground mostly covered right until April and then some. Snow usually falls when the weather is between about $+4^0$C and -5^0C. Above $+4^0$C, it usually turns to rain. Most expats who are unused to snow are enchanted during the first few weeks of snow when the city adopts a different persona and shows off its historical gems to best effect. Normally grassless stretches of parkland are hidden, as well as any old rubbish that has been tossed carelessly aside and left to create an eyesore.

Snow rarely falls solidly for more than two or three days at a time, instead usually falling and settling, falling and settling. When there is heavy snowfall, expect a build-up in the traffic and for journeys to take much longer as cars are stuck in bottlenecks, gridlocks and traffic jams with speeds rarely exceeding 20km/hr. The situation is exacerbated when traffic lights vulnerable to excess moisture stop functioning.

Occasionally (as happened in late December 1998) an unexpected warm wind from the Atlantic will lead to a widespread thaw, mild temperatures of up to $+5^0$C and messy puddles of water everywhere. The cold wind from Siberia will soon reassert its authority though, and overnight, temperatures can drop to freezing, turning huge puddles of water into impromptu skating rinks.

Also be prepared for wide temperature variation where temperatures rise from -25^0C to $+3^0$C in the matter of a week and then back down to -15^0C the following week. This change in barometric pressure is cited by many Russians as contributing to heart problems and general feelings of malaise.

Snow can be magical when it falls, far more so than rain. It comes in all shapes and sizes, which supports the Eskimo's (Inuits) need to use 22 different names to describe snow according to whether it has large crystals, small crystals, round crystals, flat crystals, and so on.

However, snow has to melt sometime and it does so rapidly during the period of the thaw which can start as early as late February or early March, when the city's streets become awash with water, so much that you wonder why they don't build better drains to cope with the deluge. Cars come off worst, becoming intensely muddy only a few days after being washed. In fact, the GAI are more likely to pull you over for a dirty car than anything else, and what really gets up their noses is a number plate that is illegible because it is covered in mud.

Traffic in winter is significantly less than in the summer, as many people choose to hibernate their cars in their mini-garages, either because they don't trust their driving ability in the snow or because they wish to preserve their cars. Those who have cars have a hard time clearing them of snow every morning before driving to work if their cars are parked in the open. Very few buildings have subterranean parking lots, as many Soviet architects did not take into account the massive growth in car ownership.

During winters the Moscow city government sprays some chemical mixture over the roads and pavements to prevent them from freezing. This can ruin good shoes, so make sure you have a pair of thick durable winter shoes that can take a hammering. Slush is assiduously cleared from the roads and sidewalks and piled up in piles on the edge of the gutter. These can just as easily turn into solid, brown ice (not a pretty sight) when the weather turns cold again.

Expat guide: Moscow   **15/Weather**

When the snow has melted and a cold snap suddenly occurs, you will come across icy conditions. Dozens of people are hospitalised every year as a result of falls on ice.

Every year several Muscovites get killed by falling icicles, whenever the chance of a thaw increases. The icicles sometimes form in stalactite proportions when they form on the edge of gutters and balconies. The City maintenance department is reasonably conscientious about removing them, and often you will notice a section of pavement blocked off with metal grilles attached by red and white plastic bunting to prevent you from walking under a dangerous icicle.

Although the first snow fell on 1 October in 1998, it didn't start falling in earnest until the first week of November. In the interim Moscow experienced a very mild period with temperatures hovering between the 8 - 12^{0}C degree mark. Once the snow started falling in earnest, temperatures started to drop rapidly. In contrast, Moscow was experience temperatures in the early 20s in the first week of October 1999.

You can be sure of a white Christmas, even if the snow doesn't actually fall. Although winter officially starts on 1 December, it feels as if Moscow has been in the grip of winter for much longer. Being the longest day, 21 December has sunrise at about 09:00 in the morning and the sun sets at 15:30 in the afternoon, ensuring six hours of daylight. The twilight of dawn and sunset are long-lived, however, and light emerges much earlier and lasts later than the above times suggest.

January 1999 was exceptionally warm, with temperatures consistently above freezing and snow in full thaw

By the time February rolls round, the snow is everywhere in evidence and winter seems to have truly set in with a vengeance. February is also a windy month, which creates a wind-chill factor several degrees below the ambient temperature, making it seem much colder.

Changing the clocks

If you can speak Russian, you will have a better idea of when the clocks are changing. If you really get left behind, dial 100 and you will find out what the correct time is. The last Sunday in October is usually the date on which the clocks are turned back one hour, while the last Sunday in March is usually the day on which the clocks are turned forward. This is the same as for the rest of Europe, but does not coincide with time changes in the US, which take place approximately a week later.

Daylight

Darkness begins with sunset at 15:30 round the winter solstice on 21 December and light returns at about 09:30 the next morning. However, soon after the solstice the sun's passage northwards changes almost visibly and daylight increases day by day so that by early February, light is visible from 08:00 and remains until about 17:00. By mid-June there are only four hours of darkness from about 23:30 - 03:30.

236

16/Pets

Having a pet in Moscow can soften the blow of a sometimes stressful existence. Muscovites are avid pet lovers and you will see them with their (often pedigreed) dogs (and sometimes cats) everywhere.

There is no law mandating against collecting dog mess off the streets or parks, and this can be off-putting to those who come from countries where it is an offence to allow a dog to litter the streets.

There is an inordinate number of Rotweiler dogs around and, scarily, this seems to be everyone's favourite breed. On many occasions these on-the-surface seemingly well-trained dogs accompany their owners off lead.

There is, apparently, significant interest in dog-fighting with 'tournaments' taking place at Serebryany Bor over weekends.

Buying pets

Remember to take into consideration whether you will be wanting to take your newly-acquired pet back home with you and what the quarantine laws are in your country. Pets returning to the UK have to stay in quarantine for six months at the time of writing, although schemes concerning pet passports and inoculations are under discussion, but whether these will apply directly to Russia is debatable.

- **Pet (Bird) market** or **Ptichy/Kalitnikovsky Rynok** *(42a Bolshaya Kalitnikovskaya Ulitsa. Buses # 5, 106 or trams #16 from Marksistskaya metro; tel: 270-5010. Open 09:00 to 16:00 from Tuesday - Saturday and from 07:00 - 17:00 on Saturday and Sunday).* The *ptichy rynok* is a long-time Moscow institution. Set on a large site off Maly Kalitnikovsky Proezd (not far from the centre), the market is open daily, and weekends are busy although the choice is better than on weekdays. Pets ranging from hamsters, dogs, cats, pythons, fish or birds, snakes and even monkeys are available at a negotiable price. Books and related equipment are also available. Animals such as dogs or cats are available from either dealers or private sellers whose own pets have had litters. When selecting an animal, take your time to ascertain its state of health and nature. Confirm availability of vaccination certificates.
- **Biofintes** *(tel: 932-8457; 14 Michurinsky Prospekt; metro: Prospekt Vernadskogo/Universitet open Monday - Saturday 11:00 - 19:30)* apart from fish, this small hobbyist shop also sells turtles, parrots, hamsters and mice as well as other pet equipment, aquariums, cages, and pet food.
- **Ermiya** *(tel: 200-5916; 24 Ulitsa Malaya Bronnaya; metro: Mayakovskaya, Pushkinskaya open Monday - Saturday 10:00 - 19:00 and Sunday 10:00 - 17:00)* sells hamsters, guinea-pigs, parrots, turtles and birds, as well as food products. Free veterinary consultations from 15:00 - 19:00.

Expat guide: Moscow   16/Pets

- **Mir akvariuma** *(tel: 291-9173; 22 Novinskiy Bulvar; metro: Barikadnaya; open every day except Tuesday from 11:00 - 19:00)* everything for the aquarist.

- **Priroda** *(tel: 253-5231; 16 Ulitsa 1905 goda; metro: Ulitsa 1905 goda)* sells turtles, parrots, fish and hamsters as well as pet food and accessories.

- **Priroda Rossii** *(tel: 930-7442; 68 Leninsky Prospekt; metro: Universitet and bus # 33; open Monday - Friday 10:00 - 20:00; Saturday 10:00 - 19:00).* This is said to be the largest pet store in Russia. It also has a number of branches around Moscow.

- **Volyus** *(tel: 163-0131; 12 Shchelkovskoe Shosse; metro: Shchelkovskaya)* Sells birds, fish, guinea pigs and turtles. Pet products and accessories.

- **Zoo na Kuznetskom** *(tel: 928-2450; 19 Kuznetsky Most; metro: Kuznetsky Most)* sells fish, parrots, hamsters, guinea pigs, pet food and equipment.

- **Zoomagazin na Arbate** *(tel: 241-7182; 30 Old Arbat; metro: Smolenskaya)* This large store sells spiders, snakes, rodents, turtles, birds, fish and kittens. You can also order the type of pet you want. All kinds of equipment.

Vets and veterinary clinics

You will find many private and government vets in Moscow. State clinics charge about 50c and private clinics charge about $2.50 for an ordinary examination. The cost of surgery depends on the particular type of problem involved, while vaccinations are cheaper if they are locally produced (about $2.50 at a private clinic) rather than imported vaccines which should cost about $8 in a private clinic. The following (recommended by expats) is a small selection of the vets available in Moscow:

- Lena Vladimirova, **Movet Clinic**, *(tel: 142-0104 surgery; 187-6907 home; 23 Ulitsa Vasilisy Kozhinoy (off Kutuzovsky Prospekt); metro: Filievsky Park)* Lena makes house calls and can speak some English. Her husband, who usually accompanies her, is fluent. Lena can treat, vaccinate and supply the correct certificates for exportation. She also issues International Health Certificates and export documentation. The clinic offers x-ray and ultrasound diagnosis and may be able to arrange boarding of dogs.

- **Eurovet** *(tel: 212-4773/4)* has recommended Western-trained vets and is located near Dinamo.

- **Ekovet-Kvant** *(tel: 278-4142 (24 hours) 19 Ulitsa Novo Khokhlovskaya; metro: Taganskaya)* offers housecalls, full veterinary services and also boards pets.

- **American Vet Center Animal Home service** *(tel: 252-2972/203-6275 (24 hours) 13 Novinskiy Bulvar; metro: Smolenskaya)* Dr Oleg Borisovich speaks some English and does 24-hour house calls. He charges about $50 to neuter a cat at home and is also able to issue the requisite documents for the exportation of your pet.

- Sergei Buguyenka (who speaks only a little English) at the **Sopiko clinic** *(tel: 288-4185; 4 Ulitsa Dostoevskogo; metro: Novoslobodskaya; open 09:00 - 21:00 Monday - Saturday; Sunday 09:00 - 17:00)* is highly rated. He also does housecalls.

- **Lena Vorobieva** *(tel: 451-0679 or pager in English 232-2222 #48312)* is rated highly as a cat veterinarian. She also makes house-calls and speaks

238

Expat guide: Moscow   **16/Pets**

some English. Lena will spay your cat at home for about $65 and neuter male cats for about $50.

- **Yuri** *(tel: 200-0388)* is recommended. Yuri works at a clinic during the day and does house calls at night accompanied by his wife Valeria who speaks good English. They offer a sterilisation service costing some $200 which includes collection of the cat at your apartment, operation plus five days of post-operative care and a follow up visit 12 days later for removal of stitches.
- **Center Veterinary Clinic** *(tel/fax: 921-6376/6565 (24 hours); 11 Tsvetnoy Bulvar; metro: Tsvetnoy Bulvar)* is said by some expats to be just as good as American clinics. It offers x-ray and laboratory facilities, vaccination and does certificates for export of pets. The clinic has a shop selling a variety of specialised dog foods and other pet products.

Sick animals/surgery

You may be required to give your own pet injections after the initial treatment by the vet. In addition, some vets prescribe herbal teas as medicine for pets. Administration by syringe might help do the trick.

Cat sterilization cost as little as $12 including anaesthesia in early 1999. The procedure lasts about 20 minutes and post-operational care takes about three days. There are some vets who charge higher fees for this procedure, some even as much as $200 though this involves taking complete responsibility for the cat during the entire operative and post-operative period.

If you require specific veterinary preparations, contact **Veterinarnaya apteka** *(tel/fax: 279-9630, 16, 5th Kozhukhovskaya Ulitsa; metro: Kozhukhovskaya; open Monday - Friday 09:00 - 19:00 and weekends 10:00 - 17:00).*

Cat club

- **The Expat Cat Club** *(contact David Boehm tel: 486-0046)* is a non-profit club open only to foreigners. It offers members help with registrations of their cats and kittens. Documents can be provided both in English and Russian. Original documents for cats from other clubs or organisations will be accepted and can be reissued in English The club also offers advice regarding everyday care of cats. It is hoped that meetings will be held about four times a year before the Moscow shows. Membership dues for the club are $30 per year. Paper work such as registrations, pedigrees etc are of course extra, but not expensive. Additional activities are being planned with participation of the members.

Cat smells/litter

Famously, a shortage of kitty litter seemed to mark the height of expat troubles during the start of the August economic crisis, judging by the postings on the Expat-list at that time. In case of further shortages, don't turn your nose up at Russian-made litter which is a lightweight, paper-based product and rated as an excellent product. It's recommended that you add baking soda to absorb odours.

239

Expat guide: Moscow 16/Pets

Dogs and breeding kennels

If you require local advice regarding specific breeds of dogs and/or how to obtain them contact the **Tsentralnyy klub sluzhebnogo sobakovodstva** (Central Dog Breeding Club) (*tel: 208-0209; 1 Seliverstov Pereulok*) is likely to be able to put you in touch with the relevant dog breeding club. You could also contact the **Russian Kennel Federation** (*tel: 459-0903*).

Finding accommodation with a pet

(See *Chapter 4 : Finding accommodation*)

Pet boarding

It is possible to put pets into boarding for about $14 a day, though many expats ask maids, nannies, or friends to look after their pets while they are away.

Ask any of the vets listed above for recommendations of boarding kennels. One establishment advertising in the news paper is Pet Hotel (*tel: 377-8897; pager: 961-3333 # 60101 or # 75113*).

Homeless animals

Apart from kind-hearted individuals, there seems to be no charitable organisation which takes in homeless animals. On occasion you might encounter a friendly stray or a litter of kittens/puppies in your neighbourhood - whether you should take them in or not is up to you, otherwise the chances are that the city authorities or winter weather will catch up with them one way or another.

Travelling with a pet

The first shots must be given at least a month before the flight, and a final veterinary examination within three days prior to the flight, though you should check well in advance with a vet in case procedures change. Cat owners should ask the Moscow Expat Cat Club to also certify that a cat is not a nationally protected breed.

Most airlines (e.g. Aeroflot, not BA, though, so check before booking) will allow a small dog to travel in the cabin with you, in a carrier, at your feet, as a cat would. Hard carriers are available, but the zip-up Sherpa bag which is approved for travel on many airlines is recommended. A netted portion provides ventilation.

You need to make a reservation for your pet and pay for its fare if you want to carry your pet in the cabin with you. Airline charges vary. Some airlines even rent out the bags e.g. Delta charges in the region of $90 for rental of a large dog bag plus an extra $150 for the dog.

Don't feed or water your pet from at least 12 hours prior to departure. This will prevent vomiting/and or diarrhoea on board. Don't be alarmed if your pet does not want to eat or drink much for about 12 - 24 hours after arrival. However, do ensure that food and water is available for when your pet's thirst or appetite returns.

240

Expat guide: Moscow　　　　　　　　　　　　　　　　　　**16/Pets**

If your pet is travelling in the cabin, remember that some passengers might be allergic to cats.

If, before bringing your pet from your home country to Moscow, you obtain a sedative from your vet at home, make sure you get a return flight supply as well. Sedating an animal might in some cases make the experience even more stressful for the pet, as it becomes disoriented as a result of weakened muscles. If the trip is longer than 14 hours, you might have to re-tranquillise half way through the trip. If your pet is in the hold and you're transferring to a connecting flight, request the airlines concerned to have the pet brought to you at the gate so that you can administer more sedatives if necessary (check with the vet how long the sedatives are likely to last in terms of your animal's weight).

Many cat owners do not even bother to use sedatives. An American vet suggested that an expat sedated her cat with a quarter teaspoon of liquid Benadryl, though you should check this out with your vet before trying it. Pet bags are sold at the better pet stores in Moscow.

Certificates needed for pets

Check with the authorities in the country to which you are taking the pet which certification will be required. Sometimes all you need is a certificate of good health by a vet in the country you are leaving, stating that it has had all the required inoculations. Remember that you will probably need to get the certificates translated.

Customs requirements

Expat accounts vary somewhat, but it would seem that entry into Russia requires proof that all the usual vaccines, and rabies in particular, are administered more than a month in advance of the flight but less than a year prior to the flight (depending on the age of the pet).

You must have a letter from a veterinarian (confirm that they are authorised to issue the documents by airport authorities) dated within 48 hours of travel (but not more than five days) certifying that the pet is in good health and has no signs of contagious disease. If you hear people talking about 'pre-export quarantine' this is said to be terminology which merely refers to the rabies vaccination.

Some Russian embassies might ask you to have the letter translated and authenticated, but expats report that even though a translation has not been provided, they have not encountered problems.

You may even be required to pay duty on your pet at the rate of ECU7/kg though some expats have managed to come away with paying less. It might pay you to do some homework via your shipper before you arrive.

Leaving Russia requires that your Russian vet fills in forms prior to your departure which you should be able to show at the airport. If the paperwork you have is in Russian, you'll need to have it translated into a certified copy for the US or UK to accept it.

Evacuation flights

Before you decide to bring your pet to Moscow, or even acquire a pet in Moscow, you will need to consider the issue of emergency evacuation. Could you bring

241

Expat guide: Moscow   **16/Pets**

yourself to leave your pet alone in your apartment with no thought of its future if you had, in the worst case scenario, to flee Moscow? Or would you be prepared to stay behind with it regardless of the risks facing you?

You probably won't have any choice on the evacuation flight you are allocated. Generally, these flights only allow one piece of luggage but even though space may be available in the cargo hold, and owners are prepared to pay, pets still are regarded as low-priority.

Quarantine in the UK

This is very much under discussion and various solutions to getting round the mandatory six-month quarantine period being considered. Contact **Precious Pets Valley Quarantine Kennels** *(tel: 44 1594 516326 fax: 44 1594 516140 www.preciouspet.co.uk)* for advice on the best method of transporting your pet and negotiating UK Customs' bureaucracy, as well as boarding for the duration of the quarantine period.

17/Travel from Moscow

Many expats say that although they love Moscow, they feel the need to escape on a reasonably regular basis. Many destinations are more accessible from Moscow because they are closer, and simply because it is worth exploring places you wouldn't be likely to explore from the US or UK or other Western places.

Over the winter season, many expats and Russians seek to flee the darkness and gloom and cold for hotter, sunnier climes, and plane seats become filled quickly, so ensure that you book well ahead. The same applies during the summer, when those Russians not affected by the crisis seek to take full advantage of sunny destinations.

The crisis has seen a number of airlines curtail flights or cease operation from Moscow, which will make it slightly more difficult to fly from Moscow.

If you want to get away from Moscow and explore Russia instead, there are a number of rewarding options, the major option being St Petersburg. Apart from that there are the Golden Ring cities of Suzdal and Vladimir, and Novgorod the Great, one of the oldest cities in Russia. Further to the south and on the warm Black Sea, Sochi offers a hot summer climate and rewarding and affordable skiing in winter. Visit *www.russia-travel.com* and *www.all-hotels.ru/index/en.html* for more information on travelling in Russia.

Nearby international destinations include the Baltic States, of which Estonia (Tallinn, specifically) receives rave reviews; Kiev in Ukraine, Romania, Bulgaria, Prague in the Czech Republic, Slovenia, as well as the Scandinavian countries are all worth investigating.

Further afield, popular destinations from Russia include Cyprus (which is like a home from home for Russians), Turkey, Israel and Egypt, all of which are well serviced by travel agents in Moscow.

Maps

The **Dom Knigi** (House of Books) on Novy Arbat has a map department on the first floor adjacent to one of the stairways going to the second floor.

Try the map store on **Kuznetsky Most**, just across the street from the Rifle Jeans Shop.

As you enter Izmailovo market head as if you are going through the market but look out on your right for a map supplier with a good supply especially of antique maps. Note that he is not always at his pitch and the best time to get him is in the morning.

Try searching for maps at various map sites on the Internet.

If you are looking for maps of Russia, a recommended supplier is : **Associated Cartographic Centre**, Irina Beskova or Sergey Beskov *(tel: 235-*

Expat guide: Moscow   **17/Travel from Moscow**

6523 or 196-0103) or **Topographical Maps** (sometimes at Izmailovo) Sergey Porfereveech *(tel: 261-0923)*.

Tips for travel inside Russia

- Don't take it for granted that tourist services which you are familiar with, will be available in cities or towns outside St Petersburg and Moscow. Internal travel in particular can be fraught by delays, disruptions caused by fuel shortages, overcrowding, bureaucracy etc.
- You will always need to have your passport and visa with you for registration at hotels.
- Do not expect reliable medical care and carry your own disposable syringes in case of emergency as well as any emergency medication that you think you might need.
- Drink only boiled or bottled water throughout Russia, although water in Moscow is drinkable.
- Do not venture anywhere near Chechnya nor to the Ingush Republic or the North Ossetian Republic.
- Do not share taxis with strangers; only enter a taxi without passengers.
- Do not expect your hotel room to be secure.
- Don't be surprised if you're asked, sometimes even at 02:00 in the morning, whether you require company for the night.
- Do not drink too much alcohol in public, as it renders you vulnerable
- Travel in groups rather than alone
- Be on your guard in underground walkways, the subway, overnight trains, train stations, markets, tourist attractions, airports.
- Keep a low profile, dress in a subdued manner, don't speak in a way to attract attention, do not flaunt expensive jewellery and generally do not try to call attention to yourself.
- Avoid drugs, prostitutes and criminals.
- Do not give or take bribes.
- Carry emergency embassy numbers with you and keep your passport with you at all times.

Russian Federation travel list

- Visit *www.onelist. com* and search for Russian Travel to subscribe to an e-mail discussion list focussing on travel in the Russian federation.

Two-tiered pricing system

For some years the practice of charging foreigners more for air and train fares as well as hotels and entrances to cultural places, prevailed. However, in 1997 President Boris Yeltsin signed a resolution stating that it was not legal to have two separate prices, one for Russians and one for foreigners. The decree arose out of the successful suing by an expat of a local airline who charged him a much higher fee than what Russians would pay for the same trip. However, despite the decree, many tourist outlets continue to ignore the legislation.

244

Expat guide: Moscow   **17/Travel from Moscow**

You could also try showing accreditation evidence proving that you work in Russia and are not a tourist.

In many instances, however, entrance charges are so small, that you should not resent being asked to pay a little extra, in the hope that this will go towards preserving that particular institution.

Travelling by train in Russia

This is recommended as the best and most cost-effective way to see Russia and to meet Russians who you would not normally meet. Russians like to eat while travelling, they particularly enjoy making toasts with vodka and telling jokes, so bonhomie, especially if you can speak Russian, seems to be the order of the day.

When travelling long-distance, you can choose between three levels of compartment: *lyuks* (luxury) two beds only, *kupe* (coupe) four beds and *platskart* which is the cheapest and least recommended option.

Services between Moscow and St Petersburg and the Baltics, for instance, offer facilities including a maintained toilet (though it's wise to bring extra toilet paper and soap), tea or coffee after boarding and before arrival (bring your own milk), snacks are sometimes provided as well, though these are not wildly exciting. On the Moscow/St Petersburg service, a restaurant car is available, though not on the Baltic service. Clean bed linen, a blanket and pillow, and a small towel are also provided as part of the tariff. Tickets for foreigners are sold at a separate window. If you are going in a group of more than five people, you may be entitled to claim a discount.

It is important to remember that to make up numbers, other passengers will be included as part of your group booking. For instance if you make reservations for ten people an extra two 'outsiders' will be placed in the last of your three compartments to make up twelve beds. Therefore, to make sure you can keep your privacy, especially where women only are concerned, make sure that you purchase all the tickets for the compartment.

If, as a woman, you need to travel alone, you would need to have a compartment to yourself. If you find yourself in a risky situation on a train (especially if you are female and travelling alone) remember that the cheaper the fare, the higher the risk. Choosing between travelling with gypsy women and drunken travellers, the second is regarded as a better bet as they are likely to fall asleep soon enough whereas the gypsy women are likely to wait until you fall asleep and then rob you.

If, as a single female traveller, you end up in a compartment with all males, ask the conductor to find you another place or look for a single man among female travellers and ask him to swap.

Compartment doors should be further secured by means of a nylon rope or cord or even a belt or tie to prevent opening overnight while you are asleep.

Your compartment will be identified by a train number, carriage number and seat number. When you board the train, the *provodnik* (a man or lady who has a compartment in your carriage and who is responsible for administration and problems on that carriage) will ask to see your ticket and will take it away to be returned the next morning. Don't be alarmed, but do make sure you do not leave behind your return ticket.

Expat guide: Moscow   **17/Travel from Moscow**

On the St Petersburg/Moscow trip, a snack cart sells (warm) beers, soft drinks in cans, chips and biscuits, but this is not always the case on the train for the Baltics. It's a good idea to bring your own bottled water and sandwiches or snacks to tide you over, as well as milk for tea or coffee

You can expect to pay porters in the region of a dollar for one or two bags and about 30c for each extra bag.

Generally, fellow travellers are found to be polite and accommodating.

Travelling by boat in Russia

It's possible to explore the waterways of the Volga both in a southerly (to the Caspian, White and Black Seas) and a northerly direction to St Petersburg by the 129km long Volga canal. The most popular route is between Moscow and St Petersburg. Boats only operate between May and September, when the water is unfrozen.

Although Russians might think the boats that ply these waterways are luxurious in the extreme, they are not likely, on the whole, to match Western standards, so don't overestimate the likely quality and service of your trip at the risk of disappointment. However, there are foreign tour companies which run their own ships, and these are likely to be luxurious and far more expensive.

Reservations for trips on Russian boats are available from the ticket office *(tel: 257-7112/19; information tel: 257-7109; open 09:00 - 19:00)* though trips are available lasting from three days to two weeks. It's a good way to see the Russian countryside while stopping off at various towns to visit historical attractions.

Sample journeys

Rostov	3139 km	22 days
Astrakhan	3039 km	20 days
Ufa	2177 km	14 days
St. Petersburg	1515 km	14 days
Nizhniy Novgorod	877 km	7 days

Journeys south to Konstantinovo, Nizhniy Novgorod, Ryazan and other places are reserved from the Yuzhnyy rechnoy Vokhzal *(Southern River Terminal, tel: 118-7811; ticket office: 118-0811; 11 Andropova Prospekt; metro: Kolomenskaya and bus #744)*

Trans-Siberian express

The trains run every day from Moscow. Since the crisis there has been some risk in taking the train, as local electricity companies have, on occasion, cut power to the train for non-payment of bills. There is also the risk of striking workers blockading the track to draw attention to their plight.

Some who have tried it say that seven days of travel on the Trans-Siberian without interruption can be boring. To break the monotony of the trip you should travel at night, stopping off at towns en route during the day. Every two or three days you could spend overnight in a hotel so that you can wash. Depending on the season, the landscape can be interesting or monotonous. The highlight of the trip is the sense of being a pioneer travelling across alien and unknown lands.

Expat guide: Moscow   **17/Travel from Moscow**

During winter the trains are warm, though the best time to travel is when the landscape has some variety, as during spring, summer or autumn. The Lonely Planet Trans-Siberian guide-book is recommended reading.

It is suggested that you reserve your trip through a travel agent, making provision for stops along the way. The trip is not advised unless you are well motivated. It is best by far to go on an organised tour.

Outside Moscow by road

There are a number of resorts within a relatively short distance from Moscow that few expats know about, but which are just as good as a long trip to shed you of the Moscow blues when you need it. Most of these places have heavy security and you simply cannot pitch up and request to look around the hotel prior to deciding whether you want to stay there or not. Instead, you have to make advance reservations, and supply the registration number of the vehicle you will be travelling in, which will allow you access to the hotel through the security gates when you arrive.

Vatutinki

Only recently opened (October 1998), this four-star hotel built by the president's department is luxurious and resembles a five-star hotel. Situated 35 km to the south of Moscow (follow Kaluzhskoye Shosse and turn right at the sign for 'OK' **before** you reach the sign indicating that you have entered the town of Vatutinki.).

The hotel features an indoor swimming-pool, sauna, basket-ball, volley-ball, tennis and indoor soccer, as well as aerobics area, disco, billiards, skating, cross-country skiing and disco. Prices start at about $40 a night for accommodation in the old hotel wing (quite Soviet in terms of decor) up to $80 in the modern section of the hotel and climb steeply during the end of the year break. Book through Marina Victorovna (English-speaking) *(tel: 334-6857/fax: 334-6870 or tel: 334-6103)*. Some of the rooms feature cookers and fridges so remember to take your own supply of beers, spirits and soft drinks to offset expensive bar bills. You can also cook your own food and request a toaster and kettle, though it may be advisable to bring your own frying pan. Crockery is provided.

Desna

The **Desna Sanatorium** *(tel: 428-1310)* is situated along the same road to Vatutinki (i.e. off the MKAD or outer ring road). Watch for the signs indicating a turnoff to the left. In winter, cross-country ski equipment can be hired, the complex has a swimming-pool and indoor exercise facilities.

Zavidovo

Situated some 120km to the north of Moscow and 7km off the St Petersburg road once you reach the town of Zavidovo, the Zavidovo resort *(General Manager: Kurt Ropers; tel: 937-9942/fax: 937-9950; www.zavidovo.ru)* was taken over by an Austrian company in March 1999. It consists of some 60 dachas, some of which are small, Soviet-style wooden dachas that are well, if rather rustically

247

Expat guide: Moscow   **17/Travel from Moscow**

equipped or larger (sleeping up to eight persons) while others are very modern, two-storey dachas which are more expensive. Accommodation is also offered within the modern hotel complex, in 42 rooms. If you are staying in a dacha, you will need to bring all your own supplies as there are no shops nearby.

The resort which is at the confluence of two rivers is set in spacious and picturesque grounds and boasts state of the art indoor squash courts, aerobic and weight facilities, basket-ball, table-tennis, indoor and outdoor tennis as well as horse-riding. Lessons in any of the sports are also available at extra cost, as is the hire of racquets and balls. The *piece de resistance* is the indoor glassed in heated swimming-pool and sauna, specially recommended in the middle of a heavy snowfall.

If you don't want to self-cater, you can eat at the hotel's restaurants.

Volen

The ski resort of **Volen** *(tel: 409-7000/7511/fax: 409-8111; website: www.volen.ru)* is situated some 47km off the MKaD along Dmitrovskoye Shosse. The resort comes into its own during the snow season with its ski lifts, ski lessons and other facilities. However, there are plans to introduce summer-time activities which will make it well worth going out to the resort during summer. Accommodation of various types is available in wooden chalets, with or without saunas, with prices ranging from about $30 - 100 per night.

Sergiev Possad

Sergiev Possad is ideal for a day trip, especially during the winter. Formerly known as Zagorsk, Sergiev Possad's major attraction is its monastery. However, in winter, it's possible to enjoy a Russian banquet-style meal ($25), a troika ride on a short circular route or on a single horse-drawn sleigh through the forest ($15) or a *banya* ($15) by contacting **Sveta Kurlikin** who speaks excellent English *(tel: 8-254 21870 or 8-254 44325)*. You can also take organised transport leaving Moscow at 09:30 and returning to Moscow at 17:30 at a total cost of $55 per person 50% discount for children.

Further afield
St Petersburg

How to get there

You can either catch the plane or go overnight on the train - a ticket on the Red Arrow costs about $150 per person in a first-class compartment for two. The train departs at 23:10 from the Leningradsky train station and arrives early the next morning (about 08:00). The trip is comfortable and sandwiches and tea are offered before bed and in the morning as breakfast. The train also offers 2nd class compartments which sleep four. There is also a day express train which takes some six hours to do the trip.

The train station in St Petersburg is in the centre of the city. Bring a supply of bottled water. If you travel on your own, note that you might have to share the compartment overnight with someone of the opposite sex, unless you buy up the extra beds in the compartment.

Expat guide: Moscow   **17/Travel from Moscow**

You could also choose to drive. The trip to St Petersburg is 700km in length and takes about nine hours. Potential hazards include road work and overzealous GAI officers who are particularly prevalent at the 40km/hour stretches, requiring much vigilance, though their fines are small. There are a number of places where one can stop for food and refreshment. The trip starts at Leningradsky Prospekt and takes you through the towns of Tver, Vyshny Volochek and Novgorod. You could even choose to stop over at Novgorod and explore this most ancient of towns.

Where to stay
- **Peterhof** ship-hotel, on Srelka Vasilevskogo Ostrova by the Tuchkov Bridge is a Swedish-run floating establishment with accommodation in cabins, offering upper-deck lounging area and restaurants. Staff will arrange to collect you at the train station and supply guides for one or more days' touring itinerary. Peterhof offers special weekend rates of $60 - 90 per person, including breakfast and use of sauna and gym (if that's your thing), but during the week rates are more expensive to take advantage of the business visitor.
- **Hotel Mercury** reasonably priced but out of the mainstream (five minutes by car to Nevsky Prospekt or half an hour by foot) offers a smallish suite including one room, two beds and separate lounge with TV, plus good breakfast. It costs about $140 per night. The hotel can arrange transport from the airport as well as train station and can organize a tour guide with car.
- **Pulfords** rent out apartments for short and long term stays and are said to be more economical than hotels.
- **The Deson-Ladoga** is recommended as being a clean, modern, Western-style hotel well away from the heart of the city. It costs $120 per night during peak season. The hotel is half a block away from a trolley bus stop that goes downtown via Nevsky Prospekt. It takes about 20 minutes to get to the Hermitage using the trolleybus. Book through Russia Travel *(e-mail: info@russiatravel.nl).*
- **Hotel Rus** *(tel: 272-0321),* off Nevsky Prospekt is basic, Soviet, clean and reasonable (around $100 per person per night) in a good location.
- The **St. Petersburg Hotel** *(tel: (812) 542-9411)* is also recommended situated on the river and costing slightly more than Hotel Rus but also around $100.
- **Elena Parfenova** *(tel: (812) 567-2255)* is an agent for single rooms in a three-room apartment or hostel recently renovated to European standard, furnished with all facilities including kitchen, microwave, refrigerator, bathroom with a shower. toilet, telephone. Bathroom and toilet are shared, rooms are locked. The apartment is in a house which is well-located right across from the American Embassy on Ulitsa Furshtadskaya in a secure neighbourhood. Each room costs $50 per person per room per night, $60 for two, $70 for three persons. Elena can supply pictures of the accommodation. As an interpreter/translator she can act as a tour guide and can arrange tours around the city and suburbs. She can also handle airport and station pick-up as well as cars/minivan with a driver. The hostel is a 20 or 25 minutes drive from the centre and a 15-minute walk from the nearest metro.

Expat guide: Moscow   **17/Travel from Moscow**

- **Marina** *(mara@lz.usr.pu.ru)* offers two beds, kitchen and bathroom at $40/night close to Nevsky Prospekt. Marina can also provide a driver from the airport/station and does English tours.

- A bed-and-breakfast establishment opposite metro Chernishevskaya, one stop away from the Moscow train station, is run by **Irina** *(tel: (812) 272-7847; basic English only).* Charges were $20 per night per person and $3 for breakfast. From the guesthouse it is a pleasant 20-minute walk along the embankment to the Hermitage.

- **Elena Igorevna** *(tel:(812) 316-3657)* offers two apartments each housing two people at $10 each per day. One is at Technologicheskii Institute station, the other at Chernaya Rechka.

- Two long- or short-term rooms for rent in St Petersburg are available from **Nadezhda Vladimirovna** *(tel:(812) 259-9826)* in her three-bedroom apartment, located near the metro stop Tekhnologicheskii Institut (two stops to Nevsky, three stops to Mariinsky Theater, a two-minute walk to Fontanka). She rents a large bedroom (two beds) for $170 a month and a medium-sized one for $140. For short stays, the rate is $10 a day. The apartment is spacious and the landlady is said to be tactfully helpful and a great resource on life in Petersburg.

- **The St Petersburg International Hostel** *(tel: (812) 329-8018; fax: (812) 329-8019; 28, 3rd Sovetskaya Ulitsa; e-mail: ryh@ryh.spb.su)* Three- to five-bed rooms at $15 - $17 per night depending on the season are available only five minutes from the main railway station. Accommodation is offered to all ages. There is a cyber café on the premises and the establishment is recommended as being clean and safe.

- **Dr Iwanow** *(care of Regina at: regina-noack@computerworkshop.de) offers two apartments for the use of foreigners.* One is situated in the old historical part of the town. The other is recently renovated with new furniture and only 200m from a metro.

- **The Oktyabrskaya Hotel** *(tel: 812-277-6330)* located at the end of Nevskiy Prospekt, Ploschad Vostanina just near the train station, has recently renovated and reportedly clean, comfortable rooms with TV, fridge, sofa and a decent bathroom. The best rooms are those overlooking the yard. A renovated double room will cost a foreigner about $45. Note that if you make a reservation by fax you may be charged a 25% booking fee. There are two parts to this hotel. Ensure that you go to the main section, across the square from the station, and not the section situated across Ligovsky Prospekt which might be suggested to you as more suited to foreigners.

Why you should go

A visit to the **Hermitage** does not cost an arm and a leg. Expect to pay extra for your camera. Remember that it would take something like 33 years to view each exhibit for about 30 seconds. Thus it's better to concentrate on certain portions of the gallery which most interest you rather than attempt to take everything in at one viewing.

    Peterhof, the summer palace of the Romanovs, is well worth a visit and is not expensive to visit. Although it is out of town it can be accessed by taxi, bus, or hydrofoil (only in summer, $15 one-way, discounted return), and suburban train (*elektrichka).* You pay extra for a tour of the palace, but note that although

Expat guide: Moscow **17/Travel from Moscow**

or perhaps because, it is stuffed to the gills with riches, children do tend to get bored.

The Peter and Paul fortress is free, but St Peter and Paul Church (containing the tombs of the recently re-interred Romanovs) inside the fortress charges a moderate fee for entry.

Visit the restored **Cathedral of the Spilt Blood**, which has a magnificent mosaic interior.

The restaurant inside the Peter and Paul fortress is highly recommended as having reasonable prices, good food and good service.

If you have a sweet tooth, don't forget to visit the bar/lounge on the main level of the Kempinsky Grand Europe Hotel (Nevsky Prospekt) supposedly has the best almond cake in town with good coffee.

Guides

Some expats find it more convenient, less costly and less time-consuming to catch the train to St Petersburg, spend a day seeing the sights and returning to Moscow on the night train.

*   **Sergei** *(tel: 812-520-2721)* will collect you from the station as the train arrives, offer you breakfast with his family and then take you to all the main tourist sights and then return you to the station in time to catch the evening train. Included in his fee of about $100 are petrol and entrance fees. Sergei speaks good English and has an excellent knowledge of the city's attraction.
*   **Helen Yanbukhtina** *(tel: 812 274-3169)* is recommended as a good and enthusiastic guide.

Sochi

Why you should go

If down-hill skiing is your thing, then Sochi is a must, with Russia's first four star alpine resort the **Radisson Lazurnaya Peak Hotel** *(tel: (095)255-3805)* in the Russian Alps at Krasnaya Polyana on the western reaches of the Caucasus. The cable car ski lift rises to 1,580 m and is reached by shuttle bus. Ski gear, snowboards and snowmobiles are available at the hotel. Groups of up to 15 can indulge in heli-skiing (banned in Europe) at a cost of $1,300 an hour.

Sochi also attracts skiers on its upper slopes during the autumn and spring, after which you can go swimming and sunbathing on the Black Sea coast. Sochi is also a summer favourite with the Russians. Being on the Black Sea, it is an affordable alternative to Turkey. At this time you can enjoy scorching temperatures and subtropical vegetation reminiscent of a Mediterranean resort, in what used to be Stalin's favourite vacation spot. It's also possible to go hiking at Krasnaya Polyana, rafting on the river, mountain biking, or horseback riding, all activities which can be arranged through the Radisson Peak Hotel.

In years to come, authorities plan to build Magicland, a 200ha, $25m-Disneyland-style amusement park at Maritinskaya Bay on the Black Sea, near Sochi.

251

Expat guide: Moscow   **17/Travel from Moscow**

How to get there

Daily four-hour flights from Moscow via Aeroflot to Sochi's airport, fares have become more reasonable since the crisis, dropping to $80 - 90 return and even to $30 one-way.

Where to stay

There are plenty of places to stay in Sochi (with accommodation costing between $15 and $150 per day), but this will depend on the season as your needs will vary. During summer you could choose one of the older Soviet-style sanatoriums where you can take mudbaths and physical therapy. Low prices include three meals a day together with therapy.

If the weather is very hot, your main criterion will be the availability of air-conditioning, and not all places have this luxury.

During winter, try the 37-room and six-chalet Radisson Peak Hotel at Krasnaya Polyana several kilometres out of town, which has prices starting at $80 a day (also offers ski and snowboard rentals). The hotel also offers chalets that sleep 4 - 8 people.

- Contact Dan Hites *(tel: (8622) 953205; e-mail: hites@sochi.ru)* for recommendations and information about bed-and-breakfast establishments in Sochi. There is a 30-person B&B 100m from the sea in Adler (about 20 minutes from Sochi though buses are plentiful). The use of a driver will cost extra. Roman and Alvena *(tel/fax: 8622 45-2593; Russian only)* and family are said to be terrific hosts and very knowledgeable about the region. The cost per person, including three meals and airport pick-up (about 10 minutes from the guesthouse) and some excursions depending on length of stay runs to under $20 per night.

- The Radisson has another hotel on the coast *(tel: (095) 255-3800)* and is said to cost some $200 a night. Situated on a slightly better pebbly beach with a hidden railway line.

- There is also the **Zelyonaya Roschcha** *(tel: 8862-297-0283/1021)* which is said to be overpriced at $150 per night, though others say that tariffs of $20 are available. You can stay at Stalin's dacha for $30 per night. The hotel has a pebbly beach.

- The **Hotel Zhemchuzhina** *(tel: 8 862 292-6084)* also at the seaside is more reasonably priced.

- **Dagomys** *(tel: 8 862 260-7630)* about $20 per night without food, is a resort area. Situated about 48 km from the airport.

Suzdal

Why you should go

Suzdal, one of Russia's oldest towns (established in 1024) is picturesque enough in the summer time and the trip there offers the opportunity to drink in the Russian countryside, while pondering the fact that this was the road walked by prisoners sent to labour camps in Siberia.

However, Suzdal is even better in the winter, when you can marvel at the transformed snowy landscape, indulge in cosy meals and ride snow-mobiles and horse-drawn sleighs while drinking in the culture of some 33 onion-domed monasteries, nunneries, and churches that seem to be around every corner.

Expat guide: Moscow   **17/Travel from Moscow**

Although it has long been designated a Russian tourist town, there are few amenities for tourists, in that credit cards are not accepted; there are no ATMs, and English is rarely spoken, though you might try German.

How to get there

You can take a bus from Shelkovskaya metro (end of dark blue line in the northeast corner of the city) costing about $2 for a one-way ticket (Moscow-Suzdal) with a change-over at Vladimir. This is a distance of 240km and it takes about four hours with about three 10-minute stops along the way. The coaches are quite comfortable and spacious and run on time, leaving Moscow 08:40 and 09:30.

Tickets can be purchased at the coach terminal from across the metro stop. At the Suzdal coach station there are taxis that take you to the hotel for about $1.50.

Another option is to take the bus to Vladimir from Kursky Vokhzal (watch out for the 'Vladimir' sign, across the road from Chesterfields). Buses leave when full until about 20:30 in the evening, costing about $2. Taxis to Vladimir run from the taxi rank by Kursky Vokhzal (directly opposite the Russky Bistro). Cost is negotiable at about $20 - 30 per car. Negotiate with the driver to take you further to Suzdal for an extra $5 or thereabouts.

A train service was recently introduced which is much faster than the regular *elektrichka* services and which would allow you to spend more time in Suzdal.

Where to stay

- **Suzdal Tourist Center** *(e-mail: gtk@tcsuz.vladimir.ru Russian only; 09 231 20908/ they should also make reservations for you elsewhere in Suzdal).* Note that the staff at the Touristic centre do not speak English and behave as if your presence is causing them a gross inconvenience. However, it's a great way to witness some authentic *Homo Sovieticus* behaviour. The hotel also has a separate (but rather downmarket) motel section from where you can rent a ski-doo or snow-mobile. The Suzdal Tourist Center is a big complex with an indoor swimming-pool, sauna, interesting shops (selling Lenin memorabilia next to condoms) and restaurant. Room rates run from $12 for the basic room to $18 for the refurbished deluxe rooms with new Western-standard bathroom, complete with bidet. The deluxe rooms are suites with television and in-room bar-fridge and glasses. Breakfast is included, but it's not the sort of breakfast you would write home about.
- Suzdal bed and breakfast **Likhoninsky Dom**
- As an alternative to the modern tourist center you can spend a night in a rustic lodge located inside one of the monasteries such as the **Prokhorov Convent** *(tel: 09-231-20908; fax: 09-231-20766) alternatively, call 241-8044 (Moscow Intercity Operator) and ask them to connect you with 20908 Suzdal, in Vladimirskaya oblast)* with comfortable rooms and modern bathrooms. A double costs some $25 and includes a good breakfast. Dinner is also available. The convent is open in both summer and winter.
- **Traktir Kuchkova Hotel and restaurant** *(09 231) 21507/(09 231) 20252)* is a more modern bed and breakfast establishment with a good restaurant in the basement.

253

Expat guide: Moscow   **17/Travel from Moscow**

Where to eat

- One of the two **Trappist restaurants** in Suzdal is located within that monastery (run by monks from the Trappist order, natch) and is open all year round. It has charming decor and atmosphere, staff are friendly and prices are cheap, food is good. Try the chicken 'pie'. To get there drive down the main street as if you're heading back to Moscow from the Tourist centre, turn right at the traffic lights after the long, single-storey shopping centre on your right opposite the eternal flame monument (on your left) head down that road until it takes a bend and park there. Watch out for GAI officers who are ultra-keen to make some money off foreign-plated cars, but who soon lose interest if they realise you can't speak Russian.

- There's another recommended restaurant, **Limpopo**, round the corner from the monastery, which is said to be cheaper (well under $10 a head) and have better food such as home-made *pelmyeni* and wild mushrooms baked in pots. The street-level bar is not impressive, but the restaurant downstairs is cosy and quaint.

- There are a number of pubs and cosy bars at the **Tourist centre** and a lively atmosphere on Saturday nights when people come out to make merry or groups from Moscow come for special celebrations. Dinner costs around $12 per person,

Must do

- Brush up on your Russian to find out when the **free concert by the Trappist fathers** in the museum above the restaurant takes place.
- Go for a **ride in a horse-drawn sleigh**.
- Visit the **monasteries.**
- See the **Pokrovsky Convent** which at one time was the refuge of abandoned wives of Tsars and other nobles.
- An agency at the Tourist center runs **snow-mobiling** rentals starting early December, depending on how cold the winter is. Snow-mobiling terrain runs along the frozen river - don't take any chances (one Frenchman fell in the water, snow-mobile and all). It costs about $50 per hour to rent the snow-mobile and a small extra for protective gloves and outfit. Helmets are supplied free. There is no ski-rental.
- **Horses** can be rented for a ride for about $5 per hour from young lads hanging around the snow-mobile area. You could also ask the snow-mobile person to contact them for you.
- Buy **artwork** at ridiculously low prices in the foyer of the hotel and on the street near the Trappist restaurant.

Novgorod

Patriarshy Dom runs tours there, although visitors report that it's not very exciting as a destination.

Baltic states

Invaluable guides to Estonia, Latvia and Lithuania are to be found at *www.inyourpocket.com*

Expat guide: Moscow **17/Travel from Moscow**

Estonia: Tallinn

Many Moscow-based expats visit the beautiful mediaeval city of Tallinn in order to renew their Russian visas. You can obtain Russian health insurance from **Ingosstrakh** *(tel: 232-3467 or 232-3468).*

How to get there
Either by train or plane. The train station is within walking distance of Old Town and the airport is only 3km out of town. If you take the train from Moscow, you will leave at 18.20 arriving at 10.00 Estonian time the next morning. The train trip ($230 adult; $124 child, 1st class, third person e.g. child, in two person cabin is free; 2nd class which holds four to a cabin costs $126 adult; $76 child) is hassle-free except for the fact that you are awakened at about 05:00 in the morning for immigration and Customs checks by Russian and then Estonian border officers, which can take a while. Note that a drug-sniffing dog occasionally comes on board. Complimentary coffee and tea are available after boarding and again in the morning. Take your own milk if you prefer milk in your tea and coffee.

Estonian Air charges $278 excluding taxes and $139 per child while Aeroflot charges $230 excluding taxes with 33% off per child.

A currency exchange which closes mid-evening is situated in the airport, as is car-hire. If you want to take a taxi, check that the meter is running. The tariff is the equivalent of about $4.

Why you should visit
To appreciate the restored mediaeval architecture in charming surroundings that feature narrow, winding, cobbled lanes, many art studios, galleries, churches and a Russian Orthodox Cathedral. In the summer, pavement cafes make for long, lazy gregarious evenings while prices in restaurants are reasonable. Though shops and boutiques offered better value for money than Moscow at one time, this is no longer the case and bargains are just as likely to be had in Moscow as they are in Tallinn. Try the large **Stockmann, Kaubamaja** and the **Viru Hotel Shopping Centre**. You could also catch a bus to the outlying **Kadaka market; Selvers hypermarket** (big selection/good prices) and the **Maksi market at Rocco al Mare** for an American style shopping mall experience.

In summer you can also visit the clean, shallow, **Piritas beach** some 15 minutes away from Tallinn by taxi. There you can hire boats and pedalos and laze at the café overlooking the yacht club and river.

In winter, particularly at Christmas time, there is much in the way of organised entertainment with Father Christmas and assorted elves in abundance.

Where to stay
- **Hotel Kristiine** *(tel: 372-6-464-600)* rated as okay, but not wonderful. Prices are about $35 for a double per night. The hotel is just a five-minute taxi ride from the Old Town, and trams and buses are easily accessible.
- **Hotel - Park Consul Schlossle,** *(tel: 699-7700; pctallinn@consul-hotels.com)* in the heart of the old town is highly recommended for helpful staff, excellent breakfast and rooms and special weekend rates; Finnish sauna and pick-up/drop-off service to the airport.

Expat guide: Moscow   **17/Travel from Moscow**

- **Hotel Viru** next to Old Town and about $100 per night per double room
- **Olympia Hotel** *(tel: 631-5315/fax: 631-567)* is about $160 per night per double room and features a health club, swimming-pool and sauna.
- **Hotel Mikhli** *(tel: 45-3704/fax: 45-1761)* near to Old Town about $50 - 80 per single is well situated on a bus route. Don't forget to ask for a room facing away from the street. They have a reasonable restaurant downstairs and offer free sauna and breakfast as part of the tariff.
- **The Barn** *(tel: 631-3252)* is a youth hostel in the centre of Old Town and rated as friendly, and its double rooms quite acceptable despite the fact that it is a youth hostel.

Baltic Service *(tel/fax: 923-5778; 3 Robnoi Pereulok)* can obtain visas and medical insurance for your trip to the Baltics.

Ukraine

The Crimea is said to be beautiful, with a stunning landscape and many historical places of interest. Kiev (known as the 'city of chestnuts' for its many flowering chestnut trees) is smaller than Moscow and similar in terms of ordinary shopping facilities.

How to get there

Either by train or plane (about $160). You will need to organise a visa, the procedure is said to be simple. Visit the Ukrainian embassy (open till 12:30, Monday - Friday) or ask a travel agent with links to the Ukraine such as Intourist to organise one for you. You will also need an invitation or hotel reservation. Faxed invitations are accepted by the embassy, while agencies may charge some $50 to obtain an invitation for you.

Note that Ukraine no longer issues visas at the airport in Kiev and you are likely to be turned away and sent back on the next flight if you manage to get that far. Once you arrive in Kiev, you may be randomly selected and asked to purchase apparently useless emergency medical insurance for $7. Some say it's possible to refuse to buy the insurance by standing your ground, while others say it is mandatory for non-Ukraine and non-Russian passport holders. It might do the trick if you have a letter typed in Russian and on company letterhead a list of the policy numbers of all insurance policies you possess, their worth, premiums and expiration dates, together with as many official looking stamps as you can find.

Border control is inconsistent, though guards are conscientious about waking passengers at the border.

If you are returning to Russia with a new visa, ensure that the conductor knows that you are foreigner so that you can obtain the all-important border stamp that will allow you to register your new visa.

Foreigners and CIS citizens are not supposed to ride together in the same coupe, so the Central Ticket office will likely refuse to sell tickets to foreigners and Russians together (should you attempt to buy tickets for foreigners legitimately).

256

Expat guide: Moscow   **17/Travel from Moscow**

Georgia

Gudauri, about a two-hour drive from Tbilisi, the capital of Georgia, is rated as a great place to visit for down-hill skiing. Visas are obtainable at the airport on arrival. Gudauri has a Western hotel, ski-rentals and cheaper accommodation in cottages on the slopes. A week's accommodation, fully-inclusive, is said to cost about $500 per person.

In **Tblisi** itself, most expats recommend **Betsy's Guesthouse** *(tel: 98-9553; 21 Gogebashvili)* which is a reasonably priced from $100 to $175 per night. The place is clean and comfortable and very centrally located. The hotel is run by an American woman, Betsy Haskell *(e-mail: betsy@2121.ge)*. The tariff includes breakfast and the dinner on the terrace in summer with a good view of Tbilisi and which attracts local and travelling expats, is recommended. A variety of different-sized rooms are charged from low to higher tariffs. The cheaper rooms do not have their own bathroom.

- **Hotel Guto** is around the corner from the Hotel Sakartvelo. It is a pink building, the hotel has about eight rooms. The rooms cost about $130-160 per night. It is down-hill from Betsy's.
- **The Bon Ton** is run by a friend of Betsy's.

The Caucasus

Consult www.one-list.com to locate a mailing list devoted to travel in the Caucasus (Transcaucasian Republics of Armenia, Azerbaijan and Georgia, and the North Caucasus region (Krasnodar Kray, Stavropol Kray, Dagestan, Adygea, Karachay-Cherkassia, Kabardino-Balkaria, North Ossetia, Ingushetia and Chechnya) of the Russian Federation, as well as surrounding regions such as Eastern Turkey, Azarbaizan Provinces of Iran, and Kalmykia and Rostov and Astrakhan Oblasts of the Russian Federation.

Czech Republic

Cesky centrum *(tel: 251-0450 ask to be connected to the Czech center)* in Moscow explains the best way to get there and where to stay and what to do once you are in Prague. They also supply a thick tome-like guidebook which explains in three languages (including English) places of interest etc in Prague.

Egypt

The following agencies are likely to offer good deals to Egypt:

- **Sinbad Tour** *(tel: 259-2930/256-0929 ask for Ahab)* is an Egyptian firm which has been found to be reliable. Most tours are offered to Russians to Hurghada on the Red Sea (where there is not much to do except scuba-dive) and Cairo, but they also have longer tours of more than a week including a boat trip down the Nile from Aswan. All accommodation is in five-star hotels. One inconvenience might be that only Egypt Air is used and it usually flies from Moscow on a Monday and returns on a Thursday. Prices are around $945 for eight days (five-star hotels, cruise down the Nile, side trips, Red Sea).

Expat guide: Moscow   17/Travel from Moscow

- **SVO Konti** *(Julia tel: 937-6607)* is a Canadian/Russian joint venture which offers a schedule that involves leaving on Sundays for a one week trip which in 1998 cost $945 for a stay of four days at a five-star hotel in Hurgharda and a three-day cruise from Aswan. Disadvantages are that Cairo is not on the schedule except for an add-on day trip.
- **Moskva Tour** *(tel: 937-5555)* has a one-week package to Hurgharda at $595 including airfare, hotel, transfers, and breakfast and dinner.

United Arab Emirates

Note that travel regulations and restrictions to the United Arab Emirates stipulate that no unaccompanied Russian women under 30 is allowed to enter the country. There's a chance that if you are a single woman, you can be arrested for being out in public with a man who is not related to you. This is because the UAE have had major problems with Russian prostitutes.

Sharjah in December is sunny and hot (30 - 33 C) most days. Packages cost about $582 and include round trip tickets, transfers, four days/four nights at four-star resort, daily breakfast and supper buffets. Remember that as Sharjah is a 'dry' Emirate, the hotels cannot serve alcohol.

Cuba

Aeroflot flies direct via Shannon, and Air France was rumoured to be planning daily flights from Paris. Visitors to Cuba will find reasonably cheap five-star accommodation, food, drink and transportation.

Cheapest fares to the US from Moscow

In the past, the travel agency 'Aeroclub' *(tel: 913-9645* ask for Kirill*)* offered the cheapest flights to the US during peak-season and with less than two weeks advance notice. It has a multilingual staff and two offices and accepts all major credit cards.

Thailand

- **Infinity** (formerly IRO Travel) *(tel: 258-5198)* offers tailor-made tours involving a range of hotels in Phuket starting from $35 in three-star hotel to $180 in five-star hotel (per person).
- **Andrews Consulting**: *(tel: 258-5198; e-mail: visa@actravel.com)* has flights to Bangkok on Aeroflot for $850. Accommodation at Pataya will set you back about $50 a day, while bungalows are available in Phuket at $150 per week.

Malta

Trips to Malta offer inexpensive weekly tour packages from $400 (including roundtrip transportation). Contact English-speaking, Maltese native *(Efrim, tel: 752-7529)*.

Slovenia

Slovenia, part of former Yugoslavia, boasts low tourist attendance, alps, seaside, lakes, great wines and food. The Russian agency, **Golden Terra,** is said to be reliable.

Turkey

Only a four-hour trip away, Turkey is a favoured destination from Moscow either staying at Istanbul or on west coast at resorts such as Antalya. Most travel agents will be able to find you a reasonably priced flight from Moscow. Visas are obtainable at the airport. There are several 'Holiday club'-type establishments on the west coast of Turkey at prices to suit most pockets.

Finding flights on the Internet

- *www.expedia.msn.uk.com*
- *www.deckchair.com*
- *www.flightbookers.com*
- *www.city2000.com*
- *www.travelselect.co.uk*
- *www.travelocity.com*

Moscow-based travel agents

English-speaking Moscow-based travel agents which expats use regularly with satisfaction include:

- **1st Travel Group Russia** *(tel: 247-1694/1416; fax: 247-1399; e-mail: firsttrv@cityline.ru)*
- **Infinity** (formerly IRO Travel) *(tel: 234-6555; fax: 234-6556; e-mail: info@infinity.ru; 13, Komsomolsky Prospekt, metro: Park Kultury)*
- **Time Travel** *(tel: 232-5844 or Marina at 956-3765)*
- **Geo Tourism** *(tel: 234-1945)* is highly recommended for all sorts of travel-related services, in particular payment for your trip by credit card over the telephone.

Home-swaps

Swap accommodation with people registering their homes on the Internet in all parts of the world. **Internet Home Exchange & Vacation Rentals** *(www.NetHomeXchange.com)* includes tips on how to begin your exchange, sample letters of introduction, checklists for a successful exchange, how to prepare your home, and much more. The site offers a data bank, with continuously updated listings. A one-year listing for each property in the Internet Home Exchange costs $39. This is a great way of taking advantage of your temporary home base in Russia, which no doubt, many people might want to visit.

18/Leaving

It seems that no sooner have you settled down in Moscow and come to grips with the system and all that entails, than you are notified that you have to leave, as a result of some crisis or other, and you then have to come to grips with leaving.

There are all sorts of issues to confront when leaving, and this does not purport to be the be-all and end-all answer to the issue. However, it's worth considering some of the issues raised here some time before you even need to leave, so that when your time is short you do not regret having considered the issue sooner.

Duty payable on goods taken out the country

Remember to get permits and receipts for anything that could be deemed an antique or work of art.

You will need to find out what the current export allowance is, as regulations seem to fluctuate depending on the day of week it is. Ask your embassy for guidance. If you are moving through a removal company, expats recommend that you ask them to handle all the paperwork regarding exportation of antiques etc, as they are best equipped to dealing with the tedious bureaucracy involved.

When exporting anything that could be deemed to be antique, your major problem areas are likely to be samovars, carpets, antiques and paintings dating before 1945.

If buying antiques or paintings, the shop should be able to tell you how old it is and arrange a permit through the Ministry of Culture.

To have a painting officially valued, you will need to contact the valuation department at the Tretyakov Gallery, which will issue you with the correct paperwork. Note that they also log the painting on to their list and you will be required to pay 100% of the official value of the painting to Customs on departure.

If you bring antiques in from the West and want to take them out again, make sure you have all receipts and certificates necessary to prove that they were not purchased in Russia.

Declaring cash when entering or leaving Russia

You can bring in or take out up to $500 without declaration. It's always worth checking on the latest allowances, given the economic situation.

When arriving you will be handed a Customs form on the plane called a *'deklaratsiya'* or Customs declaration. Forms printed in English should be available. In the section for currency simply fill in the amount of dollars and

Expat guide: Moscow   18/Leaving

other currency you have with you. Insist that the form is stamped upon entry. However, when you leave, you should not have any more hard currency on you than when you entered. It's best not to lose your original *'deklaratsiya'*. Put it in a safe place and make sure you have it when you leave the country. In theory, you should leave with no more than the amount you stated that you brought in with you. Always check what the current regulations state regarding the amount of money you are allowed to leave with *(See Chapter 12 - Staying solvent)*

A moving experience

Speak to other expats for their experiences of the moving companies to get a balanced view. It's best to get a moving company which will handle Customs documentation for you. Book a company as soon as you know you are moving, as you don't want to be fitted in as a last minute deal and dealt with in a hurry, nor without the full team at your disposal.

Despite these ratings by some expats, remember that where some have problems, others are delighted. You can't tell what kind of experience you will have until you go through it yourself. The only recommendation is to be forewarned so as to pre-empt problems. Agree a *modus operandi* in advance with your choice of mover, stipulating what will happen if goods are lost, expected methods of communication (e.g. notification of arrival times or delays; confirmation that the person you will be dealing with will not disappear on holiday and leave the task to someone else when you most need their help and knowledge of your situation). Check whether furniture will be able to get out the door once boxed, if boxed.

Past experience shows that if you choose to leave at a busy time, it's best if you book as far in advance as possible, otherwise you will likely get the dregs of service when companies squeeze in your order.

The following are companies with offices in Moscow and which have been used by expats:

- **Geologistics** Contact Brian O'Halloran *(tel: 958-2150/51)* Geologistics has 20 offices in the UK. They specialise in moving personal effects
- **Vinlund** Contact Ryan Dodd *(tel: 234-1697/187-9777; fax: 187-2067; www.glasnet.ru/~vinlund).* Vinlund is Western-managed and operated and said to be quick to solve problems, if any
- **Corstjens**
- **Allied Pickfords** *(tel: 796-9325; fax: 796-9326; 127a Varshavskoye Shosse)* Allied Pickfords is a global removal company.
- **Voerman's** Contact Paul van Willen *(tel: 240-5635/952-4937)*
- **Interdean**
- **M&M**
- **Sea-Land**
- **Hapaag Lloyd**
- **Instar**
- **Froesch GmbH** *(tel: 171 1287/5447/9694; fax: 967 1365)*
- **Intelorg Worldwide** *(tel: 745-5154)* are said to be flexible, cost-effective and to offer good service.

Expat guide: Moscow

18/Leaving

Moving small shipments

If you wish to send boxes out through the cargo services of the airline you choose to fly with, you will need to pay the airline directly. Cost for freight in the first quarter of 1999 was about $300 for 100kgs though price/kg depended on the overall quantity involved. depending on the quantity.

You will have to have Customs seal the shipment at Sheremetyevo Cargo (about one kilometre from Sheremetyevo-2). This is a very time-consuming process which will necessitate that you take a Russian-speaking person to help you negotiate the bureaucracy.

Customs will ask you to assess the value of your belongings and charge a very small percentage on the value, meaning that you should take rubles for payment of this amount. Other nominal fees involved include those covering application charges, filing fees and processing fees for instance. Be prepared to stand in the same line, several times over.

Ensure that you do not have anything likely to be construed as being flammable or explosive (such as alcohol, perfume, or aerosols etc), otherwise you will be asked to remove them.

Your goods will have to be left at the Sheremetyevo bonded warehouse at least overnight. Because security could be a problem, it's best to tape your boxes very well.

Before attempting to conduct the bureaucracy yourself, first check whether or not your airline representative will do it on your behalf.

Sergey *(tel/fax: 314-4730 (Russian/evening; 144-0765; or e-mail in English: iramo@com2com.ru)* can take your goods to the Customs division and help you negotiate the bureaucracy.

If you have less than a container-load and wish to send the goods without paying the expense of a 'hand-holding' moving company, you could try contacting freight forwarders, **Blue Water Shipping A/S** *(tel: 111-0510; fax: 111-4487; Suite 511, 46 Varshavskoe Shosse).*

If you can, deliver your well packed goods (in trunks or cases) to the freight forwarder without having to pay the extra expense of the moving company.

Contact Joseph Quinn at Sefco for further assistance or advice regarding the receiving and accepting of freight by freight forwarders *(e-mail: shipoverseas@webtv.net or http://members.tripod.com/~sefco/ easterneurope.html).*

Finding a home for your unwanted goods

You can choose to either sell items that you don't want to take with you through the Expat-list or give them away to one of the many charities in Moscow which would be grateful to receive unwanted goods in reasonable condition. The Center for Humanitarian Aid will distribute these goods to Moscow's homeless and needy children. They should be taken to 11 Novaya-Basmannaya. The entrance is on Basmanaya Pereulok behind the St. Peters & Paul Church. The Center is open seven days a week from Monday to Friday from 11:00 - 16:00 or Saturday and

263

Expat guide: Moscow   **18/Leaving**

Sunday from 12:00 - 15:00. If you can't deliver, call 261-8750 and ask for Namerud who may be able to arrange for a volunteer to collect the items.

Repatriation

Repatriation usually involves a certain amount of culture-shock, surprising as it may seem. You may find that though you think you cannot wait to get back to familiar territory, friends and services, you will miss certain aspects of Moscow to which you have become accustomed. Whether you like it or not, you will have become changed by the experience and this can involve some hardship on your return regardless of how prepared you are.

Be kind to yourself and family by allowing yourself the time, on your return, to settle in, just as you may have done on your arrival in Moscow.

INDEX

A

accident report, 61
Accidents, 61
Accommodation, 15, 25, 27, 31, 32, 36
  agencies, 33
  commission, 32
  contract, 45
  cost of renting, 31
  curtains, 37, 38
  furniture, 37, 38
  Furniture repair, 38
  landlords, 35, 40, 46
  lease, 27, 43, 46, 47
  location, 31
  Mattresses, 38
  Park Place, 34, 41, 144
  Pokrovsky Hills, 34, 41
  remont, 34, 35, 42
  Remonting yourself, 36
  Rosinka, 34, 40, 41
  size, 34, 37, 39
  Syetun, 34, 41
Acupuncturists, 173
Advantix film, 208
aerobics, 40, 89, 144, 145, 247
Aikido, 93, 141
Air conditioning and a/c appliances,
  216
Airport baggage overweight fee, 220
alarms, 58, 190
Alcohol, 175, 180, 213, 244
Alcoholics Anonymous, 94
Allergies, 176
American Women's Organisation of
  Moscow, 88
Anglo-American School charity auction
  ball, 102
Annual events, 102
Antique markets, 217
Anti-Semitism, 13, 180, 189
anti-theft device, 58, 190
Anti-Western, 13
Artistic pursuits, 138
asbestos, 37, 42
Asian Women's Group, 87
ATM, 188, 193, 194, 195
Audio cassettes, 114, 213
Australia and New Zealand women's
  support, 90

autumn, 157, 234
Availability of goods, 200
AWO, 88

B

Babysitters, 47
badminton, 149, 155
baking, 21
banking, 23, 126, 193, 194, 195, 196
banya, 141, 142, 166, 174, 225, 248
baseball, 149, 207
basket-ball, 142, 145, 247, 248
Bastille Day, 97
Beds, 215
beer, 77, 83, 84
Beggars, 187
bicycles, 20, 144, 145, 151
billiards, 142, 146, 247
blini, 81, 99, 100
Boating/sailing, 149
Bolshoi, 139, 187, 217
Book-exchange, 110
books, 110, 111, 211, 216, 218, 237
Books by post, 110
bowling, 40, 92, 142, 215
breath-test, 60
bridge, 89, 91, 92, 143
Bridge Club, 143
British Isles Business Club, 70, 93
British Women's Club, 88
broomball, 143, 154
bungee-jumping, 151, 161
bureaucracy, 222, 242, 244, 261, 263
Business culture, 224
Buying a foreign car, 57
Buying art, 139
Buying CDs, audio and video cassettes,
  English-language films, 214

C

camera equipment, 209
Camera repair, 209
Canada Day, 97
Canadian Business Association, 94
Canadian Women in Moscow, 88
Car breakdown, 62
Car hire, 64
car parks, 60
Car theft, 190

Expat guide: Moscow   18/Index

Car wash, 62
Carpet market, 214
Cat club, 239
Caucasus, 146, 257
caviar, 70, 77, 78, 81, 100
CD market, 13, 113, 114, 116, 118, 119,
    156, 189, 214, 216
Centre Culturel Francais, 89
champagne, 77, 78, 99, 213
Changing money, 188
Changing the clocks, 236
charities, 92, 94, 263
chess, 143, 155
children, 15, 18, 20, 21, 39, 40, 47, 49,
    52, 61, 63, 66, 68, 70, 74, 88, 89, 92,
    97, 102, 127, 137, 138, 140, 145,
    146, 149, 150, 151, 152, 156, 157,
    159, 160, 164, 167, 179, 181, 184,
    202, 206, 213, 216, 234, 248, 251,
    263
Chiropractice, 173
Christmas, 20, 79, 88, 98, 99, 102, 128,
    181, 212, 216, 225, 236, 255
Cigarettes, 208
Cigars, 207
Cinema, 92, 140, 215
clothes, 17, 38, 202, 203, 204, 213
Clubs and societies, 87
Coffee, 73, 84
Communication, 105
Compact disc player repair, 114
Compact discs, 113
Computers, 117
Constitution day, 101
contract, 15, 16, 17, 222, 223
Converting rubles vs dollars online, 197
cooking, 21, 48, 80, 82, 92, 212
Cooking classes, 85
cosmetics, 172, 200, 205, 212
cost of living, 11, 199
Cost of living, 198
Couriers, 134
craft supplies, 20, 23
credit cards, 23, 75, 80, 185, 196, 197,
    198, 201, 220, 253
Credit-card security, 195
Cricket, 151
Crossing roads, 52
Cuba, 258
Cultural holidays/celebrations, 96
culture shock, 21, 177, 224
Customs, 16, 18, 20, 27, 28, 110, 113,
    118, 134, 187, 196, 219, 220, 241,
    261, 262, 263
CWIM, 88

Cycling, 151
Cynepmapket/produkti/gastronom, 212

D

dacha, 47, 100, 231, 234
dancing, 90, 92, 137
darts, 143
dating scene, 104
daylight, 176, 236
de-icing windows, 59, 175
Dental services, 170
depression, 19, 21, 176
Diwali, 97
dogs, 237, 238, 240
Doors, 45
Draughts, 45
Drawing and painting, 138
drinking water, 62, 83
Drinking-and-driving, 60
driver's licence, 24, 53, 54, 55, 56
Driving hazards, 190
DVDs, 117

E

Easter, 20, 100, 138, 181
Egypt, 243, 257
electricity, 21, 42, 43, 46, 178, 234, 246
Electronics repairs wizards, 215
emergency, 19, 40, 42, 50, 61, 130, 167,
    168, 169, 170, 171, 184, 190, 241,
    244, 256
Emergency telephone numbers, 183
Employment
    Before signing a contract, 223
employment agencies, 223, 226
English-language newspapers, 111
Estonia, 229, 243, 254
European Business Club, 94
evacuation, 168, 169, 170, 184, 224,
    241
Exchange booths, 198
exchange-rate, 75, 76, 125, 196, 197,
    201, 223
exercise, 159, 182
eXile, 69, 111
Exporting souvenirs/antiques, 218

F

Fabrics and haberdashery supplies, 204
false ATMs, 188
feminism, 102, 103
Fencing, 143

266

Expat guide: Moscow

18/Index

Film-developing, 208
Finnish, 143, 199
Fish market, 76
fishing, 20, 42, 153, 182
fitness, 143, 147, 148, 182
flowers, 92, 96, 100, 102, 128, 209, 225
fluctuations, 43
Flying, 153
food, 175, 199, 209
football, 159, 160, 189
foreign stamps, 133
Fourth of July, 97
Framing artwork, 218
French, 10, 77, 88, 89, 97, 106, 109,
    110, 112, 115, 144, 170, 179, 181,
    198, 199, 206, 211
Frostnip and frostbite, 177
Fruit cordial, 84
fur coat, 19, 202, 203

G

GAI, 53, 54, 56, 59, 61, 62, 184, 185,
    235, 249, 254
garage, 40, 58
gardening, 20, 100, 212
Georgia, 257
German, 10, 41, 77, 91, 106, 107, 109,
    110, 112, 115, 143, 165, 179, 180,
    253
German Press, 112
Global USA, 44, 80, 152
golf, 42, 145, 154
Gorbushka, 44, 119, 121, 174, 213, 216
Gorky Park, 13, 68, 71, 82, 100, 101,
    148, 151, 155, 157, 161, 163, 164,
    181, 230
Greetings cards, 133

H

Haircuts, 206
Halloween, 89, 97
hardware market, 44
Hash House Harriers, 158
Hats, 203
heating, 42, 43, 165, 174, 234
HIV testing, 173
Hockey, 154
hooter/horn, 61
Horse-racing, 154
Horse-riding, 156
house-keeper, 47, 48
humidifier, 19, 44

I

Ice-climbing, 162
Ice-hockey, 162
Ice-skates, 20
ice-skating, 89, 146
Independence Day, 97
Indoor recreation, 137, 141
Influenza, 173
insurance, 23, 55, 59, 61, 64, 124, 167,
    168, 217, 219, 223, 229, 255, 256
International Women's Club, 29, 85, 88,
    91, 102, 138
International Women's Day, 100
Internet banking, 23
Internet service providers, 119
Italian, 10, 71, 92, 106, 109, 112, 115,
    181, 199, 211
Italian Press, 112
IWC, 20, 22, 29, 85, 92, 93, 95, 102

J

Japanese, 41, 74, 77, 80, 106, 141, 161
Japanese interests, 93
Jewellery repairs, 218
Jewish Community, 182
Jewish restaurants, 182
Johns Hopkins Alumni, 91
Johnson's Russia List, 123
Judo, 145
Juggling Club, 94

K

keys, 44, 50, 188, 190

L

language, 22, 51, 106, 125, 179, 180,
    206, 225
Laundry/dry-cleaning, 205
Le Club France, 89
Leaving, 220, 261
Left turns, 61
Libraries, 110
licence, 24, 53, 54, 56, 113, 133
lost, 52, 131, 132, 184, 205, 262

M

Mafia, 26, 40, 65, 183
Markets for non-food items, 213
Maslenitsa, 99
May day/Labour day, 100

267

Expat guide: Moscow

Medical and dental centres, 169
medical insurance, 23, 168, 229, 256
menus, 75, 76
Metro, 66
Mitino, 118, 213, 215
money order, 198
Moscow Business Telephone Guide,
   111, 119, 130
Moscow Country Club, 40, 42, 145,
   148, 154, 166
Moscow day, 101
Moscow Dragons Rugby Club, 102
Moscow Irish Community, 90
Moscow Mensa, 91
Moscow Oratorio Society, 91, 102, 140
Moscow Protestant Chaplaincy, 94
Moscow Rotary Club, 90
Moscow Times, 3, 32, 69, 92, 102, 111,
   158, 159
Moscow Tribune, 69, 111
Moskva Acceuil French Club, 89
Mosquitoes, 233
Mountain-biking, 154
museums, 92, 139, 200
music, 21, 92, 93, 112, 139, 218

N

nannies, 47, 48, 240
Navigator Mentor Program for
   Russian/expatriate women, 90
network, 16, 29, 89, 90, 122, 124, 159,
   222
New Age and health-food, 212
New Muscovite program, 94
New Year's Eve, 99, 225
number-plate, 58, 62

O

Obtaining dollars from a bank, 194
Old New Year, 99
Opening a bank account, 195
Opera, theatre, ballet, 139
Ophthalmology, Optics, 171
Orthodox Christmas, 99
Outdoor recreation (all year round), 156
Outdoor recreation (summer), 149
Outdoor recreation (winter), 162
Outside Moscow by road, 247

P

parking, 40, 58, 60, 200, 235
passport photos, 21, 24, 208

Paying fines, 54
Paying for travel by credit-card, 218
Pest control, 44, 176
Pet (Bird) market, 237
Pet market, 213
petrol, 61, 63, 64, 251
pets, 22, 23, 24, 31, 39, 48, 128, 237,
   239, 240, 241, 242
pharmacies, 131, 168, 172
Piano lessons, 140
Pianos, 45
Pine Forest, 41
plants, 20, 23, 24, 209
pollution, 19, 157, 176, 232
pool, 142, 143, 146
Portable ham radio
   licensing/registration, 113
postal system, 133
potholes, 56, 59
power-of-attorney, 53, 55, 57, 58
prices, 72, 75, 76, 118, 139
Pricing policy/double price standards,
   200
Professional Women's Organization, 90
Progress, 77, 78, 112, 117, 211, 214,
   217
Psychologists/psychiatrists, 179
public transport, 66, 131, 188, 208
pukh, 176, 233
Purchasing electrical appliances, 213,
   215
Purchasing serious art and antiques, 217
Purchasing sheet music, 218

Q

quarantine, 237, 241, 242
Quarantine in the UK, 242
Quizzes, 146

R

radio, 37, 112, 113, 123, 213
radio-activity, 176, 210
rain, 235, 233
Ramstore, 20, 70, 78, 79, 80, 84, 133,
   174, 198, 199, 202, 208, 211, 212
references, 16, 28, 49, 50
Registering a car, 57
Religious services and groups, 180
relocation, 15
Relocation, 125, 126
   shipper, 16, 18, 241
removals, 47
rental contract, 45

Expat guide: Moscow

18/Index

Repatriation, 264
Restaurants, 69
river boat, 67, 150, 230
Road rage, 190
Rock-climbing, 146
roller-blades, 20, 40, 155, 161
Roller-blading, 154
rowing, 155, 161, 164, 178
Rugby, 102, 158
Running - long distance, 157
Russia Journal, 111, 123
Russian art, 138
Russian customs, traditions and
    courtesies, 95
Russian food, 72, 73, 81, 82
Russian service, 202
Russian soul, 87, 103

S

SAD, 19, 162, 176
safety, 12, 13, 52, 57, 76, 127, 183, 184
Satellite television, 114
scam, 36, 187, 188
Scuba-diving, 158
Seatbelts, 60
security, 25, 28, 40, 50, 53, 58, 60, 183,
    184, 189, 195, 201
Serebryany Bor, 31, 34, 40, 41, 148,
    153, 155, 161, 230, 232, 237
Seven Continents, 78, 211
Severance pay, 222
shashlyk, 74, 82, 161, 163, 175, 230,
    234
Shoe repair, 204
shoes, 19, 48, 96, 146, 147, 204, 235
shopping, 76, 79, 112, 128, 197, 198,
    199, 200, 201, 202, 210
Shopping at the market (rynok), 76
Shopping hours, 201
Singing, 140
skateboards, 20
ski, 42, 157, 162, 163, 164, 165, 247,
    251, 253, 254, 257
skis, 20, 162, 163, 164
Skydiving, 155
Sledding, 165
sleds, 20, 164
Slovenia, 243, 259
small shipments, 263
snow, 19, 39, 58, 59, 62, 67, 90, 100,
    158, 166, 235
snow tires, 59, 62
snow-boarding, 165
snow-mobiling, 166, 182, 254

soccer, 97, 145, 149, 159, 163, 247
Society of US Service Academy
    graduates, 91
solariums, 144, 145
Spanish, 71, 90, 93, 106, 107, 115, 179
Speed limits, 59
sporting goods, 152, 153, 155, 162, 207
spravka, 147, 196, 198
squash, 144, 145, 147, 248
St Andrew's Society, 90
St George's Society, 90
St Patrick's annual ball, 102
St Petersburg, 18, 125, 133, 150, 230,
    244, 245, 246, 247, 248, 250, 251
Stamp-collecting, 140
Stockmann, 78, 79, 80, 83, 84, 98, 199,
    202, 211, 212, 255
Street names, 51
Street numbers, 51
summer, 17, 18, 19, 37, 39, 42, 43, 45,
    47, 52, 67, 72, 82, 91, 92, 93, 148,
    149, 150, 151, 152, 154, 155, 156,
    158, 159, 161, 176, 186, 188, 230,
    231, 232, 234, 235, 243, 248, 251,
    252, 255, 257
sun lamp, 18
supermarkets, 25, 77, 79, 83, 98, 111,
    200, 209, 210, 212
Suzdal, 166, 230, 243, 252, 253
swimming-pool, 40, 41, 142, 144, 145,
    147, 148, 158, 247, 248, 253, 256

T

table-tennis, 155, 160, 248
tailors, 38
Tailors, 204
Taking lifts/hitch-hiking, 64
Tallinn, 243, 255
tax, 16, 45, 46, 126, 222, 224
taxi, 64, 65, 96, 186, 190, 200, 244,
    250, 253, 255
Taxi tariffs, 65
Taxis from the airport, 65
TB (tuberculosis), 175
Tea, 73, 84
Teaching English, 107
Telephone, 130
Telephone crisis lines, 178
Television and VCR repair, 114
Television/video, 114
temperature, 19, 42, 124, 231, 232, 233,
    235, 236, 251
tennis, 40, 41, 144, 145, 148, 154, 247
Terrorism, 12

269

Expat guide: Moscow

18/Index

Thailand, 258
Thanksgiving, 20, 78, 79, 98
The German-speaking women's club, 91
Tipping, 75
Toiletries, 206, 210
tours, 29, 161, 230, 249, 254, 257, 258
traffic jam, 62, 63, 65, 66, 235
traffic light, 52, 56, 190, 235, 254
train, 200, 230, 244, 245, 246, 248, 250, 253, 255
Train, 67
trams and trolleybuses, 66
transformers, 21, 43
transport, 15, 21, 25, 64, 66
Trans-Siberian express, 246
travel agents, 230, 259
Travel from Moscow, 243
travel inside Russia, 244
Travelling by boat in Russia, 246
Travelling by train in Russia, 245
Travelling with a pet, 240
troika rides, 99, 166
Tsentr, 142, 145
turkey, 79, 98
Turkey, 243, 251, 257, 259

U

Ukraine, 210, 243, 256
United Arab Emirates, 258
U-turn, 61, 62

V

Vegetables and fruit, 212
veterinary clinics, 238

Video cassette repair, 117
videos, 20, 21, 113, 116, 117, 214
visa, 21, 24, 25, 28, 53, 54, 57, 184, 194, 208, 222, 225, 229, 244, 256
Visitors, 229
vodka, 59, 70, 83, 175, 213, 224, 245
volley-ball, 97, 149, 150, 155, 160, 247
Vomiting and diarrhoea, 175

W

Walking, hiking and nature trails, 159
Washing-machine repairs, 216
Washing-machines, 44
water, 46, 83, 174, 244
water-heating, 43
Weather, 124, 231
Websites, 123
where to buy, 109, 178, 202
Window-cleaning, 45
Windsurfing, 155
wine, 70, 84, 93, 213
Winter driving, 59
Working matters, 221

X

xenophobia, 12

Y

yoga, 145, 149

Z

ZHEK, 46, 189

270

Printed in the United States
120487LV00001B/78/A